SCOMBE GERTRUDE BELL NORA
AZIR BHUTTO SARAH   RD
OLM CARYL CHURCHILL LETTICE
NDSEY DAVIS MARY DEJEVSKY
D DOROTHY EMMET GEORGINA
NDA FOREMAN SUZANNE FRANKS
RD MARY GOLDRING MICHAEL
P HENSHER PHYLLIS HODGSON
N LIBBY HOUSTON KATHRYN
KEEN KATE KELLAWAY BRIDGET
M KILEY NIGELLA LAWSON ELIZ-
RTHY KATHARINE MOORE ELAINE
PADEL ANN PASTERNAK SLATER
BARBARA ROCHE JOHNNY ROGAN
N ANNE STEVENSON BARBARA
LEN WADDELL MARINA WARNER
D SAM WEST ANN WIDDECOMBE

OXFORD ORIGINALS

An anthology of writing from
LADY MARGARET HALL
1879 – 2001

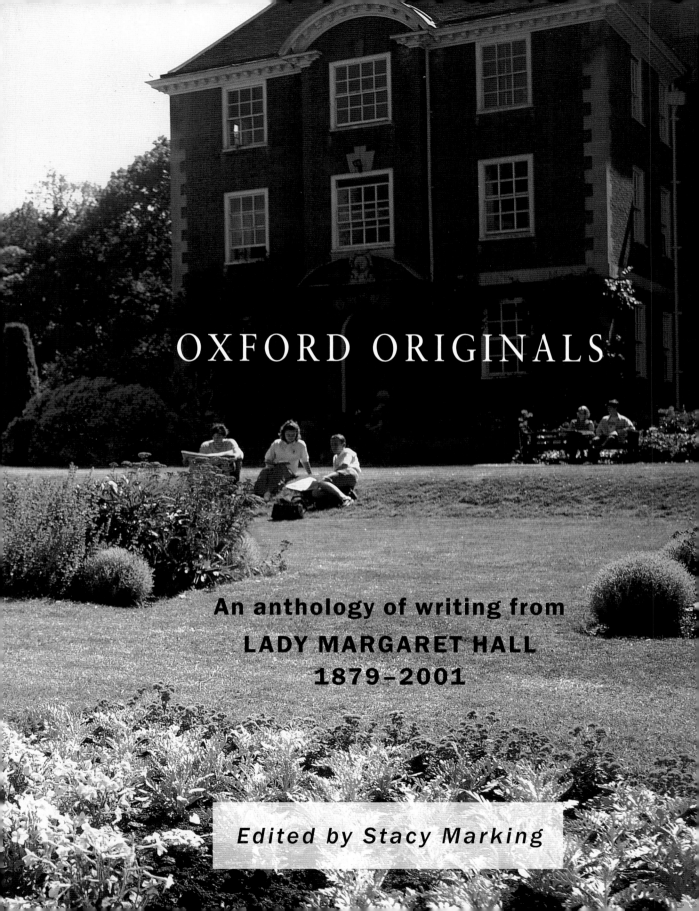

OXFORD ORIGINALS

An anthology of writing from
LADY MARGARET HALL
1879–2001

Edited by Stacy Marking

Contents

Prefaces

THIS ANTHOLOGY AIMS AT SURPRISE. I am sure that at first glance you will be surprised by the astonishing people who are in it. As I compiled it, I was constantly exclaiming, 'I never knew so-and-so was at LMH!' That initial surprise was overtaken by a sense of wonder at the extraordinary lives so many of these writers went on to lead.

That is the basis of this collection. I have included wonderful writers – not all of them well known – and writing that reveals the various, talented, unpredictable, moving, funny, powerful, eccentric and sometimes dangerous lives they have led. There are more than 180 writers and artists in here. I am proud of their number, and their talents, and of what it is we all have in common: an LMH education. What a stepping-off point! We were richly privileged, and I hope this anthology will help others to continue in our varied footprints.

'Oxford Originals': the title was inspired by a delicious piece by a non-alumna, Lady Diana Duff Cooper (see page 15) whose fashion tips were directed to the 'ladylike, yet original' undergraduates of LMH. The 'ladylike' may have long gone – hastened to its grave by the arrival of the boys in 1979 – but the 'original' is still evident in every page of this book.

It falls into three sections. I: LMH and Oxford; II: the lives people subsequently led; and III: 'Books. books, books', a celebration of the disproportionate number of LMH writers of literature, history and biography. I only hope the writers, all of them, will forgive me for squeezing their lifetimes' work into such brief extracts. I hope readers will be tempted to follow these leads to their full and original form.

LMH must account for an inordinate number of bookshelves in the British Library. May there be many more.

Stacy Marking
Editor

THE PROCEEDS FROM THE SALE of this anthology will go towards the endowment in perpetuity of a Fellowship in English at LMH. The College's English school has a reputation second to none, and our undergraduates regularly perform impressively in finals. Despite the distinction of the faculty, only one of the College's three Fellowships in English is even partially endowed, and this could jeopardise our ability to maintain our exceptional quality in this subject. The success of this book will help towards the ambitious target of £1 million.

As can be seen from our contributors, our Senior Membership contains a remarkable number of distinguished writers of all kinds and from all generations. Of course, not all read English, but it seems fitting that this collection should help secure the future of an outstanding teaching department.

This book is Stacy Marking's brainchild. I pay tribute to her editorship, and thank her for the enthusiastic and unstinting generosity with which she has given her time and her labour.

Anna McNair Scott
Advisory Council

Foreword

ANTHOLOGIES ARE FOR DIPPING INTO. This one seems more likely to be read from cover to cover. Either way, it offers in full measure what one would expect of an anthology of distinction: the pleasures of being introduced to the new, reminded of the old and swept along in a pageant of people, places and ideas.

'What will you do when you go down?' is a timeless Oxford question. Here is an LMH answer; more accurately, perhaps, a kaleidoscope of highly individual LMH answers. Not everyone had a peak named after them in the Dolomites; not everyone could get away with lines like: '"I always go to Aleppo when my sons are in prison there," the Sheikh explained.' Gertrude Bell was unique. But, as Flann O'Brien might have put it, you will find as you read on that she was not alone in that.

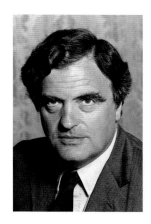

This anthology offers a rich choice of journeys: you might select one that will take you through space and time from Arabia to Zanzibar, from Antarctica to the funeral of Reggie Kray; from the trenches and field hospitals of the Great War to the travails of post-Soviet Russia; or from women's suffrage, via children's rights and penicillin, to an Italian whose assets (when confiscated by the Court) included 131 apartments, 122 warehouses, 20 factories and ten school buildings. Can his family name really have been Piazza?

The anthology format brings out not only the vitality but the great diversity of our Senior Members' contributions to the outside world. This is surely a case where feeling the width is an integral part of minding the quality. This shines out, as one might expect, from the writings by and of the pioneers; and it is much in evidence also in the writings and doings of their successors. Both LMH and this anthology offer us a real *embarras de richesses*.

Sir Brian Fall, GCVO, KCMG
Principal, LMH
1995–2001

Page 4: Brendan Neiland, RA, Lady Margaret Hall, 1998
Overleaf: Elizabeth Wordsworth (wearing cap) with the first students, 1879

I LMH & Oxford

If this awful thing of a woman's college has got to happen, you might as well go to be Head of it – John, Bishop of Salisbury, to his sister Elizabeth Wordsworth

ANNE TRENEER
LMH 1929

For purposes of study

IT WAS BLISSFUL TO SIT in the Bodleian, small, compact and unknown, in the midst of time and books. Other people in the Bodleian never seemed real to me, and I imagined myself entirely disembodied to them. It is strange that one should come to feel so much alive by being so be-spirited and de-personalised.

I loved to order books and see them mount round my desk in ramparts; books some of which had, perhaps, not been handled since Doughty (the subject of my studies) had himself handled them, possibly sitting where I sat, and dreaming of the poems he would write.

The magic words, 'For purposes of study', would bring me any book. I commanded Genii. I could intoxicate myself with books; and then dance down the wooden steps of the Bodleian, making little patterns of sound to please myself as I skipped round the corners, and out into the quad.

Who can describe the gravity of the Bodleian Quad, a gravity courteous by day, remote and harmonious as a dream in moonlight? It takes the heart with its beauty. I used to let my eyes run up the lines of its solemn walls, then drop to the worn stones under the several doorways to the medieval schools, hollowed by the tread of a multitude of scholars' feet.

The Queen is reported to have said in reply to the question, 'Why are clever women never nice?' 'They are sometimes. Lady Longford is' – Alethea Hayter (LMH 1929)

From *Cornish Years*
(Jonathan Cape, 1949)
See also pp. 34, 35, 210

'I understand', the President said, 'that Miss Drew, besides having been at Oxford and Cambridge, is also the author of a very clever book — though I feel sure you will all agree when I say that no one would think it to look at her' – Elizabeth Drew (LMH 1906)

From the
Daily Herald,
15 June 1927

OXFORD TO LIMIT WOMEN

Fixed Number For Each College

'BEASTLY SWOTTERS'

Spirited Attack on Statute That Is Degrading

From Our Own Correspondent

OXFORD, Tuesday.—Oxford to-day decided, by 229 votes to 164, to limit the numbers of women in residence at the University. A statute was passed by Congregation which will have the effect of limiting the numbers as follows: Lady Margaret Hall 160, Somerville College 150, St. Hugh's 160, and St. Hilda's 150. The number of women undergraduates in any society must not exceed 160.

Large numbers of dons and undergrads of both sexes crowded the Sheldonian Theatre this afternoon for the meeting of Congregation.

Lord Birkenhead was sitting among the doctors and voted for the statute.

BOUND TO RESIST

A spirited attack was made by Miss Margery Fry, of Somerville College, who said that women were sick of the women's question and of the disabilities of their sex, and they felt bound to resist this encroachment on their autonomy, and the privileges they had already been given.

There was not the slightest need for a women's party in the University. They wanted to be treated, not as women, but as human beings. What had they done to make themselves so unpopular?

An undergraduate had told her that one reason was that women were such beastly swotters and raised the standards of examinations.

Another reason which was given for this unpopularity was that the social life of Oxford had been changed by the advent of women in a way which

Women were such beastly swotters and raised the standards of examinations

They wanted to be treated, not as women, but as human beings

W. F. Knox (History) was one of a famous Edwardian dynasty, which included Ronnie and E. V. Knox. She published several novels and the autobiographical *A Little Learning*. She died in 1962.

WINIFRED PECK
LMH 1901

A portrait of Miss Wordsworth

YOU MIGHT AT A DISTANCE have thought Miss Wordsworth was just one of Oxford's little old ladies, quietly dressed in old-fashioned grey or black, with a hat that framed her face enough to suggest a bonnet, and a faint likeness to Alice's White Queen.

The blue eyes would light up in the square, clean-cut face, and she would perhaps tell you, with no further preliminary, how she had been thinking of the strangeness of the lilac's existence: 'So exquisite for a fortnight, so dull and shabby for the rest of the year'; or how a robin had piped so persistently outside St Giles Church that she had decided they were the real Protestants, the non-conformists among birds; or that the nightingale in the rain last night made her think of the young lady who brought all her music to a party and insisted on performing, though everyone wanted to go home to bed. Then you remembered that it was the great-niece of the poet who had been thus musing, though with a touch of humour which must have come from another strain of the family.

She told us that in her experience plain girls married most suitably because they had the sense to accept their first offers

She never added to, if she never subtracted from, the few old-fashioned rules about chaperonage and the keeping of Sunday. But in her time she accepted the appearance of the bicycle, the development of hockey, so sadly different from the game of catch in which Ruskin himself instructed the first student on his one famous visit to us. She saw our activities on the river, though indeed there was no question of an eight or sliding seats; she saw motors dash up and down to the Hall; she saw the suffragette movement absorb feminine society. She saw fashions in education, literature, social manners and dress change from one generation to another, and though she might offer laughing and pungent criticism, she had always a respect for the liberty of the individual.

It cannot have been easy for her generation to strike a balance between the old desire to protect girls from harm and the more modern demand for freedom.

From *A Little Learning* (Faber & Faber, 1952)
See also p. 23

ELIZABETH WORDSWORTH
LMH Principal 1879–1909

The first Principal's first principles

From *First Principles in Women's Education* (James Parker & Co., Oxford, 1894). Bound in a volume of *Tracts Relating to Women 1894–1910*, along with a tract on 'Employers and their Female Domestics' and 'Cupid's Code for the Transmission of Secret Messages by means of the Language of Postage Stamps'. Price 2d.

MANY WOMEN WRITERS are actually annoyed if a reviewer detects a feminine touch in their work. Why should there not be a feminine touch? Why should it be considered a compliment to any woman to be told she writes, paints, sings, talks, or even thinks, like a man? Surely it would be better for the world were she to try and be in all things her own best self.

A well-educated girl ought to be, at twelve or fifteen years old, in love with Miranda, Cordelia, Desdemona, Portia and Perdita, with Nausicaa and Andromache, and many another heroine. She ought to catch some of their beautiful feeling, their dignity – if I may use such a phrase, their eternity, that quality in them which is never out of date. . . . No girl, however well informed, is really well educated whose heart and imagination are allowed to lie dormant while facts are being ruthlessly and unremittingly shovelled into her brain.

Women can never be properly educated in gangs; they must be loved and cared for one by one, and learn to love and care for others one by one.

Mary Warnock on Elizabeth Wordsworth, *The Sunday Telegraph*, 21 May 1978

She did not really believe in education, or not in the way that the serious ladies of Cambridge believed in it. She just liked it –
Mary Warnock

LMH Reading party, 1915, from the photograph collection of Stephanie Bryan-Brown (LMH 1912)

MAGGIE BENSON
LMH 1883

From A. C. Benson,
*Life and Letters of
Maggie Benson* (John
Murray, 1917); a letter
to her mother from
LMH in 1884.
See also p. 161

Two of the daughters of the Archbishop of Canterbury came to LMH under Miss Wordsworth. The first was Nelly, who arrived in 1881 to read Mathematics and English Literature. After two years, however, 'it was felt that one of the daughters was now wanted at home to help in the constant hospitalities and intricate life of the Archbishop's palace. Accordingly Nelly was recalled from Oxford and Maggie took her place there.'

DEAN BURGON HAS BEEN PREACHING the University Sermon this morning, a perfectly outrageous sermon, all about the women's Exams., the congregation in fits of laughter nearly all through. They really laughed quite audibly. He said all the things which he said in his Letter – about women becoming men and so on. He said, for instance, that women who went in for these examinations would be 'instruments of death and channels unto evil.'

CLARA MONEY-COUTTS
LMH 1897

The Hon. C. B. Money-
Coutts was a writer and
poet. Her publications
include *The Dryad*, an
epic poem; a biography
of Angela Burdett-Coutts,
and *The Victorians*.

From *The Brown Book*
1969

WHEN I SAT IN THE SCHOOLS for the examination in Political Economy, I discovered that I was the only person in for it, and was all alone in the body of the big room, though on the platform there appeared to be several invigilators, later on all eating strawberries and cream. When I had finished my papers they invited me to join them.

MAUDE ROYDEN
LMH 1896

September 1898; from
an interview with Dame
Kathleen Courtney
(LMH 1897) by Emil
Oberholzer, April 1966.
See also p. 26

I NEVER SERIOUSLY BELIEVED that I should present myself for examination – always thought I should die, or the sky would fall, or the process of manufacturing paper and pens fall into disuse, or something of that sort.

Fashions for the Schools

19 Belgrave Square, Mayfair.

I have been asked by a young friend of mine to give a few hints to all you poor things who have 'Schools' so soon. She writes: 'It's just impossible to know what to wear, for one is so *restricted*.' But, surely, it is woman's task to *transcend* restrictions, so I am sending you a few *ideas* for different types, for, after all, it is type that *matters* in dress.

The first sketch I called 'Lady Margaret'—ladylike, yet original. I'm told a black tie is *de rigueur,* also the black and white motif; and your caps! so beautifully nicky. So in this we have just simple lines, a swathe tie and the ebony stick which, of course, is to be everywhere in August.

The next is feminine, clinging . . . I advise marocain for the gown. I'm told St. Hugh's is allowed a different uniform from the others, and I must say I *do* think knickers and gloves are an improvement. Of course, boots are a difficulty, but then there are always the jolly Russian sort with tops. (But never take your boots off. Never. Only *absolutely* never-get-there's remove their boots.) The goloshes should be carried.

Left and right: illustrations from Fritillary. LMH's own publication, The Daisy, *ran from 1890 for nine issues, until* Fritillary, *a joint venture with Somerville, was set up in 1894. This carried illustrations and advertisements as well as articles, and ran until 1931*

Lady Margaret.   St. Hugh's.   Somerville.

A secret for you. The golosh is coming into its own!

My next model is a different type. I do realise there are some of you for whom exams. are 'real and earnest and the grave is not their goal.' And this is for you, who want to get honours, not just pass. Just a rather widely-made coat and skirt, but with my own 'cavern' pockets! You see, all you have to do before the Day dawns is to slip your books into your 'caverns'—and when they ask you your verbs or your dates, you've got your grammar and history books there, all ready! Must say, I'm proud of *that* little effort.

I do hope these suggestions have helped, and the best of luck to you all. Your friend,
DIANA DUFF-COOPER.

F. Lannon (History; research at St Anthony's College, 1972–75; served on the Commonwealth Scholarship Commission, 1982–91). Her publications include *Privilege, Persecution and Prophecy*, and (with Paul Preston) *Elites in Twentieth-Century Spain*.

FRANCES LANNON
LMH 1969, Fellow 1977

A new world of happiness

THE FIRST GENERATIONS OF LMH students took pleasure in the novel experience of being women at Oxford. Eleanor Lodge (1890) called it 'a new world of happiness'. Academic work, sport, and a lively communal life presided over by the never-predictable Miss Wordsworth kept students busy and entertained. Some, like Eglantyne Jebb (1895), revelled in the 'blissful paradise of books, books, books'. Winifred Knox (1901) was at least as excited by hockey, lacrosse and tennis. Many delighted in having a room of their own for the first time, the long conversations and burgeoning friendships that lasted a lifetime. These early graduates became teachers, explorers, missionaries, writers; they campaigned for women's political and civil rights, for children's welfare and for world peace.

As women became more integrated into Oxford life, students regarded LMH as a springboard into the University as a whole, or a useful refuge from it, or both. LMH students were prominent in Oxford choirs, orchestras, politics and drama. Because the University deliberately kept women students in a ratio of about one to four with men right up to 1957 (and the proportions only changed radically when colleges went mixed in the 1970s), Oxford was also an effective dating agency. Between 1955 and 1970, more than half of all Oxford women who married, married Oxford men.

When LMH admitted men students in 1979, its social life in some ways became more self-contained. Of course, stardom on the Playhouse stage or at the Union, or gaining a sporting blue, have continued to appeal, and a host of inter-college activities. But college societies (including the Beaufort literary society) flourish. So does social life, as a spate of all-LMH marriages testifies. Students now go into business, public service, the arts and sciences, law and finance, barely able to imagine how many avenues were closed to their pioneering predecessors. But they still take with them a distinctive college experience. Talking and friendship are still where it's at – even if the college bar, clubbing and cocktails replaced cocoa long ago.

Lady Antonia Pakenham (History; CBE, 1999; Hon. D.Litt., Hull and Sussex) is a novelist and biographer, like her mother Elizabeth Longford (see page 219). She was Chair of the Society of Authors in 1972 and of the PEN Women in Prison Committee; President of PEN English Centre, 1988. Her publications include *Mary, Queen of Scots* (winner of the James Tait Black Prize, 1969); *Cromwell, Our Chief of Men*, and *Boadicea's Chariot: The Warrior Queens. The Weaker Vessel* won the Wolfson Historical Award in 1984. Mother and daughter have effectively divided up four hundred years of British biographical history, Elizabeth Longford taking the nineteenth and twentieth centuries, Antonia Fraser the sixteenth and seventeenth.

From *The Weaker Vessel: Women's Lot in Seventeenth-Century England* (Weidenfeld and Nicolson, 1984)

ANTONIA FRASER
LMH 1950

Unlearned virgins

THE PREJUDICE AGAINST EDUCATION for girls – and its dreaded end-product, the learned woman – had derived fresh impetus from the presence of a male sovereign after 1603. It had always been rather tactless to attack the learned woman with too much zest so long as that paragon of female erudition Queen Elizabeth occupied the throne. As the poet Anne Bradstreet wrote in memory of 'our dread Virago' forty years after her death:

> Let such as say our Sex is void of Reason,
> Know 'tis a Slander now, but once was Treason.

Not only were men freed from the inhibition of the 'dread Virago's' intellectual example by her death, but that male sovereign, James I, had himself a scant opinion of the female intelligence. Perhaps the frivolity of his Queen, Anne of Denmark, had something to answer for; at any rate when it was suggested that his daughter, another Elizabeth, should learn Latin, the King replied that 'To make women learned and foxes tame had the same effect: to make them more cunning.' And he forbade it.

Such sentiments would have come as a marked surprise to his English royal relations of yore: those Tudor princesses of the Renaissance, not only Queen Elizabeth herself who could translate Latin into Greek, and the famously erudite Lady Jane Grey, but Queen Mary Tudor, celebrated at the time for her knowledge of science and mathematics. For that matter James's mother Mary Queen of Scots, whose intellectual attainments have been overshadowed by her dramatic life story was, as a princess, automatically instructed in the classics. We know from the English Ambassador to Scotland that she used to read Livy regularly for pleasure after dinner.

In the sixteenth century Sir Thomas More had written: 'I do not see why learning . . . may not equally agree with both sexes.' At the end of Queen Elizabeth's reign, a classical education was a mark of elegance in the circle round Mary Countess of Pembroke: William Wotton, in his *Reflections on Ancient and Modern Learning*, wrote of that period: 'It was so very modish, that the fair sex seemed to believe that Greek and Latin added to their Charms: and Plato and Aristotle untranslated, were frequent Ornaments of their Closets.' . . . But it was in the seventeenth century that George Herbert was able to list among well-known proverbs: 'Beware of a young wench, a prophetess and a Latin woman', while women themselves were often contributing a note of ritual apology whenever they felt they had stepped outside the modest mental boundaries which circumscribed their sex.

K. A. Hughes (History; Ph.D.) is a biographer, historian and critic. She writes for *The Observer*, *The Daily Telegraph* and *The New Statesman*, and teaches at the University of East Anglia on the Lifewriting MA course. She was a judge for the 2001 Whitbread Biography Prize. *George Eliot* won the James Tait Black Prize for biography in 1999.

KATHRYN HUGHES
LMH 1978

George Eliot's girlhood

AT THE AGE OF EIGHT Mary Anne took a step towards a new world, urban and refined. In 1828 she followed her elder sister Chrissey to school in Nuneaton. Miss Lathom's establishment had been only three miles from home, and was attended by farmers' daughters with thick Warwickshire tongues, broad butter-making hands and little hope of going much beyond the three Rs. The Elms, run by Mrs Wallington, was a different proposition altogether. The lady herself was a genteel, hard-up widow from Cork. She had followed one of the few options available to her by opening a school and advertising for boarders whom she taught alongside her own daughters. There were hundreds of these 'ladies' seminaries' struggling to survive in the first half of the nineteenth century and most of them were dreadful. What marked out The Elms was its excellent teaching: by the time Mary Anne arrived, the school was reckoned to be one of the best in Nuneaton. Responsibility for the thirty pupils was shared between Mrs Wallington, her daughter Nancy, now twenty-five, and another Irishwoman, Maria Lewis, who was about twenty-eight.

The change of environment did nothing to help Mary Anne shed her shyness. Adults and children still steered clear, assuming that they had nothing to offer the little girl whom they privately described as 'uncanny'. Only the assistant governess Miss Lewis, with her ugly squint and her Irishness, recognised in Mary Anne something of her own isolation. Looking beyond the smooth, hard shell of perfection, she saw a deeply unhappy child 'given to great bursts of weeping'. Within months of her arrival at Nuneaton Mary Anne had formed an attachment to Miss Lewis, which was to be the pivot of both women's lives for the next ten years. Miss Lewis became 'like an elder sister' to the Evans girls, often staying with them during the holidays.

Mr and Mrs Evans were delighted with Mrs Wallington's in general and Maria Lewis in particular. In their different ways they both set great store by their youngest girl getting an education. Anticipating that the quiet, odd-looking Mary Anne might remain a spinster all her life, Robert Evans was determined that she would not be reduced to relying on her brothers for support. A life as a governess was not, as Miss Lewis's example was increasingly to show, either secure of cheerful. Still, it was one bit of independence open to middle-class women and Robert Evans was determined that it should be Mary Anne's if she needed it.

From *George Eliot: The Last Victorian* (Fourth Estate, 1998)

M. S. Warner (Modern
Languages; Honorary
Fellow, 2000; Visiting
Fellow Commoner
of Trinity College,
Cambridge; Honorary
Doctorates from
St Andrews and York
universities) is a writer,
and literary and art critic.
She gave the Reith
Lectures under the title
'Managing Monsters' in
1994, and the Clarendon
Lectures, Oxford, in 2001.
Her publications include
Joan of Arc; *No Go The
Bogeyman* and novels
The Lost Father (1988),
Indigo (1992) and *The
Leto Bundle* (2001),
which was on the
longlist for the 2001
Booker Prize.

MARINA WARNER
LMH 1964

Pretty maids all in a row

SISTER CLARE SHOOK OUT SOME SEED into Mary's palm from a small white envelope. 'There's some mustard and cress, Mary Blane,' she announced. 'Now see you scatter it, evenly.' They were standing by the flower-bed, which had been dug over and then divided up into square plots for the youngest girls in the Lower School to plant their own little gardens. She folded over the corner of the envelope, and put it away in the basket over her arm. 'Then, when you've planted those, I'll give you some radish seed too.'

Mary had never heard of mustard and cress, or of radishes; they didn't have them at home, a long, rumbling flight far away. 'In the Persian Gulf,' she'd told her new classmates when asked where she lived. 'It's desert. Sometimes the taps don't work at night.' There had been a stopover, the journey to her new school was so long. For refuelling, the air hostess explained to her, adjusting the notice round Mary's neck, which bore in red the letters U.M. 'There,' she said, 'you're a proper "Unaccompanied Minor" now.' When they took off again, Mary sucked two boiled sweets, one after another, to stop the knitting needles that seemed to be stabbing her through her ears. She could see the desert from the window, a tiny oasis like her model farm; the pyramids turned into toy bricks; then the sea flashed below, like the sand when her father took them for a spin in the jeep, out of the city. 'It's just a mirage!' her mother had cried out, as they drove towards a shining stretch of water.

But here, near East Grinstead, England, the rain came down the windows in long streaks, stopping, starting, stopping again and pearling, then dribbling down again, to the edge where the pane met the frame; the seeds Sister Clare gave her sprang up in the dampness the first night after she shook them out of the palm of her hand.

Beyond the children's gardens, a few old apple trees spread crookedly, their branches whiskered with lichens, in the orchard of the old house now occupied by the Lower School; one day, Mary uncovered there, in the long wet grass, a small, flat tombstone.

She wiped away the strands and puzzled out the words,

Here lies Tig
Gone to Happier Hunting Grounds
Champion Mouser
Best of Friends

She read Mouser at first as moozer; when she told Annie, who was pulling up carrots she had planted from a packet in her square of garden, to

Written for the series
*Round and Round the
Garden*, BBC Radio 4,
2000

come and see the moozer she'd found, Annie shrieked, 'It says, "mouser", can't you read?' She looked at Mary with an angled set to her jaw, one elbow out, just like a grown-up woman. 'It's someone's pet, stupid.' She turned her head and inspected Mary's garden.

Mary was nibbling a bit of mustard leaf with her front teeth in the same way as she'd seen Annie try a carrot.

'You have to make sandwiches, not eat them like that,' announced Annie, looking on. 'Don't you know anything?'

The Lower School ate on their own, at six o'clock, at one end of the huge refectory. After supper, Annie and Catherine and several others dashed to the pantry where special jars were kept, sent with them by their parents to make them grow. Mary watched from the table; her parents lived in that hot country where carrots and mustard and cress didn't spring up in the ground and cats were kicked and rotted in the streets. The girls who were to grow were issued with long spoons by Sister Matthew; they dipped them into the jars of malt and brought out stretchy strings of sticky brown stuff, which they licked yummily, poking out their tongues. The cod liver oil provoked squeals and cries and terrible grimaces, but there was a big box of biscuits – all different shapes and sizes and some with coloured icing even. One of the fathers had had this 'De Luxe Assortment' delivered, in a van with a gold coat of arms on the side.

Mary looked on and she felt a hole gape in her chest, as if you'd be able to see through her to the other side.

'Your skin's awfully yellow,' said one little girl to Mary one morning, on the stairs waiting to go into chapel. 'You most likely *need* cod liver oil.'

Matilda Crayshaw, known to all the school as Tillers, head prefect in Mary's house, was playing Lady Precious Stream in the school play; in a long silk flowered tangerine dressing-gown with scarlet revers to the sleeves, and her hair piled up and her face whitened, she hardly looked the same person as the mud-spattered hockey player in the long serge divided skirt, whom the whole school cheered at the Saturday matches.

When Mary passed Tillers in the corridor, she trembled and sometimes she had to hold her legs together. The older girl seemed to glide, like one of the angels in the Annunciation reliefs that hung all over the convent; her hair shone. The Lord God, the sisters liked to say, had given Matilda many gifts. She was probably going to be called, which was the highest privilege of all, to be a bride of Christ.

'She's my crack,' Annie whispered to Mary round the stripy curtain that half hung off the rail between their cubicles.

'She's mine, too,' Mary whispered back.

Marina Warner
in the 1960s

'Copycat.'

'I thought of it first,' Mary lied. She hadn't known about this business of cracks till now. But she was picking things up, slowly.

She had a glimmering of what the phrase might mean. It was the feeling she had, under her ribs between her shoulder blades at the back when she was looking out for Tillers. But it was also the hoping that came over her when the post arrived in the refectory in the morning and girls' names were called out. Tillers sometimes helped Sister distribute the letters; one day, when she came past the breakfast table where Mary was sitting, on her way to her own place, she bent towards her and said, 'It takes ages for a letter to come, all the way from the Persian Gulf.'

At this the crack inside Mary seemed to close up a little, under the warmth of the older girl's reassurance. Tillers was the one who could mend the hole inside her, sometimes; but sometimes, she also poked it open, too, because longing to see her when she wasn't there became so acute.

But gradually Mary started fitting in: she began to shout 'Fains I' when she didn't want to do something, and 'Pax!' when she was being tickled or bumped. She learned to 'stick up for herself' and 'pull her weight' and 'show some vim' and fling herself face down instantly on the gym floor at the command, 'Bombs coming over!' During 'Shop' which Sister John held at 2 p.m. on Saturdays in the vestibule of the gym among the smells of rubber plimsolls, hairy matting, wood polish and damp serge, she discovered gobstoppers and bull's eyes, gum drops and Smarties, fudge squares and liquorice shoelaces, Malteser balls and bars of Bounty and Milk Flake and Toblerone. It was here they were allowed to buy miraculous medals, crucifixes, rosaries and holy pictures: if you were popular, you got given lots of holy pictures on your birthday to put in your missal.

Mary screwed herself up to present Tillers with a holy picture: a tall angel was bending down to open a gate to a garden and usher through a child in a white tunic wearing a lily of the valley garland on her head:

Your own guardian angel,
I'll be your guide,
Through life's joys and trouble,
I'll stay by your side.

Her heart was beating with a kind of flip, knock, flip inside her as she ran up to the older girl who was standing in a group by the notice board looking at a new timetable, and pressed the gift into her hand.

One evening, towards the end of term, the word spread through the Lower School: tonight, there was going to be a treat. For sometimes, on special occasions, Sister Thérèse, who was in charge of the dormitory, would let the prefects visit at lights out, to say goodnight to the little ones.

From her end of the long room, Mary watched the group starting its round; none of the curtains around the cubicles was drawn and each child was sitting up in bed, waiting for the bright gaggle of older girls to reach her. Tillers was with them, of course; she was tossing back her hair under her hair band to lean over and kiss a little girl on her forehead.

There were moments when Mary felt time slide to a standstill and then inflate, very slowly, filling the space in which she found herself, barely moving, barely breathing. Seeing Tillers straighten herself and begin threading her way past the nightdress cases on the stools at the foot of each bed, round the curtain rails of the cubicles towards her, Mary remembered her mother, Jinny Blane, far away in the Persian Gulf, dressed to go downstairs for dinner, waving her beringed hands in the air, fingertips stretched to dry the frosted pink varnish on her nails, accompanied by that funny sharp smell of acetone mixed with the peachy sweet perfume she wore, her taffeta skirt rustling; she offered her lips to her daughter's forehead, her hands still held out to dry, like one of the pearl grey sea birds on the harbour front back home, unfolding its wings to catch the sun.

When Tillers reached Mary's cubicle, Mary showed her the radishes she'd pulled up that afternoon after lessons; they were lying in her soap dish, on her washstand by the bed.

Tillers picked one out and crunched it carefully. 'Mmm,' she said. 'Tastes like the real thing.'

'Would you like another?'

'I don't think so. Though it was *very* good.'

When the group of prefects had left, Annie and two of the others crept into Mary's cubicle.

'Radish!' Annie was laughing, putting her finger in Mary's soap dish, and poking the bunch. 'You gave her a radish. You don't give a crack a radish. Why d'you do that?'

Mary said, 'She liked it. She said it was very good.'

'She spat it out in her hand. I saw her. Soon as she turned away.' Annie pressed her face closer to Mary. 'Anyway, she's *my* crack.'

'Oh, no, ' Mary sucked in her breath. 'That's a lie.'

''S not a lie. It's the truth.'

Mary felt smarting behind her eyes; the hole in her chest was opening up again. But she knew now how to show some vim and so she put out her hand and stuffed it over Annie's mouth; her cheeks under Mary's fingers were oddly soft and her teeth were wet and slippery. Annie began to kick and scream; so Mary took hold of her hair by a hank with her other hand

and hung on, pulling her on to her bed to push her face downward to make her stop.

Sister Clare, when she appeared, in a flurry of dark habit and veil, separated the two girls.

'And who started this disgraceful fight?'

Annie was sniffling and purple; her face looked stoved in. Several girls cried out, 'Mary Blane!'

Sister Clare didn't wait for more; she hauled Mary towards the door and there, her knuckles whitening as she wrung her hands, her face flushed, she told her, 'I won't have special friendships, Mary Blane. I won't have you getting all over-excited and overheated . . . There'll be no more of these goodnight visits.' She cast a bitter look back towards the middle of the dormitory, where Sister Thérèse was hovering, miserably. 'What does the word of God say? That the devil has to creep on his face for the rest of eternity. With no legs. No legs. That's the devil's fate: a slimy thing that slides and slithers about. Just you remember, Mary, it's the workings of the devil, slithering about in you, that put you up to this.'

Then she raised her voice and addressed the whole dormitory of tensed, silent children. 'The older girls aren't ever going to come again. There'll be no more goodnights. Because this is what comes of goodnight kisses.'

Squeezing Mary's arm, she bent down once more to her eye level, 'I shall have to tell your parents, I'm afraid. Yes, Mary Blane, yes. I will write to them, in the Persian Gulf, to tell them of your wickedness.

'You will go back to your bed now and lie quiet and pray that your sins will be forgiven. Though Our Lord knows, you don't deserve it.'

If I wanted to marry an explorer, or bring up twenty sons, or head the suffragettes, or take up lion-taming, I would feel it worth while being so bored here – Winifred Peck to a friend from boarding school

From *A Little Learning*
(Faber & Faber, 1952)

CATHY AVENT
LMH 1939

Degrees of recognition

THE WOMEN WERE PERMITTED to take Classical and Mathematics Mods in 1880, and Schools in History, Mathematics and Natural Science from 1884; before 1894 (when examinations in all arts subjects and music were opened to women) there was a special Women's Second Examination, available in combinations of subjects such as Mathematics, Latin and French, or Logic and Political Economy. English was a subject open only to women until 1895 and Modern Languages until 1904. Among the curiosities revealed by our study of past records was the arrangement whereby some were awarded a Dublin B.A. *ad eundem*, possibly for use by teachers aspiring to become headmistresses.

From *Children of the Lady Margaret* (Oxford Society, 1992)
See also pp. 53, 54, 64

Elizabeth Wordsworth is one of the great figures in the women's movement, a cause in which she took not the slightest interest

From Georgina Battiscombe's biography, *Reluctant Pioneer* (Constable, 1978)
See also p. 93

In May 1920, women were at last admitted to full membership of the University, and in October 1920, at the age of eighty, Elizabeth Wordsworth was presented with an honorary degree.

YOU WILL BE AMUSED TO HEAR that the University has just offered me an M.A. degree *honoris causa* – which means that you need not pay any fees. It is not of the smallest use to me, at my time of life, to be an M.A. but I thought it would be ungracious to refuse, so I have accepted it and I expect the Public Orator will poke any amount of fun at me in Latin.

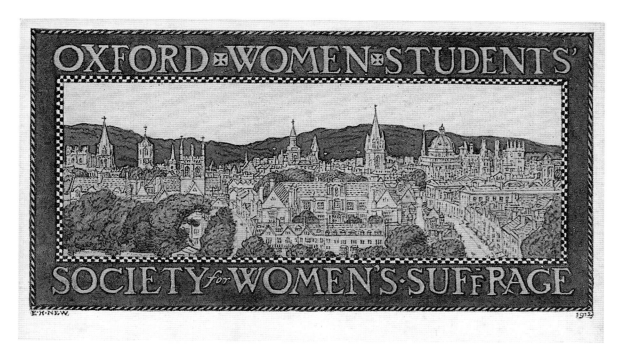

Postcard published by the Oxford Women Students' Society for Women's Suffrage in 1912, design by E. H. New

From *The Women of My Time* (Lovat Dickson, 1934)
See also pp. 70, 90

JANET COURTNEY
LMH 1885

On being an Anti-Suffragist

WE WERE ON THE WRONG TACK, I think now; we had put our money on the wrong horse. But we had no desire to stop the women's movement. We merely wanted to regulate its pace and to prevent a noisy minority from bringing us all into discredit. Probably we should have done better to turn ourselves into a right wing of the constitutional suffragists. Perhaps even we should have smiled on the suffragettes.

After all, when you want a thing very much, it does not always answer to be too squeamish about methods

S. M. Lerpinière (History; Ph.D., London, 1976) spent the war years in the Ministry of Education, and then became a Lecturer at London University and in Hertfordshire. Her publications include *Feminists and Bureaucrats*; *Women First*, and the novels *Another Shore* and *Out of the Rain*. She died in 2001.

A. M. Royden (History, LMH 1896; CH, 1930) was a famous speaker and writer in the causes of women's suffrage and the League of Nations. She was given honorary doctorates from Glasgow and Liverpool universities, and Mills College, California. She died in 1956.

From Sheila Fletcher, *Maude Royden: A Life* (Blackwell, 1989)

SHEILA FLETCHER
LMH 1942

Getting the vote: Maude Royden (LMH 1896)

IT WAS A DISHEARTENING TIME for the suffrage movement, for 1910 had seen the frustration of what had seemed a hopeful all-party attempt to shape a Conciliation Bill which would have enfranchised women householders. In response to this promising initiative, the militants had actually called a truce. However, when the government let the bill drop after a successful second reading the suffrage outlook seemed worse than ever.

The journey was so long; the goal so distant, as Maude allowed in an article entitled 'A Long Journey'. Their goal was no less than the right of every individual to develop 'to the full extent of God-given powers'. The vote was only one step towards this, 'but it is the step we are able to make now.' Who would refuse to begin a long journey because the first step was so far from the end? 'For all journeys,

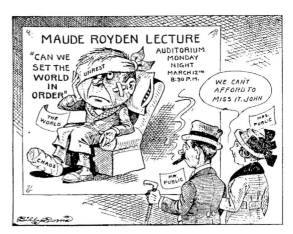

Cartoon from The Sunday Citizen, *Asheville, North Carolina*

long as well as short, there is only one step of importance . . . the next.'

Suffrage hopes in 1911 focused on a new Conciliation Bill which passed its second reading with a good majority. After that, however, the government decided to postpone further action till the following year; which was how things stood when Maude set out on a speaking tour in the USA at the end of October 1911. The tour began as soon as the *Mauretania* docked in New York. Her crowded programme meant, as she recalled, that 'most of the time I was not on a platform but in a train'.

She got on well with her audiences. In Philadelphia they were pleasantly surprised to find her appearance 'in direct contrast to that of the suffragette of the comic supplement', and her voice 'more like that of a trained actress than of a public agitator'. She revealed her ability to lift an audience to the heights of her own intense conviction, that women's suffrage was a great moral and human question.

'We claim our freedom, we women, who are physically weak, and in claiming it we claim the spiritual heritage of mankind'.

N. G. Shrimpton (Balliol; D.Phil. 1976) is a recent Chair of the Faculty of English Language and Literature at the University. His publications include essays on Swinburne, a critical edition of the poems of Matthew Arnold, and articles and reviews on Shakespeare, Bunyan, Blake, Ruskin, Rossetti and modern authors. He was a founder-director of the Oxford Playhouse Trust.

NICHOLAS SHRIMPTON
LMH 1980 Fellow

The English school: bright, particular stars

ENGLISH LITERATURE crept into the academic life of the University of Oxford in 1873, when the subject was grudgingly allowed to be part of the Pass School. Scorned and resisted as a 'dilettante' discipline, it took its major step forward in 1881 when proper papers were set on English Literature for the special women's examinations. The very first generation of Lady Margaret Hall students immediately distinguished themselves. Eliza Bradby, part of the pioneering 1879 entry, took a First in 1882, immediately establishing the Hall's prominent place in what would eventually become Britain's largest department for the study of the world's richest and most complex literature.

The Honour School of English Language and Literature finally came into being in 1894. By 1906 Lady Margaret Hall had appointed a resident Tutor in English, a writer on Chaucer and Raleigh, Grace Hadow; she was joined in 1911 by Janet Spens, whose enduringly valuable book *Elizabethan Drama* opens with a sentiment which will sound familiar to many subsequent generations of hard-driven English undergraduates: 'the student should start by being familiar with the whole of the Shakespearean canon . . .'

Right: Eliza Dorothy Bradby, who gained the first First in English at LMH

FROM ELIZA BRADBY in 1879 to the thirteen undergraduates in the 2000 entry (ten for single honours, three for the joint schools; eight from independent schools, five from the maintained sector; ten women and three men), it is the exceptional people who compete so fiercely to come here, who generate the vitality of LMH English.

Those who read English at LMH win Firsts and University prizes in disproportionate numbers. They write, direct and act in plays, publish poems and stories and journalism, play music, run societies, yet somehow still find time to read 'the whole of the Shakespearean canon'. In recent years they have provided Presidents for the Oxford Union (1988) and OUDS (1998, 1999) and editors for *Isis* (1996). They go out in the world to be everything from captains of industry to Buddhist monks, and all the roles that this anthology reveals. They are, unfailingly, the bright particular stars of their generation: the function of a Lady Margaret Hall fellowship in English, at a time in which public funding for the tutorial system is at risk, is to sustain the distinctive circumstances in which such stars can shine.

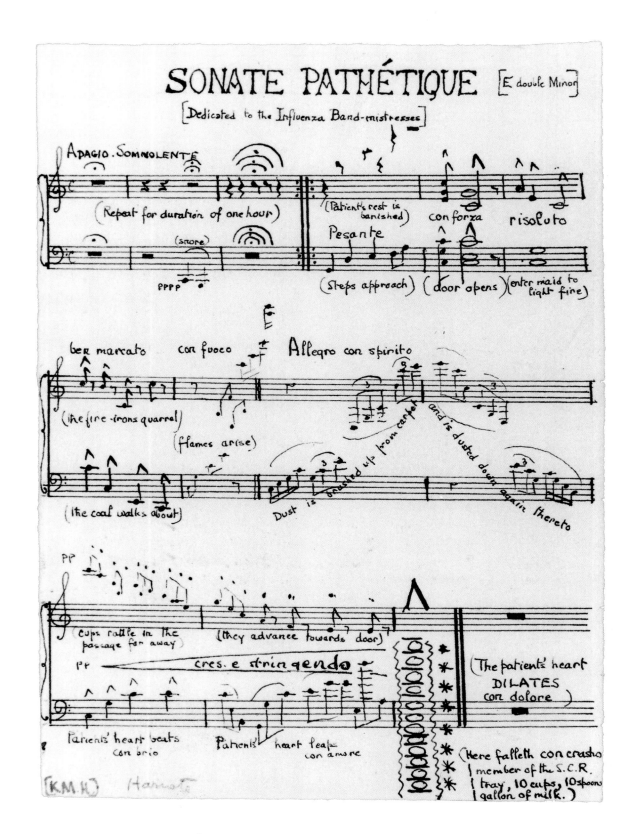

U. K. Yeo (English; pictured above at LMH in 1920) is a writer and biographer. Among her many publications are *Cordial Relations*; *The Maiden Aunt in Fact and Fiction*; *The Lotus House*; a biography of Kipling, *The White Man's Burden*, and her autobriography.

From *Queen Victoria is Very Ill* (Allison & Busby, 1988)
See also p. 30

Illustrations taken from an album of thanks after the flu epidemic, compiled by the patients of Miss Spens and Miss Lodge.
Left: attributed to Kathleen Harnett (History, 1915).
Right: Dorothy Hall (Classical Mods, 1918).
Further illustrations are on pp. 39, 150

KATHARINE MOORE
LMH 1918

The 1918 flu epidemic

My year had not had time even to get to know each other's names before the vicious 1918 flu epidemic struck us. Within a week almost all the students and most of the dons had succumbed.

My first tutorial in English History was with Miss Lodge. 'You've got it,' she exclaimed suddenly and, darting across the room, thrust a thermometer into my mouth. True enough, my temperature was up and I was packed off at once to my bed. I think every single student in Old Hall was smitten, but our two resident dons, Miss Lodge and her great friend, Miss Spens, the English don, escaped and they nursed us all. There was no treatment but bed and aspirin; doctors were reserved for the serious cases, of which there were many. I remember thinking that probably nothing like this had been experienced in Oxford since the Plague of 1665. The bells were continually tolling.

I had been ill for a little while when a knock came at my door and, much to my surprise, the Principal appeared. She came in silently and sat down. Then she said: 'I am afraid I have some very bad news for you.' It could only have been a moment or two before she spoke again, but it was long enough for me to think in terror of my family. But it was my tutorial partner, Joan Luard. Hating to give in, and ignorant of the fatal tendency of this flu to develop into pneumonia, she had held out against it too long and was already very ill when she finally collapsed and was taken to the little Hospice off Norham Road where there were slightly better facilities for nursing than at the Hall.

But she died three days later.

Now put some Benger's on the tray,
There's such a lot to do—
We've sixty invalids to-day
All through that
horrid Flu.

HENRIETTA JEX-BLAKE
LMH Principal 1909–21

*My idea of Elysium
is a place where you
get nice clothes without
having to take any
trouble over them*

KATHARINE MOORE
LMH 1918

On Henrietta Jex-Blake

THERE WERE TWENTY-FIVE students in my year at LMH which was the largest year yet. I had come up with three others from Wycombe Abbey (all to read History), which was a record. We went together that first day to pay our cheques to the Principal – £36 board and tuition for the term. She shook hands with us and gave us a brief welcome. She was Henrietta Jex-Blake, whose younger sister was Mistress of Girton. She was a stately woman and rather beautiful, and she dressed extremely well. But she was very shy and her shyness took the unfortunate form of a crisp curtness of manner which put off many people. It was difficult to maintain a conversation with her.

She gave uncomfortable duty tea parties at which one tried desperately to talk:

'I hope it won't be wet for Saturday's Garden Party, or worse still, neither one thing nor the other.'

Principal: 'It must be either wet or fine.' End of conversation!

Principal: 'And what have you been reading for amusement in the vacation?'

Me: 'Well, I've read Henry James's *Portrait of a Lady* which I liked very much.'

Principal: 'Oh, you must be very young still.' End of conversation.

M. S. Villar (Modern Languages) was Editor of *Cherwell*, and has since worked as a fashion editor with Condé Nast Publications, as an information officer with the National Council for One-Parent Families, as an orchestral administrator with the Koenig Ensemble and as a freelance journalist and arts publicist, specialising in opera.

From a script for *Woman's Hour*, BBC, 1959
See also p. 78

SUZANNE GRAHAM-DIXON
LMH 1950

Leaving interview with the Principal, Lucy S. Sutherland, 1953

PRINCIPAL: 'So, I hear you're becoming a journalist.'

Me: 'Yes, I start working for *Vogue* next week.'

Principal: 'Don't let them make you walk down Piccadilly with a tray of fish on your head.'

Me: 'Fish? On my head?'

Principal: 'We had an old student who became a journalist. On the *Daily Mail*, I think. That's what they made her do.'

Me: 'But why?'

Principal: 'I think it was something to do with the Picasso exhibition.'

Me: 'Oh. Is she still working for the *Daily Mail*?'

Principal: 'No – she became a missionary. She's doing very good work in Zanzibar.'

Suzanne Villar (second from left) with models at Vogue, 1954

M. R. Trickett (English; Manchester City Art Gallery 1945–46; Commonwealth Fund Fellow, Yale and Hull universities) was Fellow and later Principal of St Hugh's College from 1951. Her publications include *The Course of Love*, *Point of Honour* and *The Return Home*, which won the John Llewellyn Rhys Prize in 1953. She died in 1999.

RACHEL TRICKETT
LMH 1942

A fictional account of an English tutorial

AS SHE READ HER ESSAY ALOUD, Clemence was thinking that it was still hopeless, after two more weeks, trailing into the vac even, this miserable effort of saying what she meant, but that it would be over soon, and the sun through the window square burned on her ankles, wrists and forearms, reminding her how little it mattered. She had written about Byron. As she quoted, the older woman's mind stayed itself like a magnetic needle on the lines. Then Clemence was saying more confidently, 'from this it is clear that to Byron nothing matters but experience, living intensely, even though it doesn't last. After that there is nothing left except to giggle and make giggle, but even the boredom makes the other more important in retrospect.'

Her voice hesitated and stopped on an unfinished sentence; she pushed the papers aside to show where she had given up. From her long drooping hair to her indolent legs crossed at the ankle above scuffed shoes, she visibly represented her surrender, her temporary collapse. It did not seem to be noticed. The older woman's attention had been caught and held by something else.

'It's rare, isn't it,' Kitty Cameron said, 'to be able to make love seem ridiculous and tender at the same time? Though Byron's coarse about this compared with Chaucer. He does it better, don't you think so?'

Clemence did not remember about Chaucer.

'No,' she said, however, sticking to her guns, 'I don't think so.'

'Why not?'

'Because he doesn't mean it as much. He doesn't say it as if it were absolutely true. Byron believes it.'

She picked up the book and found the page she wanted.

'There, where he says "Alas, there is no instinct like the heart", the heart which may be broken . . . You can feel the conviction behind that,' she said.

'So you think Byron tells the truth, then?' Kitty asked.

There might be a catch here, but Clemence pressed on. 'Yes. I think he cares about it, too.'

'That's what Ruskin thought,' said Kitty.

A faint motion of curiosity stirred in Clemence's mind. A point had been made: she should take it down. But she forgot to ask where Ruskin said it, and Kitty neglected to tell. The discussion went on idly, the girl's mind ranging over the room. There was a blue glass jug on the desk, a glass paperweight and a pencil tray; the light blazed on them, bright and fractured, for a flash intolerable. She did not hear what Kitty was saying. At last she said, 'I'm terribly sorry, Miss Cameron, but may I go at one? It's just that I have an engagement.'

From *The Elders* (Constable, 1966) See also p. 112

K. M. LEA
LMH 1921, Fellow 1936, Vice-Principal 1947

The Scholar

I AM A CARETAKER and all my days
Go softly in great mansions,
Gathering little in converse or of praise
From their inhabitants.

Quiet as the dead – or dead it seems they are –
These great ones and my lords
For whom without command I shall prepare
And leave without rewards.

Dreary the order that no eye perceives
Sweetness unsmelled embitters
Chambers forsaken where on November eves
Impotent fire flickers.

Yet, lest there should return a single spirit
Consumed by memory
And his sharp-edged desire, to reinherit
His old locality,

Lest brute decay put out this little light
And he disconsolate
Sink into hell's dull day and fearful night,
Here will I wait.

**From *The Brown Book*
1931
See also pp. 112, 202**

*Early design for the
new library at LMH by
Raymond Erith, exhibited at
the Royal Academy, 1957*

A. Treneer (English) was a teacher and writer. Her publications include *The Sea in English Literature* and *A Stranger in the Midlands*. She died in 1966.

ANNE TRENEER
LMH 1929

Punting

PUNTING LOOKED VERY EASY to me. I got up early and wandered among the willows until a representative of Mr Timms was ready to oblige me with a punt and a pole. I stood on the punt where the girls and young men had stood and, saying nothing of my lack of skill, found myself adrift upon the Cherwell. Mr Timms's young man had the fun and I had the fury for at whatever angle I inserted my pole, and however I shoved with my un-governed strength, the punt swung round instead of moving forward. There was I, the focus of a revolving punt and of the derisive eyes of the youth who, shouting instructions at me, made me first confused and then angry.

At last I secured sufficient equilibrium to shout at my instructor in my turn to go and get his blasted breakfast and leave me to it. He said, 'Well, if you fall in and drown don't blame me.' I said I had not the faintest intention of falling in and drowning. With that I plunged my pole into the water again, slung all my weight on to it and the punt, instead of going round, shot forward at last – but without me. I could not part company with the pole. For a second I must have been exactly like a monkey on a stick, and then I was in the Cherwell. The young man's laughter was the kind you only get in Dickens; it had shaken him nearly into an apoplexy by the time I had swum on to the landing-stage, leaving punt and pole separate and at large on the river. I was hastening off without a word when he said, ''Ere, you 'aven't paid.'

For several mornings I went further up the Cherwell and primed myself with hints on how to punt. I wanted the skill to come to me when I was alone one morning. And it did. It came suddenly with pleasure and ease like a tune. And I went up the Cherwell, under the trees and over their wavering reflections; and out between the meadow banks where the cows were grazing; and past the reeds and the meadow-sweet; and I tied up for the first time for a whole summer day near a swan's nest by Water Eaton; and I came slowly drifting back at night, trailing my pole.

From *Cornish Years* (Jonathan Cape, 1949) See also p. 10, 210

If any one says LMH to me, I see the boathouse and the ladies' lace which grew so luxuriantly by the river. I hear the notes of cuckoos and pigeons – Anne Treneer

M. D. Yardley (English)
lectured in literature and
history at King's College,
London, and was
Headmistress of
Sydenham High School,
1942–66. She died in
2001.

MARY YARDLEY
LMH 1922

A Plymouth Brethren upbringing

Mary Yardley was the first pupil from a London elementary school to go to Oxford, and the first woman to gain the Charles Oldham Prize for Shakespeare studies.

We lived in a narrow world, and I lived in a narrower world than most. The restriction of our outlook was accentuated by our belonging to the narrowest of religious sects, The Exclusive Plymouth Brethren, one of whose basic tenets was separation from the world. This meant that all our friendships had to be within its circle, the arts were suspect and my library consisted almost entirely of my school prizes (fortunately it was a school very generous with prizes). My tutor at the Hall took me to my first theatre in Oxford- I did not dare tell my family. My headmistress searched for Trust Funds to supplement the college scholarship and my LCC grant. It was fortunate for me that it was all arranged before the Brethren learnt about it, for they strongly disapproved.

From *The Brown Book*
1984

My life with the Brethren was not all loss. I had acquired from early childhood a deep knowledge of the Bible and was impregnated with the beauty of its language. Moreover in my home the language I heard, similarly based, was always pure and unadulterated by colloquialisms and there was a natural dignity and simple uprightness in the hard working lives of my parents.

D. E. Smith (English) went from domestic service at Ditchingham Hall in Norfolk into the ATS during the war, and from there to LMH. She became a teacher and writer.

Ditchingham Hall was the home of Diana Athill's grandparents; her book about it is forthcoming (Granta, 2001).
See pp. 127, 229

D. E. Smith, aged 18, with the rank of Chief Volunteer at Inkerman Barracks, 1940

DOROTHY MORRIS
LMH 1948

From kitchenmaid to undergraduate

MY CIRCUMSTANCES were unusual – even in these times – for a hopeful university entrant. My father was a deep-sea fisherman turned labourer, and my academic background was no more than the elementary school in a tiny Norfolk village. I left school when I was fourteen and went to Ditchingham Hall in Norfolk as kitchenmaid, becoming parlourmaid two years later.

I joined the ATS as a Territorial in 1938 and was called up immediately on the declaration of war, once more to be in the kitchen, in army barracks. I moved out to become eventually the first ATS wireless operator trained to intercept German signals from all branches of their forces to be decoded by the Intelligence Corps operating the Enigma machine. I moved through all ranks and was commissioned.

From an Emergency Teachers' Training College – where I spent a year directly after demobilisation – I was encouraged to apply to LMH. I had nothing to offer academically, nothing at all, other than a passion for reading and the deep desire (secretly held from childhood) to write poetry. From childhood, too, I had wanted to go to university, and the child firmly believed that it would be perfectly possible to write poetry at university. Remarkably, Kate Lea let me in.

Few will have experienced so profound an illumination of a childhood dream.

From *The Brown Book* (K. M. Lea Memorial Supplement, 1995)

EILEEN ELIAS

LMH 1929

Charity clothes

THERE WERE A FEW State Scholarships, for those whom they called 'the cream', but I was, at most, top of the milk. There were also what our school governors called Leaving Exhibitions, for those going on to college. I knew they wouldn't cover anything like the total expense. For the rest, you had to scrape around by yourself. I became an expert beggar.

I scanned all the small-print handbooks in the public library in the Lewisham High Road, noting down details of funds I'd never heard of before. It was begging and scraping indeed; a bit here, a bit there. Somehow I had to make up the vast sum of £150, which would pay for tuition and keep for a year. To our family it appeared a colossal figure. There was a charity called the Girls of the Realm Guild, I discovered, that gave grants to needy students; would they give one to me, I wondered? The Girls of the Realm – I never did make out quite who they were – held a ballot for the most deserving cases. You set down your hopes and fears and monetary problems, to be printed in a circular which was sent round to the Girls, who then, with the help of their wealthy families, I supposed, decided who should have a grant of £20, or £30, or £40 if your case was an exceptional one, towards the cost of a university education for the hard-up. I pictured the Girls, whoever they were, with pencil poised above the circulars, deciding where the tick should fall, and hoped it would fall on me. It did. I was delighted when I received a really quite handsome grant.

There was the Thomas Wall Foundation too, I found out, which helped poor scholars with money. I didn't mind applying for that, for old Tommy Wall, of ice-cream and sausage fame, had been a poor scholar himself, or a would-be one, and I liked the sound of him. Rumour said he used to get the students whom he endowed to push him round the Oxford and Cambridge colleges in a bath-chair so that he could see the results of his generosity. Thomas Wall came up trumps for me.

There was another useful fund, which the Girls of the Realm also provided through some roundabout means, which helped people like me to get a college wardrobe together. Clothes were something else which put a strain

E. W. Elias (Lit. Hum.) taught evacuees throughout World War II, and then began to write about early childhood. A Quaker, she was on the Socialist Women Writers and Journalists Council. Her publications include the autobiographical *On Sundays We Wore White* and biographies of John Clare and Dr Arnold of Rugby (published in 2000). In 2001, aged 91, she married for the second time, and became Mrs Laurence Ambrose.

From *Straw Hats and Serge Bloomers* (W. H. Allen, 1979)

on our finances. You had, it appeared, to take so many things up to college with you, from dressing-gowns to bedlinen. This fund was a treasure-trove to me. Opening the long flat boxes of second-hand clothes which they sent me was like opening a Christmas stocking, for you never knew what they had found to suit your measurements: a chiffon evening dress, a flannel suit, a shawl straight from Marshall and Snelgrove's that must, I thought, have belonged to one of the Debs I'd read about. And the clothes were to go on being provided throughout my college career. I paraded in my finery before the mirror in Mother's bedroom, and thought myself incredibly lucky to be the same size as some unknown Deb.

But all this scratching around for money and clothes was apt to take its toll, that last school summer, in nerves, both the family's and mine. Sometimes I wondered if I would ever be able to take up that place at Oxford at all; the sums still didn't work out right. When towards the end of that term, a letter came from a generous old family friend, enclosing far more money than I had ever seen written on a cheque in my life – a whole £50 – I was overjoyed.

Right: drawing attributed to Evelyn Kirkcaldy (Music 1918). From the 'Flu Album', 1919

Mother stood by the kitchen table, holding the cheque in her hands, and to my enormous surprise I saw she was in tears. It was the first and only time I ever saw anybody weep for joy.

'They've got the new light stockings in Jones and Higgins,' I confided to Vera, then added, greatly daring, 'They call them flesh-coloured, I think.'

'No, they don't,' amended Vera. 'I've seen them. They're called Nude.'

I blushed. Nude was a word you didn't say. Why, people would think you hadn't got any stockings on at all, and that would be dreadful.

N. M. Binyon (History) was Scholar at the British School in Rome, art critic of *Life & Letters*, Lecturer at the Central School of Art, and an expert in typographical design and letter-carving. Her publications include *Lettering on Buildings* and *A History of Lettering*. She died in 1997.

From 'Lettering Became My Subject' (*The Brown Book* 1987)

NICOLETE GRAY
LMH 1929

Modern art at Oxford

BRITISH ART WAS JUST COMING BACK into the mainstream of European art – that is into the abstract and surrealist movements. In London people knew something of what was happening abroad, but we had seen very little work. So I decided to organise an exhibition, *Abstract and Concrete*. I invited Kandinsky, Mondrian, Miró, Gabo, etc. and English artists such as Moore, Ben Nicholson and Barbara Hepworth. Today the exhibits would be worth several million, but in 1936 Christie's were prepared to testify for customs and insurance that they were almost worthless.

I brought the exhibition to Oxford. There was no Museum of Modern Art then; Oxford was ignorant and philistine. However my tutor, R. G. Collingwood, helped to unpack and philosophers came and had fascinating discussions. After I had (with the help of friends) paid for the transport and assembled the exhibition, Lefevre, one of the leading London galleries, offered to show it. Perhaps they were right in not risking anything; I think that they sold nothing.

FIONA MACCARTHY
LMH 1958

Miss Grier acquires a Stanley Spencer

SPENCER'S PASSIONATE PLEA for integration not just with his fellow human beings but with the whole natural world of plants and animals and sun and moon has many echoes in the poetry and fiction of the period. There are obvious parallels with D. H. Lawrence, another product of the Nonconformist Biblical upbringing, with his vision of England transformed by love and truthfulness into a New Jerusalem and his struggles in finding a language to express the act of human congress that was central to this vision. *Lady Chatterley's Lover*, privately printed in Florence in 1928, was only finally published in its unexpurgated version thirty years later in Britain and the United States. In 1929 thirteen paintings by Lawrence were removed by the police from exhibition in a gallery in London and pronounced obscene. Six years later, two paintings submitted by Spencer, by then an Associate of the Royal Academy, for the Royal Academy Summer Exhibition at Burlington House were rejected by the Hanging Committee. The official letter of rejection used a standard formula that the Committee 'did not think these works of advantage' to Spencer's reputation or to 'the

Stanley Spencer, Tulip Beds, *1936. Collection of Lynda Grier*

From *Stanley Spencer:
An English Visionary* (Yale
University Press, 1997)
See also p. 61

influence of the Academy'. The subtext was that the Academy felt Spencer had become too idiosyncratic or too sexually explicit for these works to be exhibited under its aegis. Spencer, mortified and furious, resigned.

One of the rejected paintings was *St Francis and the Birds*, a picture intended to hang in the nave of Spencer's projected Church House building, and now owned by the Tate. An adoring flock of English farmyard birds surrounds a figure of St Francis based upon the memory of Spencer's father, going in his dressing-gown to find food for the hens and ducks. For Spencer it was a solemn painting of great meaning and he defended it with vigour against those who denigrated it as caricature. It was sold the day after the Academy rejected it and presented to the enlightened academic, Dr Lynda Grier, Principal of Lady Margaret Hall.

ELEANOR C. LODGE
LMH 1890

Digging for victory

OXFORD PROVIDED PLENTY of occupation 'on the land'. We gardened also with great vigour at the Hall, and I gave up games completely in order to work and supervise gardening operations every afternoon. Our best venture was a field near the Cherwell, which we dug up most thoroughly, burying the grass three spits down, and throwing up hummocks in the wettest part on which to plant vegetable marrows. We only used that ground for potatoes and marrows, and they both grew to the most amazing size, so that people used to come on purpose to admire the sight. We also dug up the grass in the Old Hall garden, and that did not do badly for potatoes, carrots, turnips, and a few other things; but our efforts in the Parks were wholly wasted. I do not know why the soil there was so impossible. We dug it up and buried grass and leaves, exactly as we had done elsewhere and we tried with nothing more difficult than potatoes and artichokes; but nothing matured at all.

Right: World War II – more of the same

From *Terms and Vacations* (Oxford University Press, 1938)
See also pp. 56, 156

LMH staff, including the housekeeper Emily Sherlock (centre above, and left), who worked at LMH from 1900 until her retirement in 1946

COOKS MAY COME and cooks may go
And maids depart in batches,
But with her eyes upon them all
Stands Emily at the hatches.

(Anonymous)

EMMA CAVE
LMH 1951

The first year photograph

THE GIRLS HAD AN OLD-FASHIONED AIR. Arranged in four stiff rows, they looked as if they were obeying instructions. On a flagged path in front, the holders of Open Scholarships sat on a bench. Behind stood the rest, lined up on three steps leading from the garden to a door into the college.

It had been mid-October in 1955, and a scattering of autumn leaves lay round the scholars' lace-up brown walking-shoes, their plain court shoes and little flat-heeled pumps. It was the era of the cardigan: either part of a twin-set – worn here, in two instances, with the traditional string of pearls – or neatly buttoned over a pale blouse. Skirts were of tweed, of flannel, of checked cloth. Flair was conspicuously absent. Only a rare outfit, only a rare face, emerged from the mass.

For this official First Year photograph, many of the undergraduates – never, then, called 'students' – who normally wore spectacles had removed them. Only one person was laughing. Evidently the joke had been a private one, for both her immediate neighbours looked serious, earnest. Such earnest expressions were numerous – though there were some modest smiles – and many girls appeared eager and aspirant, starry-eyed. But this effect was embarrassing rather than appealing, and quite sexless.

At one end of the front row lounged Castalia. She was either faintly smiling or faintly sneering. Although she wore no make-up and was certainly not beautiful, Castalia did not merge. Her small eyes glinted brightly under their heavy lids. Her thin bony nose was slightly crooked. With lean muscular legs crossed at the thigh, she presented the sole of one heavy brogue to the viewer. Her stockings, of dense mesh, suggested field sports, and a vast jersey, textured like porridge into which chopped straw had been stirred, came almost to the hem of her baggy tweed skirt. For this occasion, as for lectures and tutorials, skirts – otherwise shunned by Castalia – had been obligatory.

From *The Inferno Corridor* (Barrie & Jenkins, 1991; Arrow, 1992). One of a series of Emma Cave mysteries, subtitled 'Friendship, Revenge and Murder', it includes this description of the first year photograph. Castalia is modelled on the young Margaret Thatcher (Somerville, 1943)

See also p. 178

First year photograph, 1951, highlighting J. C. Cavendish, who writes as both Caroline Lassalle and Emma Cave

T. McLean (1969) played cricket for Oxford, and in her first year took 8 for 45 – perhaps the proudest achievement of her life. 'As it happened I was the first person to get a cricket blue both for Oxford and Cambridge, which is a lightweight achievement; the standard was low.' Her publications include *The English at Play in the Middle Ages*; *Metal Jam*, and *Medieval English Gardens*.

From *The Men In White Coats* (Stanley Paul / Century Hutchinson, 1987)
See also p. 116

TERESA MCLEAN
LMH 1969

The Oxford Women's cricket team

WE PLAYED IN POURING RAIN on a pitch lent us by one the men's colleges, miles down the Botley Road. It was more of a meadow than a cricket field, though it did have something approaching a pavilion – a grim little shed in which we sheltered when lightning stopped play. We did not have a set uniform and wore whites which ranged from jeans to shorts and, horror of horrors, divided skirts. There was nothing to distinguish Oxford from Cambridge, and team identity depended on us knowing each other. I reckoned my forte was my unusual spin bowling, but my captain unwisely ignored this hidden talent and left me out of the bowling attack, so it was up to my batting to vindicate my selection. I went in at number seven. The storm was immediately overhead, with thunder cracking round the ground, and we had nearly got the total we were chasing. There was no point hanging around: I launched some uninhibited shots, made a quick little clutch of runs, then was run out when I slipped in the mud attempting a suicidal run.

The umpire, I remember, stood in the rain with his collar up, shook his head and said 'Out!' As I walked past him he added, 'Silly girl.'

Cricket then was even more sexist than it is today, difficult though that might be to imagine. We almost always played men's teams because there were hardly any women's teams. Once we played a prep school about fifteen miles outside Oxford and it was peculiarly humiliating to be given out by a small, spotty boy.

E. Fairey (English), a teacher and lecturer, was a headmistress in Bermuda 1967–71, lecturer in garden history and a member of the Garden History Society, She became the historian of the LMH gardens. She died in 1998.

From 'The Gardens of LMH' (*The Brown Book* 1991)

EILEEN STAMERS-SMITH
LMH 1948

THE EARLY PROVISION OF TENNIS COURTS and later a hockey ground within the garden had been encouraged by Miss Wordsworth to 'promote the athletic spirit as an antidote to headache and lassitude'. Croquet was also played. Cricket however, was never allowed.

October 22ⁿᵈ   A Resolution was carried "that the Committee, feeling the strength of certain objections to the game of hockey, think it desirable that it should be discontinued for the present."

£10 towards

The LMH hockey team eventually overcame the objections entered in the log book on 22 October 1879

'R.C.E.F.U.B.'
LMH 1939

Oxford orthographics

THERE WAS A young student from Magdalen,
Whose tutor reproved him for dagdalen.
    He said 'O look heah!
    My patah's a peah.
You reahly can't tick off a "lagdalen".'

An eccentric young student of Worcester,
Once tied up his head in a dorcester.
    They said 'It's disturbin'
    You wearin' that turbin,
You look like your great aunt Augorcester.'

From Catherine Ing, ed., *An Anthology of LMH Poetry* (1942). Catherine Ing (C. M. Francis; English, 1933; D.Phil.; Henry Fellow, Yale, 1939; Lecturer and Tutor, 1945) was Fellow from 1964. Her publications include *Elizabethan Lyrics*. She died in 1983.

A lady who went into Wadham,
Was addressed by a don who said 'Madham,
    Though the quad's in a mess
    It's our own A.F.S.
Forewarned is forearmed! (Think of Sadham!).'

Anonymous poems attributed to Ruth Compton, Elaine Floyd and Ursula Blomfield (all LMH 1939–42). When they invited C. S. Lewis to come and speak at LMH, he replied in form:

Ursula, Ruth, Elaine?
They must be *noms de plume*!
So beautiful a chain
Of sounds who dare assume?

HEARD IN THE HIGH.

HILDA.   After all, one cannot expect much in the way of fashion in a gown.

MARGARET.   No, but it must be *correct*, and the quality and make are what really count.

PHYLLIS.   Your outfit looks charming, where did you buy it?

MARGARET.   At George Smith's, the Robemaker, opposite the New Theatre in George Street. He keeps a large selection and his prices are really most reasonable, it is a pleasure to recommend him.

B.A. GOWNS.	M.A. GOWNS.
27/6, 35/-, 42/-, 63/-.	35/-, 42/-, 63/-.
B.A. HOODS.	**M.A. HOODS.**
27/6 to 63/-.	32/6 to 63/-.

DOCTORS' GOWNS and HOODS.
QUOTATIONS ON REQUEST.

GEORGE SMITH

23 GEORGE STREET, OXFORD,

D. Quick (English) began acting in the National Youth Theatre, and while E. G. Thackeray Scholar at LMH became the first female President of the OUDS. She has worked at the Royal Court, the Royal National Theatre and the Royal Shakespeare Company, and recently appeared in the West End in her own translation of Simone de Beauvoir's *A Woman Destroyed*. She was nominated for BAFTA and Emmy Best Actress awards for her role in the television adaptation of *Brideshead Revisited*.

From *Waiting for Dr Quick* (forthcoming from Little, Brown, 2002)

DIANA QUICK
LMH 1964

Beautiful people

MY FATHER'S DEATH was the first thing that had ever gone wrong for me. Through my teens I think of myself as clear, undistracted, fully engaged in whatever I was doing, and confident that if I wanted to do something I could get it by concentration and hard work. And I was very blinkered. I had no critical perspective on anything. I was amazed, for instance, when Polly Toynbce, whom I'd known since the youth theatre and as a regular player in our Sunday football team (girls only allowed to be strikers), left Oxford after a year, hugely dissatisfied. I couldn't imagine that anyone could be having less fun than I was. Or wanted anything other than fun. There were some brilliant and beautiful people among my contemporaries. Emma Rothschild had won a scholarship in PPE at fifteen, and Marina Warner was in my year in my college, exquisite and already widely cultured and the belle of every social event. Tariq Ali and William Waldegrave were making waves on opposing sides at the Union and Sarah Boyd-Carpenter (now Baroness Hogg) dwelt in the sophisticated realms of journalism and Westminster. Howard Marks held sway in the druggy court from which several of my friends were exiled and then sent down when Joshua Macmillan, grandson of the former premier, was found drugged and dead in his bed. But I passed lightly by all these other student realms. I won a scholarship at sixteen and a half to a college which disapproved of acting. I adored literature but was hopelessly ignorant, and much ingenuity went on contriving to fulfil my twin passions, literature and theatre. I'd never got into the habit of watching television, and I was more or less blind to film – even when the tyro film director John Birt held auditions for a film he was making and asked if I'd be willing to strip off.

I never read a paper, didn't own a radio. I loved rock 'n' roll but I really only heard bands if they were hired to play at some ball where I happened to be doing cabaret. (I remember The Rolling Stones having to turn up for a May Ball in the middle of their first American tour, and being really pissed off. I was amused because I'd last seen Mick in the Carousel coffee bar on West Hill, Dartford, one Saturday morning two years before when he'd been agonising over whether to go on the road with the band, who'd just got their first serious gig, or stay at the London Sohool of Economics and complete his degree. They were going to replace him as lead singer if he didn't go).

BENAZIR BHUTTO
LMH 1973

Anglo-Saxon attitudes

I RETURNED TO OXFORD enthused with a sense of Asian identity – and promptly encountered my first case of racism.

'Where are you planning to stay in England?' the immigration officer asked me, studying my passport.

'Oxford,' I replied politely. 'I'm a student there.'

'Oxford,' he said sarcastically, raising his eyebrows. Fighting irritation, I produced my student identification.

'Bhutto. Miss Benazir Bhutto. Karachi. Pakistan,' he said in a contemptuous tone. 'Where is your police card?'

'Right here,' I replied, producing the up-to-date police card all foreigners were required to carry in England.

'And how do you pay your bills at Oxford?' he said with condescension.

I resisted quipping that I had brought pencils and a tin cup with me. 'My parents send funds to my bank account,' I said, showing him my bank book.

'How can a Paki have enough money for an Oxford education?' he finally said, pushing my documents back to me.

From *Daughter of the East: the Autobiography of Benazir Bhutto* (Hamish Hamilton, 1988)

II *Subsequent Lives*

LMH alumnae can be traced in a bizarre list of jobs: land agent, masseuse, flower arranger, goat and donkey breeder, small-holder, proprietor of a laundry and antique shop, potter, folklorist and 'manageress of one of London's reformed Public Houses' – Cathy Avent

CATHY AVENT
LMH 1939

War: a great career opportunity

THE 1914–18 WAR gave extraordinary opportunities to women. Apart from the nurses and VADs, LMH women became farmers and munitions workers, ambulance drivers in France, censorship and intelligence officers; some served in the Forces, others did relief work among refugees in Poland and the Middle East; one was a translator at the 1919 Peace Conference.

The expansion of careers for women after the war is illustrated by the variety of occupations recorded in the Register for the twenty years between the world wars. Our first MP, chartered accountant, factory inspector and broadcaster were among the growing number of doctors, lawyers, librarians and administrators.

While many Oxford women seized the new opportunities following the Sex Disqualification Removal Act of 1919, and chose careers parallel with those of their male contemporaries, others were clearly disinclined to take up work for which an Oxford degree would normally be considered appropriate.

From 'Children of the Lady Margaret' (*Oxford Society*, May 1992) See also p. 64

K. B. M. Jones (PPE) was a political organiser; correspondent in Vienna and singer, 1932–39; WAAF Flight Officer, and on the HQ Staff of the WRVS, 1957–67. Her publications include *Wings on her Shoulders* and *Greensleeves*. She died in 1998.

KATHARINE BENTLEY BEAUMAN
LMH 1922

Improperly dressed

THE MOST USUAL OFFENCE was that of being 'improperly dressed'. Some women persistently appeared with brooches or other forbidden articles of civilian apparel prominently displayed at roll calls or even on parade. When wearing the QMAAC coat-frock the chief delight of these offenders was to cut off the top button and turn in the collar, thereby revealing a few inches more neck. Others would sport their boyfriend's cap. Or a woman when out of sight of camp would produce a length of black braid (officer's pattern) and proceed to pin it round her cap, adding an officer's badge to complete the transformation. It was here that the WRAF patrol stepped in. Recognising that the tunic and skirt worn with the badge was that of the ranks, she would report the culprit who would then find herself 'on the mat' in the orderly room next day. The fines – of 2s 6d, 5s or 7s 6d – fell heavily on the low-paid orderly.

From *Partners In Blue* (Hutchinson, 1971)

G. Creighton (Classical Mods) was secretary to Professor Gilbert Murray, and edited *Lady Margaret Hall: A Short History* in 1923. Her three daughters followed her to LMH. She died in 1958.

R. Jobson (Natural Sciences, 1905), later Lady Holmes, insisted that women doctors of the RAMC should receive equal pay with men. She was Medical Officer with the RAMC in Paris and Boulogne, 1914–19. She died in 1963.

GEMMA BAILEY
LMH 1906

Unwelcome at the Front

Gemma Bailey describes the work of Rosalie Jobson, a newly qualified young doctor, during the First World War. She went out to France to practise medicine at the Front, but met with fierce military resistance to the idea of women doctors.

IT WAS A PRETTY SEVERE professional beginning for a young doctor. The wounded reached hospital in a terrible state, fearfully septic, with some cases of tetanus, many having received no attention since the first field dressings days before. In October news came that Boulogne was crowded out with wounded, and Rosalie Jobson went to set up an advance hospital.

The town was crammed with ambulances, jolting over terrible cobbles, and there were no surgeons anywhere; yet for two days these women surgeons were refused any work.

Eventually they started work in some sheds which had been more or less converted into a hospital. In the sheds were 800 wounded, waiting to be shipped to London, most of them untouched since their field dressings. There were orderlies, four nurses, but not one doctor; seven had been called to the Front.

> *My friend seized the chloroform bottle and I took the knife – Rosalie Jobson*

That day the two women doctors spent in dressing the wounds. By the next day a rough operating theatre had been rigged up, and the nurses dressed the slight cases, sending the serious ones on to the doctors to be dealt with in time for a hospital ship which was sailing for England at four o'clock. From nine till four they operated, extracting bullets, opening and cleaning out septic wounds, the only doctors at the hospital.

'My friend seized the chloroform bottle and I took the knife, and so we went on, turn and turn about,' she wrote. The military commission were very suspicious of a hospital run by women, and on their first visit were as near offensive as possible; but they rapidly had to climb down and admit openly it was one of the best-run auxiliary hospitals, and ever after they were very nice.

From *Lady Margaret Hall: A Short History* (Oxford University Press, 1923)

E. C. Lodge (History; D.Litt., 1928; CBE, 1932; F.R.Hist.S.; Librarian of LMH, 1899–21) had eight older brothers, and in World War I was fearless in running canteens and field hospitals in France. She was Principal of Westfield College, London, 1921–31. She died in 1936.

ELEANOR C. LODGE
LMH 1890

At the Front: France in 1918

THE HOSPITAL HAD BEEN BEAUTIFULLY EQUIPPED and prepared, but they had hitherto had little but local cases and their nurses were not equal to the sudden emergency. It was a scene of wild confusion. Aeroplanes were circling over us and the noise was terrific. Next day was a nightmare. I went round as soon as day dawned, and carried off two *plantons* with a wheelbarrow to buy all the provisions possible for the numbers which we might have to feed. We brought the wheelbarrow back full of meat, and all the patés we could lay hands on. The cook did not turn up and we were too busy to seek for her. Our *plantons* turned to and cooked splendidly, whilst we made coffee, chocolate and bouillon and prepared for a long day.

It was one continuous stream of English soldiers, for the most part wounded, all miserable, and dropping with fatigue. They had barely arrived from the Somme when the enemy began the advance. Ammunition, aeroplanes, artillery, all were lacking; half their possessions had not yet followed them; they themselves were worn out from their previous retreat. There was no resistance, our men were simply giving way and retreating helplessly. They had lost their officers, they had no one to direct them, there was no possibility of making a stand, and they were just retreating as best they could, apparently without order and without hope.

The canteen was full to overflowing, with men badly hurt or so exhausted that they could scarcely come to ask for food, and we had the same feeling of utter confusion and despair. The hospital could not cope with the numbers, and when the women had found men lying on the ground outside untended and even dying, they had insisted on the Commandant giving them a lorry and stretchers and permission to take all they could to our quarters.

The line was destroyed and no escape was possible, the small town filled with the incessant roar of lorries and cars, driving always in the wrong direction, flying from the Front. The Colonel took me on one side and said that the Germans were getting terribly near and that we might have to move at any moment. At Montmirail we halted. The town was full of wounded, and we were able to be useful, getting what information we could from the wounded English and writing it down for the authorities. For the most part the soldiers had no idea where they had been, or the name of the place where they were wounded; or when their battles had actually happened.

From *Terms and Vacations* (Oxford University Press, 1938)

See also pp. 42, 156

SUSETTE M. TAYLOR
LMH 1884

ENGLISH	RUSSIAN	PRONUNCIATION
Halt! Who goes there?	Стой! Кто идёть?	Stó-ee! Kto eedyót?
Friend	Свой (другъ)	Svóyee (droog)
I am lost	Я потерялся	Ya poteyriálsa
Where are the English?	Где Англичане?	Gdyey Angleechányey?
Over there	Тамь	Tam
Where is the enemy?	Где врагь?	Gdyey vrahg?
In front	Впереди	Ufperedeé
Where is the cavalry?	Где кавалерія?	Gdyey kavaléyria?

S. M. Taylor (Modern Languages; Baccalaureate, University of Barcelona, 1890) was an outstanding linguist, specialising in oriental languages and Spanish. The Susette Taylor Travelling Fellowship was set up in her memory after her death in 1920.

PRISCILLA NAPIER
LMH 1926

Armistice Day in Egypt

Priscilla Hayter (above, aged 11, 'miscast as the Good Fairy') and her sister Alethea grew up in Egypt before World War I. Kitchener was head of the British Residency when their father was Colonial Administrator, administering an ever less popular government.

From *A Late Beginner* (Michael Joseph, 1966; Hamish Hamilton, 1968)
See also pp. 67, 231

TO BE ELEVEN YEARS OLD, and in double figures, was stupendous, a landmark, almost a coming of age. The autumn of 1918 was also, although this seemed less momentous, crowned by the Armistice, declared on 11 November between Germany and the Allied Powers.

Cairo reacted splendidly to this event. There were fireworks, peace processions, thanksgiving services and jamborees of every kind. There was a Charlie Chaplin film in the open air, the first cinema I had ever seen, and so unspeakably and gloriously funny that Alethea and I repeatedly fell off our chairs, and our father and mother were not in much better case. The Greeks and the Italians, neither of whom had played a conspicuously glorious part in the struggle, held rival victory processions of great splendour through the streets of Cairo which unluckily encountered each other and refused to give way, and there was considerable bloodshed and many casualties.

King Fuad gave a banquet at the Abdin Palace at which there were pink sugar aeroplanes all down the middle of the table. The students at Al Azhar demonstrated, some against the British Army's continued presence and others for the hell of it, and several of them stabbed each other in the mêlée. The guns boomed out in salutes and the sirens roared in triumph, and a number of small shops were looted while no one was looking.

S. Grant Duff (PPE) was a journalist and writer in the Saar and in Prague before World War II, correspondent of *The Observer* in 1935, and Czechoslovak editor of the BBC's European Service 1941–44. Her publications include *Germany, What Next?* and *A Noble Combat*.

SHEILA GRANT DUFF
LMH 1931

The rise of the Nazis

In 1935 Sheila Grant Duff was sent by The Observer *to the Saar, which had been taken from German control after World War I, and was about to vote, in effect, for or against Nazism.*

THE ANTI-NAZIS WERE WAGING a desperate battle. The Saar was largely Catholic and the anti-Nazis had set great store by this; but Hitler and the Pope, who had been on bad terms at the beginning of the Nazi regime, were both astute enough to see that each had much to gain from an accommodation before the plebiscite took place. They had therefore signed a Concordat late in 1933 and the local Bishop of Trier advised all Saar Catholics to vote for the Deutsche Front. This was called 'realism'. . . .

It was not only avowed supporters of the Nazis who wanted to get the plebiscite over and done with as quickly as possible. It was also the earnest wish of Laval and the French Government, and it was certainly the aim of the British Government and of the British officers it had sent with the international force. . . . The non-deployment of this peace-keeping force was a bone of contention between many of the English and American journalists and the British military command. They were also critical of Colonel Hennessy, the British head of the international police, whom they accused of being a fascist.

This sort of talk considerably annoyed the British authorities. For English journalists to hold such views was considered 'disloyal', 'unpatriotic' and 'thoroughly objectionable'. It was in His Majesty's officials abroad that one met the nearest approach to the attitudes of the Deutsche Front. Just as it was 'disloyal' of British journalists to criticise British decisions, it was 'disloyal' of the anti-Nazis to have insisted on holding a plebiscite. The whole thing should have been got over without a vote. The Saar was a powder keg, one British officer assured me, and war between Germany and France had broken out in just this area before.

'For God's sake,' he declared, 'why do you and your like stir it all up now?'

From *The Parting of the Ways* (Unwin, 1982)

L. C. Holman (Modern Languages) worked for several years at the National Gallery of Art, Washington, D.C., and is an expert on war and the looting of art works. *The Rape of Europa* won the 1994 National Book Critics Circle Award in the USA.

LYNN NICHOLAS
LMH 1961

Hitler opens the Haus der Kunst

ART WAS VERY FASHIONABLE in the new National Socialist regime. In October 1933, only months after becoming Chancellor, Hitler laid the cornerstone of the Haus der Deutsche Kunst in Munich, his first major building project. Alfred Rosenberg was made intellectual head of the Party, with the title 'Custodian of the Entire Intellectual and Spiritual Training and Education of the Party and all coordinated Associations'.

The Minister of the Interior began appointing art commissioners in the provinces. Even the SS had an art branch, the Ancestral Heritage, which sponsored archaeological research worldwide in the hope of finding confirmation of early and glorious Germanic cultures. Councils of hitherto obscure artists appeared overnight to herald the Volkisch ideals; magazines proliferated: it was the hour of the opportunist . . .

. . . When the Haus der Kunst opened, Hitler spoke:

'We will, from now on, lead an unrelenting war of purification, an unrelenting war of extermination, against the last elements which have displaced our Art.' The audience entered the portals of the new museum, already dubbed 'Palazzo Kitschi' and 'Munich Art Terminal', to a stultifying display of idealised German peasant families, commercial art nudes and heroic war scenes. Despite the fact that the Führer was portrayed 'as a mounted knight clad in silver armour and carrying a fluttering flag' and 'the female nude is strongly represented . . . which emanates delight in the healthy human body', attendance was low. Sales were even worse and Hitler ended up buying most of the works for the government.

Quite the reverse was true of the exhibition of 'Degenerate Art', which opened on the third day of this Passion of German Art. In a run-down building formerly used to store plaster casts, 113 artists who had not understood Hitler's message were represented. The anti-military works of Dix and Grosz were called 'art as a tool of Marxist propaganda against military service'. Expressionist sculpture was accused of promoting 'the systematic eradication of every last trace of racial consciousness' for its depiction of blacks. Another room was 'a representative selection from the endless supply of Jewish trash that no words can adequately describe'. Abstract and Constructivist pictures were simply called 'total madness'. More than 2 million people poured through this exhibition, which was often so crowded that the doors had to be temporarily closed. Many art lovers came to see their favourites for the last time.

From *The Rape of Europa* (Macmillan, 1994)

F. C. MacCarthy (English; Royal Society of Arts Bicentenary Medal, 1987; Fellow of the Royal College of Art) won the Wolfson History Prize in 1994 with her biography of William Morris. Her publications include biographies of Eric Gill and C. R. Ashbee.

FIONA MACCARTHY
LMH 1958

An official war artist

IN SEPTEMBER 1939 BRITAIN declared war on Germany. Spencer spent the next six years working on another epic series of war paintings, 'Shipbuilding on the Clyde'. He is one of only very few official British war artists, his Slade contemporary Paul Nash being another, whose works span two world wars.

The impact of the Second World War on British life was very different from that of the Great War of 1914–18. The country was now faced with what seemed the real threat of German invasion; British cities underwent sometimes devastating bomb attacks; the Second World War effort impinged directly on many more civilian people's lives. In this sense the Second World War was a domestic war and Spencer, based at Lithgow's shipyard at Port Glasgow in Scotland, painting merchant ships under construction, was recording activities essential to national survival. To maintain supplies of food and raw materials in Britain enough new ships had to be constructed to replace merchant ships sunk by German submarines.

Spencer's vision of the artist not as the detached observer but creatively involved in the war effort itself

The upsurge of activity in wartime was the saving of an important Glasgow industry hit hard by the depression of the 1930s. For Spencer too the commission in the shipyards came as a kind of salvation at a time of intense personal disorientation. The lives of ordinary working people interested him immensely. . . .

In Glasgow he made the imaginative leap into the lives of the workers in the shipyards, inspecting their skills and their traditions of workmanship and finding a connection between the nesting instincts of the villagers in Cookham and the humanising tendencies of men in Lithgow's yard:

> People generally try to make a kind of 'home' for themselves wherever they are or whatever their work, which enables the important human elements to reach into and pervade, in the form of mysterious atmospheres of a personal kind, the most ordinary procedures of work or place. Many of the places and corners of Lithgow's factory moved me in much the same way as I was by the rooms of my childhood.

Left: Stanley Spencer,
Clyde Shipbuilding:
Furnaces, *1940,*
Imperial War Museum

Lithgow's shipyard also came to seem a Heaven, of a sort.

In his paintings of the First World War, Spencer had glorified the menial: the sacred unobtrusiveness of water bottle filling, locker washing, laundering, kit inspecting, map reading. He now focused his attention on the grave and exacting technicalities of ship building: plumbing, riveting and rigging; furnace building; welding, burning; constructing the template; bending the keel plate. Spencer saw the work as worship. He observed: 'Everything I see is manifestly religious and sexual . . . it is not that coils of rope suggest haloes it is just that all these men, hawsers, strings, as in all forms have a hallowing effect of their own . . . it is part of their nature.'

The 'Clyde Shipbuilding' project was conceived on a monumental scale. Spencer's proposal was for a frieze seventy feet long, composed of three tiers of elongated panels, each illustrating one of the major occupations of the shipyard. Each composition was built up from many hundreds of quick life drawings, executed in the shipyard, often on a convenient long roll of toilet paper. A *Daily Telegraph* reporter described how he produced a roll of pencilled sketches from his coat pocket, unrolling the thirty-five-feet drawing down the length of the table in his Port Glasgow lodging house. Spencer referred to these as 'scrappy notes but they are more useful to me than elaborate finished drawings'. At the next stage he produced more carefully composed and finished drawings which he then squared off. The drawings were transferred at full size to the canvas. The huge murals are composed of a multitude of independent groupings, which gives them the miraculous sense of simultaneous events so familiar from paintings by Bellini or Carpaccio. It could be said that in Spencer's 'Shipbuilding' canvases, Old Masters and Socialist realists meet. Spencer's self-identification with the workers manifests itself in the multiple self-portraits he included in the series, emphasising his vision of the artist not as the detached observer but creatively involved in the war effort itself.

From *Stanley Spencer: An English Visionary* (Yale University Press, 1997)

Oxford girl undergraduates, who are including in their subjects special studies to fit themselves for war duties in the Services, Civil Service, censorship, B.B.C., etc. In addition, they carry out A.R.P. duties and grow their own vegetables!

ON GUARD

Of the 160 girl undergraduates at Lady Margaret Hall, more than a third are trained fire-fighters and do a regular spell of duty. Here is Miss R. Brown, one of the first girls to volunteer, complete with stirrup pump and steel helmet.

One of the buildings guarded by Miss Brown and her fellow fire watchers is the library, where some of the girls are seen studying. It was designed by Sir Reginald Blomfield, and contains 2,000 volumes valued at £10,000.

Printed and Published for The DAILY SKETCH and SUNDAY GRAPHIC, Ltd., by Allied Newspapers, Ltd., Withy-grove, Manchester, 4.—SUNDAY, MARCH 8, 1942.

H. M. Pipe (History) taught history at Camden School 1949–57, and was Headmistress of Orpington Grammar School 1957–78. She has written a play about Frances Buss; was Editor of *The Brown Book* 1980–89; and, with Cathy Avent, joint editor of the LMH Register, without which this anthology could not have been compiled.

From *The Camden in the 1930s* (Camden School, 1994)

C. Avent (English). After five years in the WRNS, she joined the Education Inspectorate, specialising in career advice.

From *Careering Along* (Educational Explorers, 1975)
See also pp. 24, 53, 54

HILDA PIPE
LMH 1939

Bombs . . .

IT WAS THE SUMMER OF 1939, and customary for the prefects to take themselves out to dinner at the end of the school year, so we met that night at a restaurant. When we parted we promised to meet again in ten years' time, but where should it be? Lighthearted and euphoric, we decided that the centre of the Thames would be a suitable spot, but we never kept our promise.

Ahead lay six years of war, the school's evacuation, the building taken over as a rest centre for those bombed out of their homes and decorated with garish paintings of flowers, and then a bomb dropped on the building that we were to have inherited. But, as a lady governor said: 'They can't kill the Camden!'

CATHY AVENT
LMH 1939

. . . and bigamy

I JOINED THE WRNS ostensibly to do photography because I was not tall enough to be an M/T driver, but on arrival at the training depot was asked by the petty officer if I had 'Matric maths'. There were several of us in a group who had all left university a month before, and somewhat haughtily we outlined the honours degrees which we had so proudly and recently obtained. This was of no significance except that it meant we had at least taken mathematics to the age of sixteen.

One group of WRNS was sent to Great Baddow in Essex to work at Marconi's research laboratories in a category of rating known as classifier. There was only one male rating at this 'Wrennery', the stoker. To fill this post, the Drafting Commander at Chatham chose a man who had been sent home from the Mediterranean to await trial on a charge of bigamy.

We were paid 10d a day. Some of us hit upon the bright idea of earning a little extra money by going pea-picking on local farms which were used for experimental work in connection with tractor design. Despite my own rural background, I was as innocent as my companions when told by the gypsies, who formed the main temporary workforce on these farms, that the sack of peas which we were attempting to fill would probably fall over unless we steadied it with several large stones in the middle.

E. M. Houston (English)
is a poet and writer,
performer and climber.
Her publications include
*Stained Glass Raree
Show* and *At The Mercy*.

LIBBY HOUSTON
LMH 1960

Post-War

In 1943
my father
dropped bombs on the continent

I remember
my mother
talking about bananas
In 1944

when it rained,
creeping alone to the windowsill,
I stared up the hill,
watching, watching,
watching without a blink
for the Mighty Bananas
to stride through the blitz

they came in paper bags
in neighbours' hands
when they came
and took their time
over the coming

and still I don't know
where my father
flying home
took a wrong turning

From *Selected Poems:
All Change* (Oxford
University Press, 1993)
See also p. 236

*Flight Officer
A. M. Houston,
died 8 April 1943*

L. U. Cooper (Classical Mods; OBE, 1978) was a founder of the Writers' Action Group, which eventually secured Public Lending Rights for authors in 1978. Her publications include a biography of R. L. Stevenson and many novels, among them her first and highly acclaimed novel *National Provincial*, and *Unusual Behaviour*. She died in 1994.

LETTICE COOPER
LMH 1916

An air raid

I KNEW, HOWEVER, AS SOON as the raid started that it was going to be a bad one. I felt very frightened. It's much harder when fear has eased off a bit. It comes back like a wave and nearly knocks you over. I heard a stick of bombs drop soon after the siren, and I am afraid I got flustered, though I have always tried so hard not to.

The guns were banging away, and presently there was another stick of bombs, beginning fairly near and going farther away. We all counted them – one – two – three – then a little longer gap – four. Mrs Everyman jumped up and fetched the other two children into the kitchen. It isn't reinforced, but it is very solid, and well below the level of the road. Of course the only place that is probably any real good is under the stairs; but there isn't a great deal of space, and it is so cold standing on the stone floor in the passage.

After the second stick the raid seemed to shift farther off, and we all got rather drowsy sitting by the hot fire. Suddenly there was a whistle, not a very long one, and the floor heaved under our feet. I knew – I don't know how – that it was a stick coming towards us. I jumped up and leaned over Peter in a futile attempt to keep him safe. We could never decide afterwards whether it is true or not that you don't hear the whistle if the bomb lands very near you. The whole room seemed to come up through my stomach. There was a loud explosion, and then a long crash of falling stone. The black-out blew in, the glass cracked, the lights went out. The room was full of smoke and choking dust. Peter shrieked, 'Mother!' on a high note of terror. I heard my own voice say, 'It's down, it's over,' then Mrs Everyman's voice, much steadier than mine, 'It's all right, sonny. Mother's here.'

The room was full of smoke and thick with dust. But the walls and the heavy furniture had all stood firm, and we six human beings were untouched.

Mrs Everyman had lit several more candles and had kettles boiling on the fire. She had fastened the blackout down somehow over the empty window-frames and was vigorously sweeping up. The raid was still going on, but I felt that we were now immune. We had had it. We had had it and we were still alive.

From *Black Bethlehem* (Victor Gollancz, 1947)

P. G. Hayter (History) was a writer, biographer and poet. Her publications include a novel, *Imperial Winds*, and her collected poems, *Coming Home from the Sea*. She died in 1998.

PRISCILLA NAPIER
LMH 1926

Plymouth at war

During the war years 27 Plymouth-manned warships were lost at sea by enemy action. The civilian population suffered heavy casualties from German air-raids: 1,200 people were killed and many thousands had terrible injuries. One-third of the total population were driven from their homes by the bombing. Priscilla Napier's play uses a Chorus of Plymouth women.

WARDEN

Sometimes they come down gunning in the open.
Lie flat and still. Cover your head with your arms.
Unless you know the voice that's telling you
Never believe the News.
Knowing the voice, do what you're told to do.
(And, ladies, kindly learn to mend a fuse.)

Stay where you are if an invasion comes
And don't go cluttering up the vital roads
Like the poor bloody French;
Nor spreading any alarms.
Should you require to kill a parachutist
Employ your old Two-two;
And dig your family a garden trench.
You heard me then. Cover your head with your arms.

Never say die.

READER

Rumours and runlets, whispers in the air,
Terrors and torments, channelled underground,

MRS LEA

They say, they say, there's Germans everywhere,
They say the *Royal Oak* was sunk by spies
And what the wireless tells you is all lies.

MRS TAYLOR

They say the Fleet's not coming in again,
Not till the war is over, and they say
The rich are sending kids to USA,
Not yours and mine, oh dear no, ours'll stay
And take what's coming to them. And they say
There's Germans on the moor and starting fires!

From *Plymouth at War: a verse play*, written over the years 1939 to 1945; reissued 2001
See also pp. 57, 231

First – but still counting . . .

B. J. L. Warnock
(Jurisprudence; QC,
1986; Honorary Fellow,
1991; DBE, 1997) was
called to the Bar in 1963.
She was a Member of
the Criminal Injuries
Compensation Board,
and one of the
prosecuting counsel in
the Guinness trial. She
became Director of the
Serious Fraud Office in
1991, and the first
woman Director of Public
Prosecution in 1992.

S. Desai (PPE; called to
the Bar at Lincoln's Inn,
1958) was the first
woman judge in the
Bombay High Court,
President of the Indian
Federation of Women
Lawyers, and Chief
Justice of Kerala. In
1994, she became the
only woman Judge in the
Supreme Court in India.
In 1999 she became
a member of the
National Human Rights
Commission, which
deals with some 50,000
complaints a year.

From 'The Path to the
Indian Supreme Court
Bench' (*The Brown Book*
1997)

BARBARA MILLS
LMH 1959

First woman Director of Public Prosecutions

IF ASKED ABOUT BECOMING a 'first woman' by another woman my instant reaction is to say 'Don't do it'. . . .

The proof of true equality will be when a woman is appointed to a top position and no one comments on the fact that she is a woman.

SUJATA MANOHAR
LMH 1954

First woman judge in the Indian Supreme Court

WHEN SHE WAS ASKED how it felt to be the second woman on the US Supreme Court Ruth Ginsberg replied, 'It feels nice. But it will be nicer still when people stop counting.'

We have not stopped counting in India. I am the only woman on the Indian Supreme Court – out of a total of twenty-five judges. The High Courts have about a dozen women judges out of a total of around four hundred.

I started practice as a lawyer in the Bombay High Court in February 1958, after reading PPE at LMH and then qualifying as a barrister from Lincoln's Inn. There were only four or five women practising in the Bombay High Court then. Nobody took women lawyers seriously – they were birds of passage, waiting to get married.

A. M. Hudson (D.Phil.;
Reader, British Academy,
1983–86; FBA;
F.R.Hist.S.; Professor of
Medieval English from
1989). Other publications
include *English Wycliffite
Sermons* and *Lollards
and Their Books*.

From *Heresy and Literacy
1000–1393*, ed. Anne
Hudson with Peter Biller
(Cambridge University
Press, 1994)
See also p. 208

ANNE HUDSON
LMH Fellow 1961

The just laywoman

The Tracts of Walter Brut, a Lollard whose views are apposite even now.

WALTER BRUT'S VIEWS WERE OUTSPOKEN and in many ways extreme:
. . . war and legal execution were against the Christian insistence on charity;
oaths were illegal; the just layman – and, more outrageously to his readers,
the just laywoman – was a priest and had a duty to preach publicly; and,
most flagrantly of all, since the church allowed that a layperson of either sex
might in extremis baptise, there was no outright bar to the possibility that a
woman might consecrate the host.

M. I. Lusk (PPE; BD
Edinburgh) spent the war
years in the Scottish
Home Department. She
became a Deaconess of
the Church of Scotland
and was ordained
Minister in 1978. In 1988
she became Moderator of
Edinburgh Presbytery.

From *Wrestling with the
Church* (Arthur James,
1994)

MARY LEVISON
LMH 1941

First woman Queen's Chaplain

*Mary Levison first stood at the Bar of the General Assembly of the Church
of Scotland in 1963 and petitioned unsuccessfully that women should be
declared eligible for the ministry. She was eventually ordained in 1978 and
became the first woman Queen's Chaplain of Scotland.*

THAT WE HAVE ACHIEVED what we have without giving offence and with
a minimum of conflict is a matter for satisfaction. Wrestling there has been,
but that is a different thing from fighting and campaigning.

EDITH LANGRIDGE
LMH 1885, acting Vice-Principal 1895, Warden of the LMH Settlement

A first-rate engineer

Edith Langridge designed the church which was started in 1905 in Barisal, India. When the drawings were sent to the architect in Liverpool, the men in his office protested: 'It is ridiculous for you to tell us these plans are done by a woman – they are the work of a first-rate engineer.'

FATHER STRONG KNEW EXACTLY what he wanted. He asked me if I could draw. So I said, 'Yes, just plans and objects.' He wanted the central object to be the high altar with a canopy, and with a high chancel arch to enshrine it, so that was soon on paper. It was to have a nave and two aisles, each half the width of the nave. The builder said what the size of the pillars should be to carry the weight of the superstructure. And then I sketched what the inside of the church when built would be like . . . It was these sketches, that seemed natural to me, which surprised the architect . . .

No one ever said less and accomplished more – Janet Courtney

Mother Edith with the Duchess of York, 1928

A. J. M. T. Barnes
(Natural Sciences; DBE).
Consultant obstetrician
and gynaecologist at
the Elizabeth Garrett
Anderson Hospital, she
became the first woman
President of the BMA.
Her achievements, too
numerous to list, include
the distinctions MA, BM,
BCh, DM, FRCP, FRCS,
FRCOG, Hon. FRCPI.
She died in 1999.

JOSEPHINE BARNES
LMH 1930

Doctors' dilemmas

ETHICS AND THE LAW have a delicate reciprocal relationship. What is legally acceptable may not always be ethically acceptable and vice versa. The research scientist has a responsibility to take account of both.

Medical ethics means 'the obligations of a moral nature which govern the practice of medicine. They are the common possession of the medical profession and members are expected, both by fellow doctors and by the society in which their patients are found, to adhere to them.'

The ethics that are common to all professions are 'knowing', 'doing' and 'helping'. These are known as the three 'social values' in a recognised concept of a profession.

I am not a feminist –
I like men too much

The difficulties inherent in medical research are compounded by the high costs incurred, for example in developing a new medicament. Public interest in medical matters has been enhanced by the media and the public in general is better informed and less trusting of the motives and actions of the medical profession than formerly. Nevertheless, it is important that all research and all new treatments involving human beings from the moment of their conception should be conducted on the highest moral and ethical principles.

It is, however, not altogether evil that society puts brakes on the speed with which modern research is conducted and still more brakes on the clinical applications of such research.

The Declaration of Geneva, the Declaration of Helsinki and the discussions in the responsible press and on radio and television not only inform society, but permit society to have a voice in regulating the work of medical researchers.

Dame Josephine Barnes,
with Elliot Philipp and
Michael Newton, 'The
Ethical and Legal Aspects
of Medical Research',
from *Scientific
Foundations of Obstetrics
and Gynaecology*
(Heinemann, 1986)

The Hon. M. A. Fremantle (Natural Sciences), later Dr Margaret Jennings, conducted research at the School of Pathology, Oxford; was University Lecturer at LMH, 1945–72; First Florey Research Fellow 1952. With H. W. Florey, she published over 36 monographs and books, including *Antibiotics and General Pathology* – and, Reader, she married him. She became Lady Florey in 1967 and died in 1994.

From the obituary in *The Brown Book* by Edith Bülbring (LMH 1960, Fellow, then Emeritus and Hon. Fellow until 1976), Professor of Pharmacology at Oxford. She died in 1990.

From G. MacFarlane, *Howard Florey: The Making of a Great Scientist* (Oxford University Press, 1979)

MARGARET FLOREY
LMH 1924

The discovery of penicillin

AS A MEMBER OF THE TEAM working on penicillin, Margaret Fremantle [Dr Jennings] assisted Howard Florey in the thorough preliminary testing in animals of the toxicity, absorption, distribution in the body and elimination of penicillin which was essential before its efficacy could be tried against an overwhelming infection in the living animal. This crucial experiment was finally carried out on eight mice on 26 May 1940, and clearly showed that penicillin could protect against an otherwise lethal dose of virulent bacteria. That day has justly been described as one of the turning-points in medical history.

The work was carried out against the background of the fall of France, the evacuation from Dunkirk and the Battle of Britain, when at one point the threat of a German invasion seemed so imminent that vital records were buried to escape detection and spores of the penicillium mould were rubbed into the linings of everyday clothes of the scientists, where they might lie unsuspected until the danger had passed. Margaret's engagement in these experiments is recorded, and her name is included among those listed on the plaque in the rose garden facing Magdalen College, in front of the Botanic Garden, which commemorates the Oxford work on penicillin.

One of the turning-points in medical history

DURING JUNE AND JULY 1940, Florey pursued his systematic animal experiments designed to show how much penicillin had to be given, and how often, in order to protect animals from various doses of virulent organisms. Because he was working to fine limits he had to use large numbers of mice to get significant results. Margaret took over the preparation of suspensions of living bacteria and their injection into mice for therapeutic tests.

On 1 June she began, early in the morning, to inject a batch of 75 mice each with a lethal dose of streptococci. One hour after each injection Florey gave a dose of penicillin to 50 mice, the remaining 25 serving as controls. The doses were graded, in order to determine the minimum protecting dose. He repeated the penicillin injections at two-hourly intervals for twelve hours, finishing at 2.30 a.m. Within two days, 17 of the 25 controls were dead, but only 1 of the 50 treated animals. But, by ten days, 25 of the 50 treated animals had died, and 21 of the 25 controls. It was clear that penicillin treatment could protect, but that it must be continued for a longer period.

On 1 July another experiment had been done using 50 mice. This time the dose of streptococci had been increased threefold, the severest test so far. Twenty-five animals received no treatment, the rest were given injections of penicillin every three hours for the next two days and nights. Florey and Kent lived in the laboratory throughout this time. Every three hours each night an alarm clock woke them, and they gave 25 injections. This time the results were beyond question. All 25 of the control mice died within sixteen hours. All but one of the treated mice were alive and well ten days later.

Dr Margaret Jennings (Lady Florey) at the School of Pathology in 1944, photographed by the Ministry of Information film unit, which was recording work on penicillin

M. C. Robinson (Natural Sciences; BM; DCH; FRC Psych.) was a Member of the Mental Health Act Commission. She was a doctor at Lulindi Hospital 1949–59, and consultant at Durham 1970–86.

M. C. ROBINSON
LMH 1939

Rural hospital life

LULINDI HOSPITAL IS BUILT IN BRICK, but had at the time of my arrival a grass and bamboo roof which was threatening to collapse. After two years the complete re-roofing of the hospital with reputedly trouble-free asbestos cement sheets, instead of the grass and bamboo, made the hospital lighter and pleasanter, eliminating the trouble and expense of constant repairs to the thatch.

There are between 200 and 300 out-patients and over 120 in-patients a day. We have epidemics of measles, German measles, whooping cough, meningitis, Asian 'flu, chickenpox, mumps and dysentery all in simultaneous progress, and every possible dangerous complication of these, particularly pneumonia. The usual tropical diseases abound such as hookworm, bilharzia, yaws, malaria, trachoma and leprosy and the additional variety of animal mauls and crocodile bites. A recent development has been the tuberculosis work, and the ubiquitous and never lessening incidence of venereal disease.

About 180 operations are done each year and the number of 'incredible' cases grows; one of the most extraordinary was a man who had been shooting pig on his rice plantation when a large piece of his home-made gun flew back and lodged in his brain. This piece of metal, of peculiar shape, weighed 36 ounces and was extracted with very great difficulty and trauma from the inner recesses of his brain; the man, however, made a slow but complete recovery with the aid of penicillin, and is now normal in every way.

From 'Rural Hospitals in Tanganyika' (*The Brown Book* 1957)

E. N. Floyd (English), an
award-winning television
scriptwriter, published
The Descent of Woman
in 1972 to enormous
acclaim; it has been
translated into nine
languages. She followed
this with four further
books on human
evolution, which
she describes as
'progressively less
popular but more
scientific. Within the last
three years my ideas
have been taken a little
more seriously by
professional scientists,
and I have made
presentations of them
at Oxford, Cambridge,
Harvard and other
universities.'

ELAINE MORGAN
LMH 1939

The cost of a naked skin

Elaine Morgan examines the evolutionary 'faults' in the physical attributes of human beings, and explores the theory that our ancestors may have lived at one time in an aquatic environment.

DARWIN COULD NOT CONVINCE HIMSELF that being naked could possibly make a primate fitter to survive. This is what he had to say about it:

> The loss of hair is an inconvenience and probably an injury to man, for he is thus exposed to the scorching of the sun and to sudden chills; especially due to wet weather. No one supposes that the nakedness of the skin is any direct advantage to man; his body therefore cannot have been divested of hair through natural selection.

Most modern evolutionists – some of them more Darwinist than Darwin himself – would find it impossible to accept this statement. They start with the axiom that man evolved on the savannah, they observe that he has lost his body hair, and they conclude that nakedness must, therefore, have been an efficient adaptation for life in that milieu.

Practically all the contemporary theories about nakedness begin with the oversimplified concept of a torrid savannah and an overheated ape. It is perfectly true that the days are hot there, but in the nights the temperature can drop as low as 11°C.

In 1989 the BBC sent a series of outside broadcast crews to spend an entire day on the savannah, sending back live pictures of the wildlife to be slotted into the viewing programme at intervals during the day. Some magnificent shots of wildebeest, lions and elephants were obtained. But the most memorable shot was the final one of a couple of broadcasters muffled up to the eyebrows trying to keep their teeth from chattering. As one reviewer summed it up, 'The weather broke, the light went, and Julian Pettifer nearly died of exposure.'

If our ancestors had kept their coat of fur they would have been better insulated not only against the cold of the night but also the heat of the day. All desert animals have retained their fur. In hot countries, shaving off even a portion of wool from a sheep's back leads to an immediate rise in its internal temperature and the rate of panting. Desert-dwelling humans like the Bedouin keep their heads and bodies covered when out in the sun, just as northern peoples cover themselves with clothes when out in the wind, in both cases attempting to replace the natural protection that we have lost.

From *The Scars of
Evolution* (Souvenir
Press, 1990)
See also p. 48

Larger and totally aquatic mammals, like whales, manatees and dolphins, have shed all their fur and replaced it by the fat layer more appropriate to an aquatic existence. Large and partially aquatic animals like seals and sea-lions which go ashore to breed, often in very cold latitudes, have of necessity kept the fur, which is the best insulator in air, and supplemented it with the layer of blubber which is the best insulator in water. But even among seals – especially those which have been aquatic for the longest time – the balance of benefit seems to tilt in the end towards hairlessness.

The largest species, the elephant seals (bulls measure 17–19 feet and weigh up to 8,500 pounds), spend about forty days out of every year completing their annual moult. Their skin is thick, and the process of shedding the dead cells which continuously flake off from it is hampered by the fur. The hair comes off in large strips and patches still attached to the outer skin, giving them an exceedingly moth-eaten appearance, 'as if they were coming apart at the seams'. For the second largest seal, the walrus, the attempt to hang on to a mammalian fur coat was obviously not worth the candle. It is completely hairless except for a rather splendid moustache.

Because the largest aquatic mammals are the most naked, it is sometimes urged that our own ancestors would have been below the body size at which hair loss becomes the best strategy in water. But there are several examples which counter that argument. One or two species of river dolphins are comparable in size to humans. So is the marsh-dwelling tapir – the nearest thing we have to an aquatic horse. It is an excellent swimmer and diver, has a proboscis like an incipient elephant's trunk, and its hair is very sparse.

There is one major barrier to acceptance of the idea that our ancestors may have lived at one time in an aquatic environment. The barrier is psychological rather than logical. It overturns at a stroke too many of the preconceptions we have grown accustomed to living with.

MARY GOLDRING
LMH 1940

Technology and the thief of time

LAST YEAR THE SCIENCE MUSEUM, as a bit of a lark, built Babbage's original calculating engine, 140 years after he designed it. It is 7 feet high, weighs 300 tonnes and actually works. Any of the parts in it could have been built by Victorian craftsmen, but it happens to have 4,000 parts in it. It's questionable whether Victorian technology was up to replicating that number with the necessary accuracy so, although the mathematics were faultless and the drawings accurate, it has taken 140 years for the back-up technology to catch up.

There are other reasons for delay, such as the 'Cinderella' syndrome. Babbage may have been a victim of that, too. You can have a technology nobody wants and fusion is one of them. Manned space travel, I would say, is another. So are agri-chemicals: a lot of things that could be done for crop yields are not done because people don't like to see dead birds. Cars are not as fast as they could be. And at very experienced companies the executives themselves make stunning errors. I don't know who remembers when both ICI and Courtaulds spent millions developing smoking material that didn't contain tobacco. It smoked! Nobody liked it! And a whole tranche of development had to be junked.

One of today's Cinderellas, who might yet dance, could be the fast breeder reactor. Nothing much wrong with the technology of the reactor core, it works like a dream. What goes wrong with the fast breeder is the pipework outside, where heat from the reactor is transferred to the boilers via hot sodium. Inside one pipe, the sodium, and outside it the hot water, and never the twain should meet – unless you want to vaporise a large part of the Firth of Forth. The pipes leak. Welding them is a major, structural, engineering problem. I will bet that if, improbably, the banks wanted some kind of sodium water technology, or the toy makers or the people who make lap-top computers, that metal-working problem would have been solved in a matter of months because there would have been a mass market demand. People who make pipes and weld pipes would have had a real profit incentive to throw resources at it, instead of sending a few people with Elastoplast up to Dounreay. They would have seen the possibility of a lot of money, and there is nothing very wrong with that.

Here I think we have emotional hang-ups. Our approach to new technology is tangled up with our attitude to mass production and specially to consumer goods, and there is a deep-rooted feeling that gentlemen do not make consumer goods.

B. W. Edwards (English), was a teacher, a buyer at Peter Jones, and a benefactor of LMH.

BEATRIX WARR EDWARDS
LMH 1916

The Compleat Draper

Beatrix Warr Edwards described her job as the 'Late Buyer of Handicrafts at Messrs Peter Jones Ltd, Sloane Square'.

> Polonius: Do you not know me, my lord?
> Hamlet: Excellently well, you are a fishmonger.

From 'The Compleat Draper' (*The Brown Book* 1924)

IF YOU CAN FACE THIS RETORT from all who care to patronise your establishment you are born with the right spirit for shop-keeping.

You must be just so well-bred as to prevent an ill-bred customer from guessing that you are well-bred at all; just so ill-bred as to snub admiring young men sufficiently to retain your own self-respect and their custom; just so indulgent to old people as to satisfy them and yet save yourself from wasting more precious time on them than the business can afford. A good hostess should make a good shopkeeper, a hermit or a scholar never.

G. D. Browning (History) writes the *Weekend Guardian*'s column on office politics.

GUY BROWNING
LMH 1983

Ten cast-iron ways to organise yourself for rapid decisive action

1   START WORK half an hour earlier
2   Work in small digestible chunks
3   Think in the morning, do in the afternoon
4   Guard your diary against unwelcome intruders
5   Get organised before you get an organiser
6   If you're not adding value, delegate
7   Don't go to a meeting without a timed agenda
8   Travel only if you'll return richer or happier
9   Keep your desk and your conscience clear
10 Plan tomorrow but act today

From *Double Your Salary, Bonk Your Boss, Go Home Early* (Virgin, 1997) See also p. 98

SUZANNE GRAHAM-DIXON
LMH 1950

Careers advice from OU Appointments Board, 1953

ME: I want a job in journalism.

Adviser: Oh? And have you any experience?

Me: Well, I'm Assistant Editor of *Cherwell* and I've had some diary paragraphs accepted by *Time and Tide* and I won a fashion competition in the *Daily Telegraph*. I think I'd rather like to be a fashion editor . . .

Adviser: Fashion? [said as Edith Evans says 'Handbag?' in *The Importance of Being Earnest*]

Me: Yes. I want to go to London and Paris and Milan and New York and meet interesting people and . . .

Adviser: I have just the thing for you [producing leaflet] if you like meeting people. You should train to be a Hospital Almoner.

From *The Oxford Dictionary of Twentieth-Century Quotations* (Oxford University Press, 1998)
See also pp. 95, 172

I had the necessary qualifications: inexhaustible stamina, insatiable curiosity, and a thick skin – Nora Beloff on being a journalist

I managed to acquire some experience of writing by practising what Lord Beaverbrook described to me as 'the black art' – journalism – Elizabeth Longford

M. L. Rawlings was an
actress in stage, film,
radio and television.
She translated Racine's
Phèdre, and was Vice-
President of Equity, the
Voluntary Euthanasia
Society, and The Actors'
Charitable Trust. She
died in 1996.

MARGARET RAWLINGS
LMH 1925

Going on the stage

*The acclaimed actress Margaret Rawlings was the daughter of a missionary,
and was raised in Japan until in 1920 she was sent to school in Oxford,
where she met poets such as John Masefield and Walter de La Mare through
her talent for verse speaking. She won a State Scholarship to LMH in 1925.*

IN MY FIRST TERM JOHN MASEFIELD invited me to act at his amateur
theatre at Boars Hill.

The college refused me permission.

'Oh, no. I'm afraid dramatic performances are not allowed outside the
college.'

'But,' I said, 'there are none within the college.'

'Oh, yes, there is a College Dramatic Society.'

I found it was defunct but resurrected it and was responsible for two
productions.

Then, one day, I got off my bicycle near the Martyrs' Memorial to speak
to a friend, an undergraduate at Corpus, and said:

'I've made up my mind. I'm leaving LMH and going on the stage.'

'How will you start? Do you know anyone?'

'No.'

Then the friend said: 'Well, I know Esmé Percy. Some of us, members of
the OUDS, were in the crowd scenes of the Hell scene in *Man and Super-
man* when the touring company came to the New Theatre.'

Managers in those days recruited crowds and walk-ons from amateur
societies when they needed them, and the young men were delighted. There
was no Equity, the actors' union, and no one minded being unpaid or just
given expenses.

The chance to be on a stage and directed by Esmé Percy was quite
enough. He was a great actor and director. So I got a lift to London and
went to the stage door of the Kingsway Theatre where he was rehearsing a
repertoire of Bernard Shaw plays before going on a long tour of England
and Scotland. I gave the name of the young man from OUDS and sent a
message that Mr Percy had promised to see me. I waited a whole morning.
He came out at 2 p.m. and said:

'Oh, Lord, yes. You'd better come and do something.'

So we went down to the stage and I did my Cleopatra speech. He told me
to go and see Charles Macdona, the manager and presenter of the tour.
After a long wait I was admitted to his office and he said:

'Do something.'

From *The Brown Book*
1986

So I did my audition. He said:

'I don't think much of that,' and I said:

'You couldn't expect me to do it well with you walking up and down jingling keys in your pocket, sir.'

I don't know whether it was the 'sir' – we always addressed our male tutors as 'sir' – or whether Esmé Percy had confidence in me, but the next morning I got a letter saying: 'We can offer you the parts of Jennifer in *The Doctor's Dilemma* and Gloria in *You Never Can Tell*, and other parts and understudies as required, for £4 a week, starting date for rehearsals three weeks ahead.'

I went about in a dream. I conscientiously wrote out a fair copy of an essay on Sainte Beuve I had been researching after complaints that I seldom attended tutorials. I went along and knocked on the door of Miss Grier's apartment. She had often urged us not to be afraid to bring our anxieties to her, at no matter how late an hour. I told her I had decided to leave. She was aghast. She said:

'I am *in loco parentis*. What am I to do?' (A letter to my parents in Japan would take at least a month.)

I said: 'I have accepted the job.'

She was very kind and tried to dissuade me. She said:

'But if you are not a success what will you do?'

And I said: 'I shall work in the theatre, at anything – in the wardrobe or as a dresser.'

Neither of us knew anything about employment.

LMH theatricals, 1887

M. J. S. Waddy (English) is a writer, journalist and film-maker. As *The Guardian* correspondent in Latin America in the 1970s, she was expelled from Bolivia as a Maoist spy, but returned in 1997 to witness the exhumation of Che Guevara's body. She worked in television on many current affairs series, including *This Week*, and wrote and directed an award-winning film about Sigmund Freud in 1990.

STACY MARKING
LMH 1956

The Turkish Myrna Loy

THERE WERE REALLY ONLY THREE components of the 23 Turkish movies I was in: a goodie, a baddie and a belly dancer. The first two were always male, the third always fat. My producer considered himself rather adventurous including a foreigner at all. He was hoping to broaden his market, but I realise now that my comic foreigners satisfied a xenophobia as deep in the Turks as in the English.

My name was altogether too foreign. The producer walked around me during my first, ill-fated death scene (the one where they discovered my comic potential) and stated that I was not unlike Myrna Loy. So that was my billing: the Turkish Myrna Loy. I scarcely knew who Myrna Loy was, and wondered whether this was a generic rather than personal billing; was I one of a chain of Myrna Loys?

Once I was despatched to open a cinema on the Anatolian plains. It was an open-air cinema, with a screen hanging over a low stage, and lines of narrow benches on which sat impassive men, chewing sunflower seeds. They had never heard of me, nor of Myrna Loy, and could not give a damn about either of us cutting the ribbon and declaring this cinema open. But the film was *Some Like It Hot*, and the date was 5 August, the anniversary of the death of Marilyn Monroe. She first appears well into the film, with an incomparable, incandescent walk along the platform of the Chicago station. The taciturn audience rose spontaneously and stood under the night sky in silent homage.

From 'The Turkish Myrna Loy', *The Guardian*, October 1982

L. M. Davis (English) joined the Civil Service in 1972 in the belief she had chosen an Equal Opportunities employer. In 1985 she reconsidered that view and became a historical novelist. Pragmatism led her from the Civil War period to the Romans. She wrote *The Course of Honour*, followed by the long-running 'Falco' series of detective stories. Other details, some true, may be deduced from this story.

Lindsey Davis's many awards include the Authors' Club Best First Novel Prize, the first Crime Writers' Association Ellis Peters Historical Dagger, a Book Trust selection for presentation to HM The Queen, and the 1999 Sherlock Award for Best Comic Detective.

LINDSEY DAVIS
LMH 1968

The Short Story *(a hitherto unpublished short story)*
With critical apparatus

I SHALL NEVER FORGET my first offer from a publisher.

He stood there: David Warner's Hamlet, without the ragged knitted scarf. He looked nervous. It would surprise people to discover he was a decent swordsman. It would certainly surprise me.

He had eaten a substantial portion of my paella, and there was not much wrong with that, apart from the fact I could never make it turn out bright yellow. I get restless over paella. The business of steeping the saffron filaments niggles me. It has a faint unethical tang, like ivory and ambergris. I reckon that saffron is overdue for a radical exposé, then an old liberal-thinker will feel obliged to give it up. If the stuff squeaked when picked, it would be off-limits already. Sometimes you do see photographs of crocus fields, inset in a text describing the hapless bulbs being stripped of their glowing filaments in mid growing-cycle for Sunday supplement cooks. The harrowing article usually appears about three adverts before the cookery page.

Even in 1973 (for this is a period story), I used to dread that those dried wisps of stamen floating in the egg-cup of warm stock represented decadence, heralding the fall of civilisation as I had hoped to know it. In my heart I believed anything so expensive must be bad.

As you were then. I had things on my conscience, and there he stood. He was serving up some smart talk about off-set Litho and I should have rapped back a witty rejoinder on Letterpress, but instead I was putting away the tablemats and wondering why saffron never even works. He had founded a student newspaper, I heard. I was consoling myself that his stomach enzymes were not City and Guilds examiners; so long as they had had nourishment, what was a little matter of presentation? Why shouldn't paella be a pale shade of grey? It could be a local speciality from Croydon. It could become much sought after, once the great saffron exposé made the other colour unacceptable.

'So long as you can type it yourself,' he said. I wished he would stop playing with my salt cellar. It was a silly design, peculiar to the times – a squat troll in a funny hat – but it was a household utensil, not a toy. 'If you have any short stories or articles,' he offered, 'I dare say we could publish them for you.'

There are times when a girl does feel used. This child, I thought (myself six months older, so already in work), will never make a newspaper magnate. I knew this to be his ambition that year. He saw himself as the heartless editor, Walter Burns, spurring me to the typewriter like Hildy Johnson at full leap in *The Front Page*. I had seen the film, though not courtesy of laddie here.

'We can print anything – drawings or whatever you like to paste together,' he went on. 'If it's on A4.' How did anything ever get written when all people had was quarto paper and a fountain pen?

Four years I had known him. Four years exactly on January the Twentieth. I knew the date as certainly as I knew he did *not* know it. All that time he had been looking down his long nose at my attempted grim revolutionary play, my flirty verses, and my three-volumed sentimental novel (yes, I had written my autobiography at the age of twenty-one, in order to leave myself free to enjoy what remained of my life without the burden of constantly taking notes). Perhaps it was too much to expect a person with a nose so finely sculpted to reserve it just for breathing through.

So! He would deign to take my efforts now, build his own reputation, maybe earn his own fortune – as a favour to me. Print anything, would it? How about: I DON'T WRITE SHORT STORIES, DAMMIT?

I maintained an aloof calm. 'Short stories have never been an interest of mine.'

'With a very small circulation, of course,' he carried on, in case I was in any doubt about the exclusive nature of his new magazine. There came upon his face a look of gentle wariness that endeared him to many a fool of a woman; I was one of them. It hardly took Batman and Robin to work out that the students were so desperate for material they would print my old shopping lists if I entitled them *An Examination of Middle-class Attitudes*. Which they were of course, with all that saffron.

He was still standing there. I had made available to him four chairs and the laundry box. If I thought standing was a sign of respect, it would have irritated me even more, but this was just intellectual inefficiency. He could not decide which seat to choose.

I was reaching for my H. E. Bates hat. His problems were over if he only kept his nerve. I owned four ringlock files of satirical memoirs, a historical novel I had worked on for ten years, several folders of lyrical descriptions, half a page of miscellaneous dialogue for characters not yet invented, and a scurrilous ode. Not to mention the will to pen whatever he wanted from scratch. How could he go wrong? All he had to do was ask for help in a civilised fashion. Put on his spotted bowtie and allude to latent genius; acknowledge (within reason) that the scribbled jetsam in the cardboard box at the back of my wardrobe might give his so-far ill-defined magazine a transfiguring boost.

'It shouldn't entail much. How many words to a page?' he pondered.

I held my peace. I was already offering him pungent description, cogent thought, an abiding love for language and its lilt, and swift astringent aphorisms; technicalities were his affair. If he wanted to be an editor he would have to learn to count. 'Perhaps ten thousand words?'

'Ten thousand words,' I snapped back, betrayed into showing an interest, 'is a full-length essay on William Hazlitt, padded out with half-page quotations from all the Nineteenth Century Essayists!' He did not ask if I happened to have one, unfortunately.

He made no immediate reply, either impressed by the speed of my estimating or else bracing himself for the next cajolement: 'Ought we to wash the dishes?'

'There is only room for one in my kitchenette.'

He capitulated gracefully.

'The trouble with short stories,' I told him, 'is that you need to start by finding a twist for the end.'

I could tell he could see me making plans: a paragraph of atmospheric description (clawing fog in Croydon?), a section of 'wickedly accurate social observation' (government architects in Croydon?), rooks beating a turgid autumn sky over a newly harrowed field (*not* Croydon; NB check: does harrowing happen in autumn?), a timeslip, a railway train (better still, a railway bridge disaster), and something nameless and formless to leap upon the hero at the end . . .

After that, overtime, daywork rates, overalls, tax relief for electric light, and royalties. Royalties? No. No chance from Little Lord Beaverbrook here.

'I would have to obtain permission from my Department,' I mentioned, with the nonchalance of a wage earner in a neat pleated navy skirt addressing a mere aran-jumpered scrounger. This may have been my mistake. One does not, if one has an eye to the main chance in publishing, flaunt one's contract of employment at one of next year's unemployed graduate statistics. Give him time, plus the right input from his wealthy relatives, and this one might be heading up his own imprint eventually. 'I could make enquiries, or just stay anonymous. Just so long as you don't use anything for a political purpose – ' His was a *student* magazine and even in my brief career I had already signed the Official Secrets Act three times. 'Or advertise my official status.' I had no status, believe me. But I was already wondering whether I had enough wide-line file paper to start drafting a piece that evening.

It was not that I relished relating, say, the first erotic experiences of a spinster librarian or something creepy narrated by a Victorian doctor to an ingenue one windy night in a dilapidated Scottish castle. What I had in mind was reducing the scale of my long-projected bombshell paperbacks about 'Fingers' Mulligatawny, the loveable spiv from Ashby de la Zouche. I had a difficulty with Fingers, the only reason he and I were not enjoying wildfire cult success; he relied for his appeal on not only his stooge 'Thumper' Golightly, his sidekick Cosmo the jobbing builder, his eternal antagonist 'Smiler' Reifenstall, and his own interesting characteristics – an offbeat dress sense and apt quotations from Shakespeare in unlikely situations. The hold-up was that Fingers needed rip-roaring, ring-a-ding plots. Shrink him to a short story, and there would be so much less doorbell-dinging plot to invent.

'Is this salt pot made of pewter?' Laddie was still twiddling my troll, oblivious to the seething cauldron of creativity he had stirred. 'You would think it would be poisonous. What kind of alloy is pewter, I wonder?'

I looked it up in my dictionary ('tin and other metals'). Nobody could say this wordsmith lacked the tools of her trade. He seemed satisfied. He was studying philosophy. He dealt with the world's great unsolved questions; I could not expect him to produce answers as well.

While he kept puzzling about alloys, I tidied away the cruet myself. I would have to take the initiative. Plead with him to give me my big break, beg him to let me do for him what Byron did for John Murray. After all, I would never make a cook. I lurked in that bedsit kitchenette thinking, 'tarragon and garlic, cinnamon and paprika', so carried away by the silkscreen glamour of the names that I forgot to sprinkle any in the pan. It was a safe bet Wordsworth was never left to watch the bread rise in Dove Cottage, and wasn't Coleridge known to have let the baby's milk boil over in front of his eyes? So hold the front page, Harmsworth! A girl who had once set an apple pie on fire in a Baby Belling should admit it when her imagination was being misapplied.

'That was a very large meal!' he commented, stretching himself in the little armchair with distinct finality; as a columnist, my moment had probably passed. I could see how it was. Having polished off the paella, he had now lost interest.

I told myself I was lucky. A narrow escape. Those press barons with their air of Puck-like mischief all have malevolent hearts. The acquisitive bastards let you sell your soul because writing is the only job you know or care to know. They milk your inspiration, drain off your youthful creativity, then they terminate your contract and have your sandwich box hurled after you as they have you thrown into the street. I was well out of that.

'Have you had quite sufficient to eat and to drink?'

'Yes, thank you.' He would never make an editor. He was always so polite.

I wrote him his story. He had had his meal and gone, and I had finished washing up. I sat down and poured out for him the best that I could, typed it myself, double-spaced, on A4 paper, then, in case he had a deadline, I posted it first class.

The twist in the tail was what I should have foreseen. The lad *was* a real press baron: he promptly turned it down.

Critical apparatus (fragments of)

A draft letter to Barbara G. Peters of Scottsdale, Arizona, found among papers marked 'To Do':

My dear Barbara,

A contribution for the Poisoned Pen Press to illuminate 'the writer at work'? Here in 'The Short Story' the writer actually has a Real Job!

By chance I can even offer some critical notes. Ms Micheline Mildley Batz, M. Phil. (disputed), a compatriot of yours, recently sought my co-operation with her thesis. I was delighted. I love to help graduates make their names with intrusive biographies. The crazier, the better. Plans were at once afoot to make available to her every disk, draft and diary from my archives. I was the more thrilled to learn that she had contributions from the magisterial Professor Baillie-Wicke of Oxford and controversial TV pundit Prof. Zuazua (from that very, very new university), plus of course my favourite academic, Internet guru Dr Alaric Szchnout.

What a disappointment when Ms Batz was found so unexpectedly deceased ('the foul play is not being investigated' – a police spokesperson). Lamentably, the thesis is now missing, allegedly munched up by Penthesilea, her pet pot-bellied pig, and no one has come forward to finish her labours. However, her mother has sent me the remaining papers . . .

We need to talk terms, dear B. I see that your draft contract mentions 'two mauve towels' . . . *(tails off. Contract failed due to the impossibility of arranging payment of 10 per cent of two towels to Davis's Literary Agent)*

<u>Some notes from Dame Flora Baillie-Wicke</u>

1] The reappearance of 'The Short Story' is enormously exciting. Here at last is confirmation that Davis did produce a three-volumed novel, a welcome addition to my life's work on authors' missing manuscripts. This reference can, I contend, only be to '*"Buzz, Buzz!" – Hamlet*', the tantalising autobiography of which Davis claimed in 1995 at Boulder, Colorado, that it had been 'quite properly torn into 1-inch squares* and thrown away'.

2] Major questions remain unanswered. What happened to the great unpublished poet, author of *'A Bientôt, Mate!'*? What could have caused the decent government administrator in the navy skirt to abandon the index-linked pension for the notorious uncertainties of popular fiction? But we cannot fail to see the influence of LMH Eng Lang and Lit in the homage to fine writing – and the thoroughness, by which 'writing' is extended to mean payment and terms! My colleague Professor Borivej ZuaZua comments: And 'overalls'! What a discovery!** This insight into the author's customary attire while writing . . . (*remainder lost*)

3] The incident at the heart of this story is a conversation which can only have taken ten minutes. We are at the conclusion of a meal, about which we know very little (Was there wine? Who laid the tablecloth?). We proceed from the clearing of the mats to the re-cupboarding of the cruet. During these operations a conceit is created: the author, while protesting her inability to write short stories, is drawn into producing one. But where is it now? When 'Little Lord Beaverbrook' turned it down, what happened? Spiked? Returned? Simply 'lost in our post-room and we regret any inconvenience'? And could we learn more of the unsatisfactory figure of 'Laddie' from the great lost poems, which must have featured the great lost men in the author's life? Even more tantalisingly – where is that pewter troll salt cellar? Further research is urgently needed. (*Dame Flora has applied for funding; we await her future animadversions on these fascinating issues*)

Comment from Professor Borivej Zuazua

My normally astute colleague 'Faffy' Baillie-Wicke is barking up completely the wrong bongo tree.

I am, frankly, surprised that 'The Short Story' has been released for publication. I understood it to have been embargoed at the Public Records Office, under special Security provisions. I have been trying for fifteen years to obtain sight of this document!

Internal evidence reinforces my hypothesis that 'the Falco novels' are an elaborate cover. The postulated 'Fingers' Mulligatawny, unrealised hero of unwritten books, with his picaresque associates and 'ding-a-ling' plots, foreshadows actuality. The author we call 'Lindsey Davis' was originally recruited for the notorious 'Department of Health and Social Security'. There she adopted the conventional disguise of 'filing clerk', with putative responsibility for the second half of the alphabet. In order 'to avoid bumping into a fellow clerk in the confined rows of filing cabinets' she learned to recite the alphabet backwards: so useful for code! This story dates from a later connection with the discredited 'Property Services Agency'. There she allegedly worked on the consultancy for 'The Green

Cross Code Man' (clearly a paramilitary pseudonym) and 'the rather meta-physical contract for the hole into which the new British Library was put'. Curious details indeed. That the 'PSA' operated from Croydon has long been questioned. 'Ashby de la Zouche' may be significant. So did the trained cipher expert vanish into X (*manuscript censored*) while a series of novels was produced by a crack team of civil service drafters in order to provide a phantom existence while the operative ran dangerous missions in volatile countries? The 'Literary Agent' with whom she was provided is now generally recognised to be her Intelligence Control. The meaning, in that context, of '10 per cent of two mauve towels' has yet to be deciphered . . .
(Professor Zuazua has applied for funding)

By e-mail from Dr Alaric Szchnout:
Baillie-Wicke and Zuazua! How do these guys get tenure?
1) 'The Short Story' has been in the public domain for years; it was read aloud at a crime bookshop in London in (?) 1997.
2) This may <u>not</u> be authentic Davis. Cf computer analysis: key phrases associated with her accredited work never appear: e.g. Vespasian, Forum, Falco. Sausage, a trademark term, absent in any form, including Lucanian.
3) Suspect allusions. Heavy-handed Sixties detail. The notorious 'troll' salt cellar, cf also 'quarto' paper, 'bedsit kitchenette', 'radical' thinking, supposedly dangerous student newspapers, and the much-discussed 'David Warner's Hamlet'. Undigested historical research, inserted to lend spurious 'authenticity'.
4) 'Spy' postulation now regarded as loonie.
The Szchnout theory: Only training for popular fiction is Eng Lit and Lang. 'The Short Story' shows classic profile of old-style LMH Eng student: intelligence, determination and curiosity, educated to research material, produce opinions, and state views in clear, convincing form. Use of dictionary clinches it: indisputably OED.

But modernity beckons. This author has volunteered to lead my Virtual Dissertation team. Students have for some time been permitted to escape studying the literature of the past (which they find alien and difficult); now they gain a degree more gently, through reading genre paperbacks. Many find themselves e-mailing the websites of still-living authors, with anguished pleas for last-minute help with written work. This process will be rationalised: instead of students struggling, the author will herself write a dissertation on her work for submission in their degrees. Details of this natural progression in simplified scholarship may be found at www.the FingersProject [*Webpage currently under construction*]*

*Nothing changes . . . (LD)

M. A. Doody (English; Professor of Literature at Notre Dame University) has published works on Samuel Richardson and Fanny Burney, and *The True Story of the Novel*. She has written one detective story set in Oxford, and her 'Aristotle' detective stories are bestsellers in Italy, France and Germany. She is currently working on *Aristotle and the Mystery of Life*.

MARGARET ANNE DOODY
LMH 1960

THE CORPSE PAID none of us any heed. He lay at ease on a fine carved couch, his feet towards the gate. He looked a good deal better than when I saw him last. The women had well performed their grisly task of washing that corpse, and Boutades, though pale, looked as proper and pleased as if he had died in his bed. His white grave-cloth was immaculate – how unlike the khiton he wore when he had last received us – and the women had carefully wound the woollen fillets all the way up the throat, so that no wound was visible. This unusually extensive swaddling had pushed his chin up and gave it an arrogant jut. Lying there with the obol in his mouth, he looked almost smug. The women had crowned him with the customary vine-leaves which added a touch of the bacchanal oddly sorting with the manner of his going. Poor Boutades! I remembered the huge amphora which would never again offer him a drink . . .

The hired mourners struck up a fine threnody. They sang heartily, probably encouraged by generous refreshment from the kitchen as well as handsome payments. The prothesis had been so normal and so well-conducted that I felt somewhat cheered after saying my farewell, as if life might return to its ordinary ways. This feeling was indeed foolish. . . .

From *Aristotle Detective* (Century, 1978; reprinted 2000)

G. Williams (History), who also writes under the name Jennie Melville, is the author of over fifty novels. Recognised as the inventor of the woman police procedural novel, she is Secretary of the Detectives Club, and her many awards include the Silver Dagger of the Crime Writers' Association. She is cited by Lindsey Davis as an inspiration.

GWENDOLINE BUTLER
LMH 1944

DRESSED IN DARK CLOTHES, her head muffled up in silk and muslin, for she wanted to look well, Fanny Burney made her way out of the castle through a side gate which even her maid did not know of, and which she had learnt of through listening to Mrs Schellenbarter complaining that it was never locked and guarded as it should be.

Nor was it tonight, Fanny thought, hurrying in the moonlight down a winding slope into the town. She was going to the theatre on her own. She knew that she was behaving in a way young gentlewomen did not behave but she meant to write for the theatre, because that way came fame and money, and therefore she must learn the ways of that world. In fact, she wanted to, because she wanted freedom, freedom from family and the ordered rule of men. You could be respectable and be a woman in the theatre, she thought of Aphra Behn, you did not have to be like that licentious actress, Mrs Robinson.

She knew it was rash, setting out alone for the theatre, when two women had already been murdered. . . .

From *The King Cried Murder!* (CT Publishing, 2000)

C. Pateman (PPE; D.Phil., 1971) was Senior Lecturer at Sydney University, and Professor at UCLA from 1990. Her publications include *The Disorder of Woman: Democracy: Feminism and Political Theory* and *The Problem of Political Obligation*.

From *The Sexual Contract* (Polity Press, in association with Blackwell, 1988)

CAROLE PATEMAN
LMH 1965

The sexual contract

A WIFE, AS FEMINISTS have continually emphasised, is not paid a wage for her labour; she is not employed. Furthermore, employment is part of the public civil world, and a wife labours in the private home. Perhaps, then, despite the fact that a wife receives no pay, she is more like a servant, who also is a domestic labourer. A wife is now usually the only other adult member of the family, or if there are others they, too, rely on her labours.

In the past, a wife's position in the master's family was never exactly comparable to that of other subordinates. The wife of an American slave-master, for example, had her own jurisdiction over slaves, even though she was also subject to her husband. The most apt characterisation of the position of the wife was that she was the first servant of the master; or, more generally, as many of the early feminists insisted, a wife was merely the first servant of the master of the family. Mary Astell's pointed comment was that a woman 'has no Reason to be fond of being a Wife, or to reckon it a Piece of Preferment when she is taken to be a Man's Upper-Servant'. Lady Chudleigh summed up the matter neatly in 1703:

> Wife and servant are the same,
> But only differ in the name.

J. E. Hogarth (Philosophy; OBE) broke new ground for women: she was Superintendent of Women Clerks in the Bank of England for twelve years; Chief Librarian of *The Times* Book Club from 1906; Head of Indexing at *Encyclopaedia Britannica* in 1910, and Chief Welfare Supervisor at the Ministry of Munitions during World War I. Her publications include *Oxford Portrait Gallery* and *Women of My Time*. She died in 1954.

From *The Adventurous Thirties* [1830s] (Oxford University Press, 1933)
See also pp. 25, 70

JANET COURTNEY
LMH 1885

The role of women: 'Church, Child, Kitchen'

THE MORE I STUDIED THE DECADE of 1830, the more I wondered, not that the women's movement has got as far as it has, but that it has not got farther. It looked a century ago as though women must march straight on to triumphant equality. But history has a way of recoiling upon itself – its advance is spiral, not straight. Still a spiral mounts.

Just how and why the check came is a little difficult to determine. But it seems to have come with Queen Victoria. Admirable example as she was in her own person of a woman's ability to rule, she had no greater belief in the capacity of the rank and file than have other exceptional women.

It counted for much that Queen Victoria had married a German. What better way to prevent illicit feminine influence than to embrace his ideal of wifely submission and call women back to 'Church, Child, Kitchen'?

C. M. O. Fawcett has always painted, doing illustrations for *Isis* while sudying and having one of her four children during her final year at LMH (Boris Johnson, MP and Editor of *The Spectator*, is her son). Her first exhibition was held in the Maudsley Hospital, and since then she has shown in Brussels and New York. Commissioned portraits include the actress Joanna Lumley, the SDP 'Gang of Four' and the editor of *The Times*. This self-portrait is part of the LMH collection.

CHARLOTTE WAHL
LMH 1961
Self-portrait

A. C. Hayter (History; OBE, 1970; FRSL; Heinemann Award RSL, 1962; Leverhulme Award, 1966; British Academy Rose Mary Crawshay Prize, 1968) was on the editorial staff of *Country Life*, 1933–38. In the war she worked on postal censorship; and then for the British Council, 1945–71, in Athens, Paris, Belgium and Luxembourg. She was a Governor of the Old Vic and Sadler's Wells theatres. Her publications include *Opium and the Romantic Imagination*; *Coleridge's Journey to Malta*; and *Horatio's Version*.

From *Elizabeth Barrett Browning* (Writers and their Works, no. 182, British Council, National Book League, and Longmans, 1965)
See also p. 227

ALETHEA HAYTER
LMH 1929

A poet not a poetess

WHEN WORDSWORTH DIED, just half way through the nineteenth century, and a successor for him as Poet Laureate had to be found, the claims of Elizabeth Barrett Browning to succeed him were seriously canvassed. It was suggested that a female Poet Laureate would be particularly suitable when a woman was on the throne of England; but the influential Athenaeum flatly stated that in any case no living poet of either sex had a higher claim than Mrs Browning's. This seems to us a startling pronouncement to have been made the same day – 1 June 1850 – on which *In Memoriam* was published, and Tennyson in fact got the Laureateship.

The suggestion that a female Sovereign should have a female Poet Laureate seemed foolish enough to Mrs Browning. She thought of herself as a poet, not a poetess; she considered that poetry should be judged by its merits, not by the sex of its writers. 'When I talk of women, I do not speak of them to a separate, peculiar and womanly standard, but according to the common standard of human nature,' she said. But it has never been possible for critics to disentangle Mrs Browning from her sex. She was always being classed by her contemporaries as the top woman poet (generally bracketed with Sappho), not simply as a good or very good, or fairly good, poet. No such woman writer would probably come again for a millennium, wrote Sydney Dobell in 1850; but he went on to say that no woman writer, not even Mrs Browning, would ever write a great poem.

'She was a woman of real genius, I know; but what is the upshot of it all? She and her sex had better mind the kitchen and the children,' said FitzGerald.

Elizabeth Barrett Browning was as much obscured as a poet by her sex and her personal legend as Byron was by his. It is therefore difficult to assess her achievement as objectively as that of other nineteenth-century poets such as Patmore, or Clough or Meredith, with whom she might reasonably be classed; but she has in fact much more in common with them than with Christina Rossetti or Emily Brontë.

E. G. Harwood (History; OBE, 1964; FRSL). Her biography of John Keble won the James Tait Black Prize in 1963; other publications include biographies of Elizabeth Wordsworth, Queen Alexandra, Charlotte Yonge and Christina Rosetti.

From *Mrs Gladstone* (Constable, 1956)
See also p. 24

GEORGINA BATTISCOMBE
LMH 1924

An unsung career

WOMEN ACHIEVE FAME, and with fame a biography, because they are notable as artists, authors or actresses, as explorers or aviators or social reformers, as saints or courtesans, but never because they are notable as wives. Yet matrimony remains the most unusual, as it is by far and away the most popular, of feminine careers. Why then does it go unhonoured and unsung? Even the Christian Church seems to countenance this attitude: the calendar is liberally besprinkled with the names of virgin saints, but the number of 'godly matrons' can be counted on the fingers of one hand. Many famous women are, of coure, married, but they are famous for reasons which have nothing to do with their marriage. Elizabeth Fry, for instance, would have been equally renowned had she remained Miss Gurney, and Elizabeth Barrett Browning's claim to fame does not rest upon the fact that she was Robert's wife.

Marriage, however, can of itself become a woman's life work, and there is no career more exciting than marriage to a great man. Catherine Gladstone is a remarkable instance of a brilliant woman married to a brilliant man and finding in marriage the ideal outlet for her energies and talents. Her husband was one of the greatest men of the century, and she herself possessed something of this quality of greatness. Her beauty, charm and originality made her an outstanding figure in any company; she was a little of a genius and rather more of a saint. In her own right she deserves remembrance, but she is chiefly important as affording a new means of approach to the somewhat baffling and distant figure of Gladstone himself.

Without Catherine, William Gladstone's life would have been comfortless and unhappy; without William, Catherine's life would have been emptied of its essential significance.

MARY WARNOCK
LMH 1942, 1946, Research Fellow 1972

Mary Warnock had a 'supremely happy childhood'. She was the youngest of seven children, born seven months after the death of her father in an outbreak of diphtheria.

MY MOTHER, WHO MADE NO SECRET of her preference for boys over girls, must have been greatly disappointed that her two youngest children were both girls. She told me, when I was about three years old, how deeply she wished that I had been a boy. I think, even at that time, I partly understood; but it did not make me at all sorry for her. I felt, if anything, a bit indignant that she should overlook the advantages of having me (ME) as a daughter. I was, I think, a self-pleased child, perfectly content to be who I was, even if others might wish me to be different, as they often did.

It is perhaps worth remarking how supremely self-centred children are. Having been told by well-meaning adults that my father was in heaven, I did not think it in the least odd that in church everyone should address their prayers to him: 'Our Father, which art in heaven . . .'

From *A Memoir: People and Places* (Duckworth, 2000)
See also pp. 13, 194

Mary Warnock on the beach, aged five

B. M. Strachey (History)
worked for the BBC
1940–74, becoming
Chief Planner of the
World Service in 1964.
She travelled widely,
including a trip
to Australia in a
windjammer and to
India on one of the
first Overlander buses.
She died in 1999.

BARBARA STRACHEY
LMH 1930

Barbara Strachey came from an extraordinary matriarchy. Her grandmother Mary Pearsall Smith eloped with Bernard Berenson; her great-aunt Alys was miserably married to the philosopher Bertrand Russell; her mother Ray was a pioneer feminist; her father Oliver was a brother of Lytton Strachey, and her aunt was married to the brother of Virginia Woolf. Her biography of the Pearsall Smiths was based on over 20,000 family letters. Here she describes herself as a baby.

BARBARA'S BROTHER CHRISTOPHER was all sensitivity and intellect, who was heard explaining to his nurse at the age of five what a gradient of one in four meant, and who used to insist on playing imaginary three-dimensional noughts and crosses in his mother's bed in the early morning. But it was Barbara, as the eldest girl, who was favoured by the older generation. Her mother Ray said of her when she was a baby: 'Barbara . . . is a monster. She grows and grows and has the appetite of – her mother and grandmother – and a great brick red face and bellowing voice and stamping feet, and the energy of Uncle Horace in a "happy" mood.' This was the kind of child her great grandmother would have approved of, and so did her grandmother, even though she was hard to manage. Mary, happily recognising her own image no doubt, wrote to Bernard Berenson, 'I find that I feel the greatest elan of instinctive love for Barbara when she is naughtiest, screaming "I want, I want" and beating one with her little fists. It is such a vigorous asser-tion of her separate personality that it vivifies all mine.' Unfortunately such approval – such fellow-feeling, perhaps – was not conducive to discipline.

From *Remarkable
Relations* (Victor
Gollancz, 1981)
See also p. 232

NORA BELOFF
LMH 1937

WOULD THE SOVIET UNION be run more rationally and less harshly if women rather than men were in charge ? My legal textbook had nothing on women's rights as, in principle, there is full sexual equality. But principle is one thing and practice another. The males dominate every institution from the Politburo down to the smallest factory or farm.

Men are in short supply and, having chosen a wife, they expect to be looked after. The women thus combine full-time jobs with bringing up families, cleaning the house, standing in queues and very often sharing the kitchen with others. No wonder they employ go-slow tactics in their reproductive tasks.

From *No Travel
Like Russian Travel*
(Allen & Unwin, 1979)
See also pp. 95, 172

S. H. Franks (PPE) went
on to Harvard as a
Kennedy Scholar in 1978.
For ten years she was
a BBC TV producer, and
is now an independent
journalist, lecturer
and producer. Her
publications include
*Race and Affirmative
Action*; *Writings on the
Wall* and *Dished – The
Rise and Fall of BSkyB*.

SUZANNE FRANKS
LMH 1975

Having none of it

WOMEN ARRIVED AT THE PARTY too late. By the time they were poised to join the workplace en masse the conditions and rules had made it an unrecognisable and constantly changing environment. They have transformed their lives and found a new identity, not instead of, but in addition to their old one.

As soon as there is any suggestion that men might also change a little or expand their identity into new areas, we hit panic mode: talk of crises, men as victims and the grumbling of a backlash against women in work. The prospect, let alone the reality, of change brings shudders and warnings about how powerful women are destroying men. This argument resonates in the most unexpected quarters. Indeed even erstwhile ardent feminists (such as the author Fay Weldon) blame women for reduced sperm counts and argue bizarrely that what we really need is more unequal pay for women. No one explains how a handful of women in senior jobs plus a growing number of low-paid service workers threaten to emasculate society, but they conclude (rather like the Promise Keepers movement in the United States) that if women would go back home, then the world would return to the way it always was, crime would reduce, families would be healed and we would all be happier.

If work brings salvation, whilst conditions become tougher, then politicians need to understand that that other convenient political icon, the family, will start to falter. Educated young women with aspirations and ambitions are opting out of motherhood. In Britain more than one in five women born in the Sixties are 'voluntarily childless' and the proportion is projected to rise, whilst in Catholic family-loving Italy the fertility rate has sunk as low as 1.2 and in very few Western countries is it still above the magic 2.1 'replacement level'. There is growing anxiety across Europe and Japan about the imbalance of an ever-greying population and fewer children. Yet there is no official recognition that the declining birthrate might just have something to do with the absence of social support for parenting.

From *Having None of It:
Women, Men and the
Future of Work*
(Granta, 1999)

Anne Stevenson is a poet and literary critic. Eight collections of her poetry were published by Oxford University Press between 1974 and 1996, including *Collected Poems, 1955–1995*. Her latest collection, *Granny Scarecrow* (Bloodaxe Books, 2000) was shortlisted for the Whitbread and Eliot prizes.

From *Between the Iceberg and the Ship* (University of Michigan Press, 1998)
See also p. 180

ANNE STEVENSON
LMH Research Fellow 1975

The complete woman

THE TROUBLE IN Sylvia Plath's *The Bell Jar* seems to be this: throughout most of her life Esther has pulled herself to the top of her society – at school, at college – by native intelligence and stupendous willpower. Now, suddenly, she finds that she is a victim of forces beyond her control, forces that are also desires. She wants to be a complete woman, but in most womanly roles she can't excel. Why can she not cook, take shorthand, dance, play the piano, translate languages, do all the things in the world women are expected to do to help men? And why, on the other hand, do the things she can do (write, win academic prizes, win scholarships) seem not to matter to other people, particularly men – or, if they do matter, lead to disillusionment?

L. E. Miller (English) is a writer, critic and literary journalist for *The Times*, *The Daily Telegraph* and *The Observer*, and was Deputy Literary Editor of *The Independent*. She is the daughter of A. E. M. Davies (LMH 1958), and is married to the tenor Ian Bostridge. *The Brontë Myth* is her first book.

From *The Brontë Myth* (Jonathan Cape, 2001)

LUCASTA MILLER
LMH 1985

Putting the writing first

BOTH CHARLOTTE BRONTË and Sylvia Plath were ambitious for literary fame but would come to be remembered, in their different ways, as icons of female suffering. Like Charlotte's more than a century ago, Plath's private life has become a very public tragedy, overshadowing her works in the collective imagination. Both may have fed their personal experiences into their art, but this process of transfiguration would often be ignored in favour of a gossipy desire to know and possess the background 'truth' – a desire so compulsive that, in the case of Emily  Brontë, the obvious inaccessibility of the 'truth' did not prevent biographers from inventing it. We have to decide where the cultural value of these artists lies. It is time to turn the tables and put the writings first.

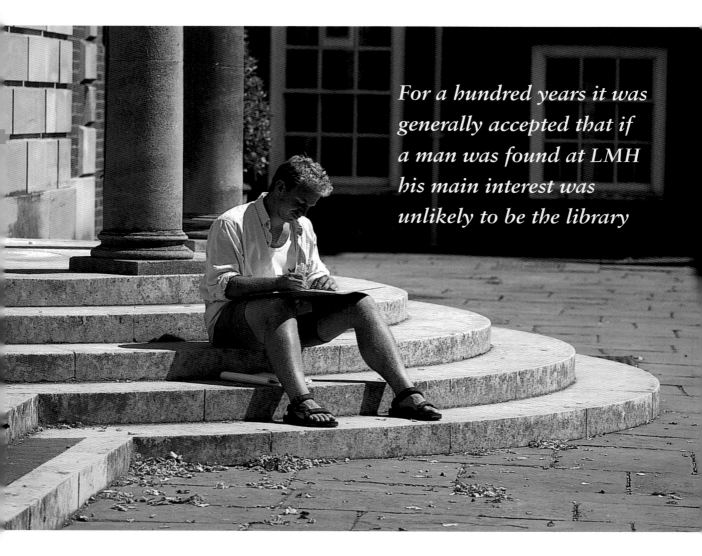

For a hundred years it was generally accepted that if a man was found at LMH his main interest was unlikely to be the library

It took some time before many of the venerable women dons could accept that men had a right to be in the building – Guy Browning on the arrival of men, The Times, 9 October 1979

C. C. D. Robson (History) filmed in Afghanistan behind Mujahideen lines in 1986, before becoming an advertising account executive. He is now CEO of an eBusiness solutions provider ranked in the top five in Europe.

From 'Afghanistan – Empty Valleys, Full Hearts' (*The Brown Book* 1989)

CHRISTOPHER ROBSON
LMH 1983

In 1986 Christopher Robson spent a year with the Mujahideen.

IN TERIMANGAL YOU CAN BUY Kalashnikovs and rocket-propelling guns. This town in northern Pakistan is where weapons are distributed to the Afghan resistance, and the region is closed to foreigners. I was dressed as an Afghan with a woollen cap, baggy trousers and an embroidered rug around my shoulders, preparing to slip through the border into Afghanistan.

At nightfall we crossed by jeep, bumping haphazardly through the darkness to our first guerrilla base. We passed a gun emplacement as we arrived at a hut made of dried mud and built into the hill. Several bearded Mujahideen were sitting cross-legged against the walls on which Kalashnikovs and other weapons hung like sides of ham. We were now in the war zone, and next morning we heard the first ominous humming of two helicopter gunships.

Our guide Habibullah declared prophetically at the beginning of each valley that Jekadalek, our final destination, lay beyond the mountain. Yet as we struggled over each new mountain I began to doubt it really existed. By day my mouth was so parched that I could hardly speak, by night it rattled in the cold as we stumbled without sleep over the mountains. Occasionally we rested; lunch was nan bread soaked in oil, for dinner it was soaked in sour milk.

When we finally arrived, the valley was littered with the wreckage of war. Houses were empty or destroyed, the graves for the Mujahideen were sickeningly abundant and bomb craters lay everywhere. Many were full of water, young soldiers swimming in them. All around were unidentifiable steel carcasses and large unexploded bombs. Several Mujahideen were now sitting joking, their rockets finished. They seemed oblivious to the war that continued around them, and it had not occurred to them to leave: this harsh and mountainous countryside is their home.

The following day we were bombed. Five Russian SU-24s swept down on our position. The Mujahideen scattered to gun posts to hide, or merely to watch. I started filming out in the open as two planes began their dive. They descended lower and lower: their retaliation would be swift. But the Russian bombs landed harmlessly below us. The apparent inefficiency of some of the most sophisticated military technology in the world astounded me. Within an hour the guerrillas were swimming in the bomb craters, and I sat feasting off the grapes that coated the valley floor. I began to understand why the Afghans are so superstitious and why they hold their fate to be in the lap of the gods.

S. C. Kiley-Worthington
(PPE) was war
correspondent of
The Times in Africa,
then moved to be
correspondent in Israel
2000–1. He is now
a features writer and
foreign correspondent for
the *Evening Standard*.

SAM KILEY
LMH 1984

My agony and some ecstasy in reporting Africa

Shot in the arm after being mistaken for one of the South African invaders in Lesotho in 1997, Sam Kiley recalls seven years of fascination and frustration in the land of his birth.

SO WHY DO I DO IT? Why do a job that gives you classic 'post traumatic stress disorder' (shell shock) dreams? That gives me the ability to divine the time of death by smell? Why, after seven years, am I still covering Africa? I'd love another posting. But typecast as a 'war correspondent' (for light relief I've been sent to Bosnia, the Balkans and Iraq), it has been difficult to persuade *The Times* that I can do anything else. There is not much of a queue for my job either.

There is an old saying that Africa is like a poison. One visit to the Dark Continent, and you will never, really, leave. It stays in the blood and the infection is incurable. On Wednesday a little more of Africa entered my blood stream when I was shot in the arm in Lesotho.

Agony and ecstasy. Beauty and bestiality. Life and death. In Africa there is nothing trivial, nothing ordinary. Africa is a world of absolutes. And the longer I live here, the less I understand. This continent's history keeps repeating itself as farce and tragedy in ever tighter revolutions.

Few, if any, of the iron age cultures of Africa that are being forced to develop into democracies in the technological age, when they got the wheel only 150 years ago, will survive far into the next century. How could they? The West had 2,000 years to evolve through its dark ages, disasters and genocide into modern states – and as the Balkans have shown us, they are still little more than a chimera.

Africa, now in its dark age, most certainly is a basket case. The 'new breed' of African leaders I thought I had found two years ago – the alliance of Ethiopia, Eritrea, Uganda, Rwanda and others who rid Zaire of Mobutu Sese Seko – have proved as idiotic and incompetent as their predecessors. Eritrea and Ethiopia are now locked in a border war. Rwanda and Uganda have sparked off another civil war. So, I think most of Africa's leaders should have been drowned at birth. And I prefer my own culture to the primitive world of tribalism.

So what do I like? Well, I love Africans – individually. Most have a Monty Pythonesque sense of the absurd. A well-timed joke can secure your life, or an interview with a president. And they are often heroic. I shall never forget a teacher and a young lieutenant in Mobutu's army. Abandoned by their Government about a hundred miles south of Kisangani in the middle

From *The Times*,
26 September 1998
See also p. 162

of the jungle, these two men kept working. The soldier probably had a few days to live as Tutsi rebels approached his village. But he worked tirelessly to prevent Hutu extremists from laying waste to his village. He carried no weapons. He should have fled with the rest of his men. But he stayed, and kept the Hutus at bay with gentle persuasion and a charismatic kindness. He is probably dead now.

The teacher had not been paid for fifteen years. Yet his school educated more than a hundred children. They paid in food and clothing. They wrote on pieces of dried bark. Having taught himself English by listening to the BBC World Service, he had passed it on to his pupils. 'They are part of the global economy,' he explained. I nearly wept.

In Mogadishu I was sitting in the lavatory when the wall opposite me began to echo to the sounds of bullet impacts. A clan squabble outside had turned nasty and would soon involve anti-aircraft cannon. I crawled into the corridor, lying flat on the ground as the building seemed to sway with the impact of a rocket-propelled grenade.

I have always wondered what it would be like to be shot. It hurts

Then Ali, the hotel cleaner, came wandering down the stairwell with his red plastic bucket, sponges and bottles of Ajax. 'Ali! Take cover! What do you think you're doing?' I yelled. 'The second floor,' he replied and carried on cleaning.

Earlier this month, having spent four weeks in Kinshasa covering the rebel attack on President Kabila's capital, I left the city by ferry for Brazzaville. It had been a miserable trip, nothing but bad news and bad vibes. Volleys of rifle fire were used to drive crowds of potential stowaways back as the ferry pulled away. A young man was caught without a ticket, beaten up, stamped on and jammed under a bench by soldiers.

Then the drumming began. A troupe of youngsters from Brazzaville had been in Kisangani for a music festival when the war broke out. They had taken a month to get back to Kinshasa, and two weeks to get out. Street kids mostly, they owned only the tracksuits they were wearing, which where, incidentally, immaculate.

Each of them could get a full musical scale out of their wood and skin drums which they slung between their legs as they somersaulted, twirled and pounded with entranced joy and passion. They were rude, lewd and beautiful, and played for the entire 30-minute crossing without pause or payment.

They had not given up on Africa. They could not. I silently pledged that I won't either. Then I turned my face away from my colleagues, and wept great blobs of salt water into the mighty River Congo.

A. M. Weaver (History), while still at LMH, set up the sports department of Oxygen FM, the student radio station, and won the Guild of Motoring Writers' Award. Before sitting finals he was commissioned by a now-defunct magazine to set up a motoring page; subsequently he became a road test assistant for the magazines *Autocar* and *What Car?*

ALISTAIR WEAVER
LMH 1995

Le Mans et lemons

IT'S 8.23 P.M. AND THERE ARE SEVEN MINUTES in which to pre-qualify for the 1999 24 Heures du Mans. A bright yellow Porsche 911 GT2 crackles into life and explodes out of the pits. Its pilot, Gary Ayles, has never driven the car and has no clutch. The 911 snaps sideways as he accelerates out of the pitlane, crash-changing the gears. He swings right and disappears from view.

Back in the pits, the team stares helplessly at a tiny monitor mounted high on the wall. It displays only the miserable truth that in almost seven hours since the session started, the car has yet to complete a flying lap. A solitary mechanic stands transfixed by the two-way radio, headphones on, microphone at the ready. Suddenly he becomes animated: Ayles is complaining that something is flapping under the car. There is a mutual sigh of resignation that seems to echo off the bare pit walls.

Two minutes later Ayles limps back down the pit lane, the engine dies and the car is pushed back into the garage. There is frantic activity, bodies peering desperately under the car. The burst of energy is met with an equally sudden realisation that there is no time. Ayles clambers out, shakes the hand of team owner Gerard MacQuillan and retires to the back of the garage. Welcome to the world of the gentleman racer.

MacQuillan had arrived at the Le Sarthe circuit hoping to pre-qualify two cars. The first, a normally aspirated 911, was to compete in the LMGT class and the second, a more sophisticated turbocharged 911, to compete in the GTS category. Introduced in 1995, pre-qualifying has become a noisy, ritualistic yardstick for the race ahead. For the larger teams it's one of the first opportunities to gauge themselves against the opposition. Well prepared and much practised teams like Toyota treat the experience almost like an extended test session, never needing to approach the extremities. For the smaller teams, pre-qualifying is a nervous, tense and often frustrating business. It can mean the unravelling of a man's dream.

From 'Le Mans et lemons' (*Autocar*, 26 May 1999)

J. W. Allen (English and Modern Languages) is ITN's man in the pit lane. His publications include *Schumacher: Driven to Extremes*.

JAMES ALLEN
LMH 1985

The Formula, the figures

THE TOP TEAMS IN THE GAME, like Ferrari, Williams and McLaren, operate on budgets of over £80 million per year. Lunacy? Perhaps, but if you consider that each one of the 17 races every season is watched by a world-wide TV audience of over 350 million then you can see why sponsors queue up to be involved. Apart from the Olympic Games and the soccer World Cup, no event comes close to reaching that kind of global audience and those events happen once every four years. There will have been 68 Grand Prix races by the time they swing round again.

There is so much to get excited about in Formula I. The cars are incredibly fast; on some circuits they cover the equivalent of a football pitch every second, and they are beautifully engineered. The engineering side are where most of the Oxford alumni working in F1 are to be found; metallurgists, composite specialists and designers, all looking for new ways of making racing cars lighter and faster. The electronics are equally amazing. The more technologically advanced cars carry almost one mile of cable on board to transmit the data from over two thousand sensors around the car to the central computer. In 1998 the Ferrari team installed a satellite dish on the roof of its transporter so that their engineers in Italy could watch this telemetry in real time.

SAM WEST
LMH 1985

Hamlet the worrier

Sam West analyses his performance as Hamlet in the Royal Shakespeare Company production.

THIS IS VERY MUCH A Hamlet age. Hamlet in a Tony Blair age. If Tony Blair isn't good casting for Claudius who smiles and smiles, who is?

Doubts, cynicism, moral relativism, these are the norms now. It is hard to notice the bitterness in Denmark because there is so much sugar coating the pill. Hamlet is a character that exists in opposition, but it is hard to stand up to something that seems quite liberal.

Hamlet is a man for our times because he distrusts himself. He is a worrier, not a warrior. Steven Pimlott described the play the other day as being like *Gladiator* with Woody Allen playing Russell Crowe.

See also p. 248

M. P. Giles (PPE), writer
and editor, was Paris
correspondent for *The
Economist*, then their
London-based
International Finance
Editor. He is currently on
the senior management
committee, responsible
for the Economist Group's
publishing, television and
conference businesses.

MARTIN GILES
LMH 1985

Cyberlaundering

AN ITALIAN COURT RECENTLY CONFISCATED assets worth 1 trillion lire
($590m) from Vincenzo Piazza; they included 131 apartments, 122 ware-
houses, 20 factories, ten school buildings and 250,000 or so shares in a
Sicilian savings bank. Not bad for a builder with a declared income in 1989
of 1.9m lire. The Italian authorities reckon that Mr Piazza, who was
arrested three years ago on charges of associating with the Mafia, moon-
lighted as a money launderer for Sicily's crime lords. This is just one of
several cases which suggest that money laundering – that is, disguising the
origin of criminals' cash and then transforming it into apparently legitimate
investments – is still a big business.

But if there is one thing that money launderers hate it is cash; physical
cash, that is. Shipping huge wads of banknotes is a logistical nightmare. It
also raises the risk that couriers will be intercepted and the loot traced back
to its source. Transferring money electronically is both quicker and easier.
Hence concerns in law-enforcement circles that new forms of electronic
money could render obsolete traditional methods of tracking tainted money,
which rely heavily on the policing of bank transactions.

Electronic money systems come in three different forms. There are
stored-value cards, which allow customers to load money on to a micro-
chip-bearing piece of plastic. This can then be carried around like a credit
card. There are computer-based systems, for example those involving payments over the Internet. And there is talk of hybrid systems which allow
smart cards and network-based payments to work together.

Although these new gizmos are still under development, financial regula-
tors and policemen have been studying them intently. And they have raised
several questions to which they want answers. One is whether limits will be
placed on value that can be held on chip-bearing cards. The anti-laundering
brigade also wants reassurance that crooks will not be able to set themselves
up as e-money issuers. And they want to know whether all transactions in
whatever system will be logged at a central point, so that investigators can
reconstruct an electronic audit trail if necessary. At least one card-based
system currently being developed by Mondex, a company owned by Master
Card, is designed to allow money to be transferred directly between cards,
without leaving such a trail.

From 'Cleaning up dirty
money', *The Economist*,
26 July 1997

P. J. Hennessy (English) has been a political and economic correspondent at the House of Commons since 1992 for the *Daily Express* and the *Evening Standard*. He is one of the first men to follow his mother, E. A. Browne (LMH 1953), to LMH.

PATRICK HENNESSY
LMH 1982

Scoop!

Patrick Hennessy's front-page scoop – the first account of Labour's pledge not to raise income tax rates if elected – owed much to his close friendship with Gordon Brown's former adviser Charlie Whelan.

SHADOW CHANCELLOR Gordon Brown today pledged that Labour would not increase the basic or the top rate of income tax in its first term of government. The five-year promise, by far the most far-reaching ever made by a would-be incoming Chancellor, staggered the Tories as well as many Labour MPs and activists. Mr Brown's pledge was reinforced by an equally ambitious clampdown on public spending, with no increases on current Tory plans for two years.

Mr Brown was using a speech in London tonight to end months of speculation by setting out Labour's tax and spending election blueprint.

The main points were:

• No changes either to the 23p basic rate, or the 40p top rate of personal income tax for the lifetime of the next parliament.

• A new starting rate of income tax, replacing the current 20p rate, to be introduced when resources allow.

• No extension of VAT on food, children's clothes and shoes, books, newspapers and public transport fares.

• No increases in total state spending above the levels already set by the Tories for two years.

The move ends months of shadow cabinet wrangling over personal income tax – the single issue which most experts believe cost Labour the last election.

Critics of Mr Brown's tax plans, however, said ruling out personal income tax rises did not necessarily mean voters would escape Labour raids on their wealth.

From 'Labour Fires Tax Exocet', *Evening Standard*, 20 January 1997

J. Rogan (PGCE) has written 18 books, mainly on music subjects, including *Timeless Flight* (on The Byrds); *Death of a Supergroup* (on George Michael); *Morrissey and Marr – The Severed Alliance*, and a biography of Neil Young.

From *Starmakers and Svengalis* (Futura, 1988)

JOHNNY ROGAN
LMH 1980

A history of British pop management

EGO, AMBITION, GREED, POWER, corruption, faith, dedication, love and uncanny luck have all played their part in motivating the myriad figures of British pop management. What emerges most clearly, however, is the tendency of managers to reflect and even determine the political pop climate in which they function.

The Fifties was an age of managerial autonomy mirroring the power that the four major companies had over the fate of so many artistes; the Sixties was an age of entrepreneurial expansionism in which managers and groups rivalled each other for creativity and charisma; the early Seventies represented the rejection of the old-style tycoon, ushering in a period when accountants and solicitors replaced romantic visionaries thereby ensuring that the only sparkle left in British pop was that of artificial glitter; the late Seventies and early Eighties heralded the return of the young, inexperienced manager and saw an equally frequent turnover of musical styles and subcultural fashions.

From *I'm a Man: Sex Gods and Rock 'n' Roll* (Faber & Faber, 2000)
See also p. 147

RUTH PADEL
LMH 1965

I'm a man: sex gods and rock 'n' roll

ROCK IS AGGRESSIVE, MASCULINE, artist-led. Rock has to have edge, attitude, or 'guitars in it'. Pop is European harmony: the Beatles Schubertian legacy. Rock is all Africa and rhythm (Hendrix, the Stones). My 13-year-old daughter thinks rock happened in the Middle Ages when I was young, and there isn't any now. Rock is what there was Before Us. (Itself a rockist belief, if ever I heard one.)

R. A. Swett (English) has written three bestselling novels: *Special Relationship*, which contains a thinly disguised portrait of a Bill Clinton-like US President; *Perfect Strangers* and *Just Friends*.

ROBYN SISMAN
LMH 1968

The President-elect

FOR THE TEAM, IT WAS JUST A PUBLICITY gimmick. Jordan Hope was to be packaged as Kennedy reincarnated – young, energetic, idealistic, with a gorgeous wife. Only no bad stuff. No Marilyn Monroes, you hear? And please, no Lee Harvey Oswalds, Rick had added. But for Jordan that moment nearly thirty years ago when he and John F. Kennedy had clasped hands was sacred. He had a vision to carry on where Kennedy had been stopped dead in his tracks just three months later – but in his own style and on behalf of his own generation.

'Time to go, Jordan.'

Time. It was a rarity to get even five minutes alone. How was he going to slip his leash for several hours? What would it be like to see Annie again?

'We have nothing to fear except fear itself.' This had been Jordan's mantra since the day he had got his college scholarship, and it had served him well. He repeated it now as he put on the pressed dark jacket and sober tie that had been chosen for his forthcoming speech, just as yesterday's jeans and corduroy had been judged appropriate for California. He flashed himself his heart-throb smile in the closet mirror while the surface of his mind automatically reshuffled the familiar phrases. Change. Hope. The economy. The deficit. Maybe his stetson joke, if the mood was right. Dallas meant oil, banking, the aerospace industry. Dallas meant Neiman Marcus and the Cowboys. Dallas meant Kennedy.

But while the autocue played in his head, the wheels of memory whirled and clicked on another loop. Oxford. The summer of 1970. Moonlight on the Cherwell, the throbbing rhythm of the Doors, and Annie silky and warm and under his hands.

Annie. Of course it had been her voice, that actressy huskiness softening the crystalline consonants. Typically she had come straight to the point. The curious thing was that, amid the flood of disbelief and despair that engulfed him, Jordan had also felt an unmistakable surge of elation.

'Jordan, I have a son. He thinks you're his father, and he's coming to find you.'

From *Special Relationship* (Heinemann, 1995)

N. Gerrard (English) is a journalist and writer. She co-writes with her husband Sean French: their *Killing Me Softly* was a bestseller.

NICCI GERRARD
LMH 1977

Sexual reading

THE CONTENTS OF MY HUSBAND Sean's bedside table long ago spilled on to the floor: a pile of novels, some short stories, several volumes of poetry, a leaning tower of maths and science books, a thumbed *Ancient Greek Made Easy*, the New Testament, a sprawl of biographies and essays and philosophical reflections. Currently, I'd estimate Sean is 'reading' about 50 books seriously. A further 500 or so that he has started and intends one day to finish are kept in a special bookcase close at hand.

Books are Sean's way of organising, understanding and to a degree controlling his world. In his bedroom down the hall, my son also lies in a circle of books – football annuals, adventure stories, chess manuals, joke books, an introduction to logical paradoxes. He loves knowing things and displaying his knowledge.

I had an idealistic sense that literature cut through the gender divide but, in reading and writing, men and women are different. Men write novels that feel like fact. The heart of their books, its source, is often an idea, a theme. They are satirical, sarcastic, sceptical; women sincere and often sentimental. Men thrive on aperçus, aphorisms, jokes, asides, digressions, nudges and winks to the reader. They feed us information. They like talking about cosmology. They show off in their writing, putting their logo on the text, never allowing the reader to forget them.

I always felt irritated and restricted by that old saying: 'Boys will be boys and girls will be girls.' But the evidence stacks up against me: girls concentrate, boys don't (five minutes is their apparent attention span), girls play imaginary games and boys tumble and fight. Girls collaborate and boys compete. Girls talk about feelings and boys talk about facts. Girls are interested in people, boys in ideas. Girls like stories, boys like lists, girls like fiction and boys like fact.

From 'Sexual Reading', *The Observer*, 27 September 1998 and *The Persephone Quarterly*, 1999

JULIA GOWAN

LMH 1953

Lesson

RAIN IS OUTSIDE.
Grief, or something they give that name
is somewhere inside
not very far away.
Tears already this morning
then thank God a joke
and the sky lifted
momentarily.

I have explained something to the class,
with care to be precise, and if possible helpful.
Criticism, I explain, is like the surgeon's knife
that probes the source of disturbance.
Appreciation
is love. I do not tell them
that it is love that runs out, runs out
to meet its beloved.
They must learn accuracy first. They are boys.

There is silence now, warmth,
a gentle creaking of chairs, desks,
someone whispering, something lurking. No fear, however,
They work. At a poem –
'Schoolroom on a wet afternoon'.
The word 'bereaved'
gentle and blank
chooses my eye from the page.
Rain is outside.

A boy looks up and smiles. He
hides away a paper dart. I smile back.
This often happens.
Nothing is complete in itself. Not even grief.
Not even life. Or death.
Rain is outside.

M. Rushworth (English) combines studies at LMH with being a writer and poet, contributing to *Cherwell* and organising the LMH Arts and Drama Festival.

MATT RUSHWORTH
LMH 1999

THEY SAT BESIDE one another that day,
The rock-pools were empty and the
Wind stayed very light;
I emptied my buckets on to the sand,
The contents were bland,
Nothing anyone should note.

* * *

The lights go out
One by one,
Over the stones,
Across the beach.

Drained of the shadows of buildings,
The darkness thickens over the sand;
All around us
The day falls in.

The adults are going to
Talk near the sea.
All except one.
Left to be our guard:
They take off their shoes and dance.
The waves hit them only on their feet.
I watch and want really to run down too.

I want to be older or smaller.
Dancing in the waves or crawling in the sand,
When they put down their buckets and cry.
She moves straight over, sighing.

I can dance and I never cry,
Though sometimes when it rains
I'll mix the raindrops in my eyes with tears,
She never sees, though I want her to sometimes;
It's when I don't want to walk,
When I'm cold and wet and I walk behind.

From 'On the beach, a child' (LMH Arts and Drama Festival, 2001)

C. B. Drazin (Classical Mods) has also written *The Finest Years: British Cinema of the 1940s*, and a study of *Blue Velvet*.

CHARLES DRAZIN
LMH 1980

The cuckoo clock speech

THE CORE OF ORSON WELLES'S performance in *The Third Man* was the dialogue scene with Joseph Cotten at the Great Wheel. The style of the film changes to accommodate his larger ego. Welles is not the kind of actor to stay silent any longer than he has to – he barges in on Cotten's lines in a manner that is reminiscent of the overlapping dialogue in *Citizen Kane*. As nearly all the actors did, he tailored his lines until they felt comfortable, but in substance the scene was played as scripted, until it came for Lime to take his leave of Martins. Then there were hoots of laughter as Welles tried out a few extra lines of his own:

> In Italy for thirty years under the Borgias they had warfare, terror, murder, bloodshed – but they produced Michelangelo, Leonardo da Vinci and the Renaissance. In Switzerland they had brotherly love, five hundred years of democracy and peace, and what did that produce? . . . The cuckoo clock.

'Fine,' said Reed, and the cuckoo clock speech was shot.

Ever since, it has been quoted as an example of Orson Welles's brilliance. In fact it was stolen. As Bob Dunbar, who worked on the film, said, 'It was Orson who remembered the gag about the cuckoo clock. He didn't invent it, he just remembered it. I remembered it too, and I was supposed to find out where it came from. We were going to shoot in half an hour. How the hell was I going to find out? Go to the British Museum?'*

In fact, it was a member of the National Film Theatre audience who gave Charles Drazin the probable source of the joke: a lecture by James McNeill Whistler in 1885.

From *In Search of The Third Man* (Methuen, 1999)

Sharing food . . .

Miss Lea said briskly, 'I have never been one of those academic women who think there's some distinction in not knowing how to boil an egg' – Rachel Trickett (LMH 1942)

B. Flower (Classical Mods) was Craven scholar; tutor and lecturer at LMH, then at University College, London, and from 1941 at Glasgow. She died in 1955.

BARBARA FLOWER
LMH 1931

VI. 2. FLAMINGO. Pluck the flamingo, wash, truss, and put it in a saucepan; add water, dill, and a little vinegar. Half-way through the cooking make a bouquet of leek and coriander and let it cook with the bird. When it is nearly done add *defrutum* to give it colour. Put in a mortar pepper, caraway, coriander, asafœtida root, mint, rue; pound; moisten with vinegar, add Jericho dates, pour over some of the cooking-liquor. Put it in the same saucepan, thicken with cornflour, pour the sauce over the bird, and serve. The same recipe can also be used for parrot.

2. ANOTHER METHOD. Roast the bird. Pound pepper, lovage, celery-seed, grilled sesame, parsley, mint, dried onion, Jericho date. Blend with honey, wine, *liquamen*, vinegar, oil, and *defrutum*.

From B. Flower and E. Rosenbaum, trans., Apicius, *The Art of Cooking* (Harrap, 1958) See also p. 118

M. L. Camber (Modern Languages) was a journalist for *The Times* and is now an artist, playwright and poet in New York. Her publications include *Voices of Paris*, *Badlands* and *The Art of Love*. She is currently producing a series of film portraits of major film directors.

MELINDA CAMBER-PORTER
LMH 1971
Sharing Food
watercolour, 1986

113   SHARING FOOD

N. L. Lawson (Modern Languages) is a cookery writer and broadcaster, and post-modern Domestic Goddess. Her publications include *How To Eat: the Pleasures and Principles of Good Food* and *Nigella Bites*, in conjunction with her 2001 television series.

NIGELLA LAWSON
LMH 1979

On baking cakes

I DO THINK THAT MANY OF US have become alienated from the domestic sphere, and that it can actually make us feel better to claim back some of that space, make it comforting rather than frightening. In a way, baking stands both as a useful metaphor for the familial warmth of the kitchen we fondly imagine used to exist, and as a way of reclaiming our lost Eden. This is hardly a culinary matter, of course: but cooking, we know, has a way of cutting through things, and to things, which have nothing to do with the kitchen. This is why it matters.

The trouble with much modern cooking is not that the food it produces isn't good, but that the mood it induces in the cook is one of skin-of-the-teeth efficiency, all briskness and little pleasure. Sometimes it is the best we can manage, but at other times we don't want to feel like a post-modern, post-feminist, overstretched woman, but rather a domestic goddess, trailing nutmeggy fumes of baking pie in our languorous wake.

So what I am talking about is not being a domestic goddess exactly, but feeling like one. One of the reasons that making cakes is satisfying is that the effort required is so much less than the gratitude conferred. Everyone seems to think that it is hard to make a cake (and no need to disillusion them), but it doesn't take more than 25 minutes to make and bake a tray of muffins or a sponge layer cake, and the returns are high: you feel disproportionately good about yourself afterwards. This is what baking, what all of the book, is about: feeling good, wafting along in the warm, sweet-smelling air, unwinding, no longer being entirely an office creature, and that's exactly what I mean by 'comfort cooking'.

Part of it too is about a fond, if ironic, dream: the unexpressed 'I' that is a cross between Sophia Loren and Debbie Reynolds in pink cashmere cardigan and fetching gingham pinny, a weekend alter-ego winning adoring glances and endless approbation from anyone who has the good fortune to eat in her kitchen. The good thing is, we don't have to get ourselves up in Little Lady drag and we don't have to renounce the world and enter into a life of domestic drudgery. But we can bake a little – and a cake is just a cake, far easier than getting the timing right for even the most artlessly casual of midweek dinner parties.

This isn't a dream; what's more it isn't even a nightmare.

Oh, that being a domestic goddess were really just a piece of cake!

Anne Simor (LMH 1958), from *The Brown Book* 2001

From *How to be a Domestic Goddess: Baking and the Art of Comfort Cooking* (Chatto & Windus, 2000)

Molten chocolate baby cakes

THESE ARE THE ACCEPTABLE FACE of culinary cute: their intensity guarantees the triumph of chic over prettiness. And what's more, they're easy to make. You can make the mixture up a few hours in advance and put it ready and waiting in the prepared tins in the fridge until you want to cook them, which must be the moment you want to eat them. You might think that preparing the tins sounds fiddly, but in fact the job is just demanding enough to make one feel uncharacteristically competent in a Blue Peter kind of way, but not so much that any actual dexterity is required.

(This recipe comes by way of the great James McNair, America's gastro compendium made flesh.)

50 g soft unsalted butter, plus more for greasing
350 g best dark chocolate
150 g caster sugar
4 large eggs, beaten with a pinch of salt
1 teaspoon vanilla extract
50 g plain flour
6 individual pudding moulds, butter baking parchment

Unless you are making these in advance, preheat the oven to 200°C, gas mark 6, putting in a baking sheet at the same time. Lay three of the moulds on a sheet of doubled baking parchment. Draw round them, remove, and then cut out the discs as marked. Press them all into the base of the tins.

Never worry about what your guests will think of you. Just think of the food

Melt the chocolate and let it cool slightly. Cream together the butter and sugar and gradually beat in the eggs and salt, then the vanilla. Now add the flour, and when all is smoothly combined scrape in the cooled chocolate, blending it to a smooth batter.

Divide the batter between the six moulds, quickly whip the baking sheet out of the oven, arrange the little tins on it and replace in the oven. Cook for 10–12 minutes (the extra 2 minutes will be needed if the puddings are fridge cold when you start) and as soon as you take them out of the oven, tip out these luscious baby cakes on to small plates or shallow bowls. Serve these with whipped double cream, crème fraîche, crème anglaise or ice cream.

Some recipes take a little longer . . .

From *Medieval English Gardens* (Collins, 1981)

JENNY PERY
Jug and Apples
wood engraving,
2001

TERESA MCLEAN
LMH 1969

Comfort me with apples

THE BEST WAY TO EAT APPLES was cooked and sweetened. They were sliced and dried in the sun, sealed in earthenware jars and buried under the ground, and put in honey, wine-must, brine or vinegar pickle to preserve them. They emerged from these treatments strong-tasting and in little pieces, all ready for the pot, wherein they were cooked into sweet porray for the favourite medieval desserts. Among these were apple tart, made with spices, figs, raisins, pears and saffron; apple muse (mousse), with almonds, honey, grated bread, saffron, sweet spices and salt; apple and parsnip fritters, with ale, saffron, almond milk and salt.

Raw, as they came off the trees, apples were deeply symbolic, as the instrument of the Fall. Pears did not have the same symbolic importance as apples because they did not have the same role in the Genesis story or the Song of Songs, where the lover sings 'Comfort me with apples, for I am sick with love.'

OLIVE LODGE
LMH 1905

Turkish delight, or 'Ratlak lokum'

PUT 7 KILOS OF WATER in a large cauldron over the fire to heat, at the same time adding a quarter of a kilo of citron or lemon powder, and 7.5 kilos of soft white sugar, and stir up well with a wooden spoon three feet long.

Fill another bowl with 5 kilos of water and 7 kilos of potato starch, before adding 2 more kilos of water, and mixing well.

When the water in the cauldron is hot, pour into it through a sieve the potato-starch mixture from the bowl; and, when it boils, keep stirring it with the long wooden spoon for three hours. Then pour the sticky mixture into wooden trays that have been well dredged with a mixture of sugar and flour, and leave till next morning. Now cut into squares. Other flavours may be used, attar of roses being particularly good: chopped walnuts, almonds, or hazelnuts make a pleasing variation in Turkish delight.

From *Peasant Life in Jugoslavia* (Seeley, Service & Co., 1941)
See also pp. 118, 175, 176

M. M. Murphy (Modern Languages), consultant and writer on wine and food, was the author of *The Country Cook* and *London at Table*.

MARGARET COSTA
LMH 1935

Sorrel

LEAVES ARE IMPORTANT IN COOKING all over the world. In England cabbage, spinach and lettuce leaves in particular are familiar enough – if not for apple pies – but, for me, it is the long, dark, arrow-shaped leaves of the wild sorrel that grows, ignored, in great profusion all over our islands that are the most delicious leaves of all.

We know so little of the wild foods of our country. In Morayshire I have picked basketfuls of yellow chanterelles, in Norfolk too; in Hampshire, wild raspberries. I have collected nuts and seaweeds and samphire, ormers and mussels, and cockles as small as a child's thumbnail. And everywhere the most neglected of all the wild harvests – the leaves; uncurled bracken shoots, dandelion and young nettle leaves – these picked with gloves on – and sorrel. Look for sorrel from April to October wherever you live and you will find it sheltering under the long grass in most damp meadows; I have even picked it on Hampstead Heath. You cannot mistake it; the lively, lemony, bitter taste fills your mouth at a single bite. You can grow it too with very little trouble and gather it and cook it nearly all the year round, but the broad-leaved French sorrel the seedsmen sell has a milder, less surprising flavour.

Athough the sharp sour flavour to which sorrel owes its name might be thought to be an acquired taste, I have not yet met anyone who did not like its lively refreshing tang from the very first bite of a raw leaf, taken to distinguish it from dock which it much resembles. It can be cooked in almost all the ways suitable for spinach and lettuce. Indeed, when I cannot get sorrel I often try to simulate its flavour by adding lemon juice to lettuce soup or to spinach.

Bound with a little beaten egg and flavoured with lemon juice or perhaps a very little finely grated shallot, or a little tarragon, sorrel purée makes a very good stuffing for fish, particularly mackerel. Another very popular way of serving it as a vegetable in France is to fritter the leaves: dip them in a very light batter and fry them in very hot deep olive oil. The fritters can be eaten on their own with a squeeze of lemon juice or be served with pork, veal or roast chicken. For the batter, add a bottle of light ale gradually to two tablespoons (30 ml) of seasoned flour to make a thin cream, and then fold in a stiffly beaten egg white.

From *Four Seasons Cookery Book* (Thomas Nelson, 1970; Grub Street, 1999)

OLIVE LODGE
LMH 1905

Bosnian recipes

Rose-leaf slatki

USE ABOUT THIRTY HEADS of red roses (damask roses). Take a handful, so arranged that the paler parts near the stalks are held by the thumb and first finger, ready to be cut off and thrown away. Cut the remaining bundles of red petals into thin strips, like tobacco, and put them into a clean vessel with one oke (about 2.5 lb) of white sugar. Mix the rose leaves and sugar up and down by hand; then crush and squeeze them between both hands, and afterwards add about one oke (about 1 to 1.5 pints) of water. Heat for at least an hour – till the water boils. Then add cream of tartar to give it a good colour. Otherwise it is quite dark-coloured. Put into jam-jars and cover.

Inferior jam, for cooking or for children

Pelmez is made by adding water to several pounds of either rose-hips or damsons or plums, and boiling them, without sugar, for hours, till they become like thick jam.

Another recipe for rose-hip pelmez is to clean the hips, then add water, and heat till it boils and bubbles, when sugar, in the proportion of one kilo to three kilos of hips, must be added. The whole is then boiled for about two hours. Store in well-covered jars.

From *Peasant Life in Jugoslavia* (Seeley, Service & Co., 1941) See also pp. 116, 175, 176

BARBARA FLOWER
LMH 1931

XVII. URTICAE. Urticam feminam, sole in ariete posito, adversus aegritudinem sumes, si voles.

XVII. STINGING NETTLES. Take the wild nettle, when the sun is in the sign of Aries, against illness, if you wish.

From B. Flower and E. Rosenbaum, trans., Apicius, *The Art of Cooking* (Harrap, 1958) See also p. 112

E. C. Sykes (FRGS; RSA Silver Medal; Secretary of Royal Asiatic Society, 1920), although accustomed to a comfortable diplomatic life with her brother, the British Consul in Persia, decided to travel to Canada and work as a home-help. It was a task for which she was very poorly suited but her book about it reveals a brave attempt, in contrast to her more conventional travel books, *Persia and its Peoples* and *Stories of the Shah*. She died in 1939.

ELLA C. SYKES
LMH 1881

Home-help on the prairie

Ella Sykes, accustomed to a life of travel and comfort, undertook a six-month trip to Canada in 1911 to work as a home-help. Unlike most home-helps, she travelled First Class, with a berth in the Pullman to the Pacific, taking with her a camera and a folding india-rubber bath.

IN ORDER TO SUCCEED, a girl must be skilled in something that the country needs, such as teaching, stenography, dressmaking, poultry or vegetable-raising, a knowledge of the domestic arts being absolutely essential. I do not recommend an educated woman to take up home-helping as a profession, save in certain districts, as that calling is too often only another name for maid-of-all-work or drudge, £5 a month being usually the highest salary for incessant work and little relaxation. But if she can cook, bake and wash, a girl need never starve, and a few months of domestic work will not be time wasted, as she will learn the excellent Canadian methods of doing things, which will help her considerably when she starts on work more to her taste.

The Matron of the 'Home of Welcome' interviewed me after the meal, and I explained that I wanted a post on the prairie as home-help, but that I was neither competent nor experienced. She looked at me sadly as she said, 'What a pity it is that Englishwomen are taught to do nothing properly.'

It was curious how completely I had now merged myself into my part. It was no longer acting. I knew the despairing feeling of hunting for work and finding none, and I had a pang of disappointment as girl after girl went off to her post, and I, the incompetent, was left behind without one. I filled up the time with washing my clothes, thus learning the use of a wringer and a washing-board, and the right way to hang garments on the line, and was humiliated to find that I did everything the wrong way if I followed the light vouchsafed me by Nature.

Sometimes I used to wonder whether it were indeed I who was cleaning out rooms on my hands and knees, or rubbing clothes on the washing-board, or ironing, or replenishing that voracious stove with pieces of wood. I must confess that though I gave my whole mind to my work, yet I found the life very monotonous, and it was hard at first to be ordered about, and not be mistress of my own time.

Dismissed after three days, she worked one week's notice – ten days in all.

From *A Home-Help In Canada* (Smith, Elder & Co., 1912)
See also pp. 121, 135

A. K. Chisholm (History),
is the biographer of
Nancy Cunard and
(with her husband,
Michael Davie) of Lord
Beaverbrook. She is a
reviewer for the *TLS* and
The Spectator, has judged
the Booker Prize, and is
on the council
of the Royal Society of
Literature.

ANNE CHISHOLM
LMH 1959

Rumer Godden in India

IN INDIA IN 1915, to be a trusted servant in a British household was to be privileged, envied and secure; no doubt there was sometimes arrogance on one side and resentment on the other, but in the memoirs and autobiographies of the old India hands there is no mistaking the respect and liking felt by many for the people who helped them run their daily lives. Families and servants lived closely together; rules and routines were carefully observed but within them a kind of intimacy grew. And for British children, especially in a relatively easy-going household like the Goddens', the servants were their first and best friends.

Rumer noticed, remembered and celebrated many times in her Indian writings the house and garden at Narayanganj and the cast of characters on her childhood stage. The children were looked after by a flamboyant Eurasian, Nana, who told them tall stories about her mysterious origins and the cruel nuns in the orphanage where she had grown up. She also told them that their parents were snobs for requiring her to wear the usual nanny's uniform, and taught them music-hall songs – 'Swanee River', 'K-K-K-Katie' – which they sang until their father could bear it no longer. They adored the dramatic Nana, with her near-mahogany-coloured skin and knee-length blue-black hair, despite her fierce temper and appalling sulks, but although Eurasian nurses were sought after – they were educated, Christian, and could speak English – they were looked down on by both races, and the lilting, sing-song Eurasian accent was considered as undesirable as it was contagious.

Outside the nursery, the household servants were all men. There was the magnificent Azad Ali, a towering figure in immaculate white tunic and pleated turban, who stood behind Arthur Godden's chair at meals, poured tea and drinks, carried trays into the garden and delivered letters on a silver salver. His staff were Muslims: Mustapha, the handsome young khitmagar, waited at table, and Abdul, whom the children disliked because he was ugly and told tales, was the nursery bearer. Their father's personal bearer was a Buddhist from Sikkim; mountain people, it was said, made the most loyal servants. Guru, the gatekeeper who kept watch on all comings and goings and ran errands to the bazaar, was a Hindu, as were the gardeners, who were high-caste Brahmins. Nitai, the sweeper, who cleaned the family's bathrooms and lavatories, was an Untouchable. Then there were the syces, Arthur's smart, uniformed grooms, and the cook, and the cook's boy; altogether some fifteen people to wait on a family of six.

From *Rumer Godden*
(Macmillan, 1998)

M. E. Lee (English) was a university lecturer in Lagos. Her publications include *Ladder of Bones* and *The Gilded Buddha*. She died in 1976.

ELLEN THORP
LMH 1925

Leopards, rabbits, a pangolin and a bear

THE HOUSE IN BURMA was always overflowing with pets, animals who shared our board, and not infrequently our beds: leopards, rabbits, a pangolin and a bear.

The leopards, pretty and dainty as kittens while young, but who early on indicated a tendency to be red in tooth and claw; when they were old enough to fend for themselves we set them free in the jungle, to the great indignation of some members of the station who considered we ought to have shot 'such dangerous brutes'.

Illustration by Ella Sykes
See also p. 119

The pangolin was a queer scaly creature whose enormous ever-flickering tongue decimated the fly population; I cannot pretend he was a great success as a pet; we never penetrated beneath his scaly armour and discovered whether he had loving and loveable instincts. He pined, so we let him loose in the jungle.

Bhalu was a black bear. A forest ranger brought him to Daddy, a little forlorn bundle of black wool, whose mother had been shot. He was old enough to be reared on milk and mashes. He grew up to be a jolly, friendly bearlet, and enjoyed a game of hide and seek as much as we did, and lolloped around after us wherever we went. He lived under a crab-apple tree and loved the small sour apples which fell around him. He used to gather a pile of these apples, then plump himself down on his little tail, and with feet well splayed out and the heap of apples between them would sit there and devour them, throwing cores, stalks and leaves about him in a manner which would have made an anti-litter official weep.

He adored being bathed and had his own beloved zinc bath, and after he had been washed, he used to empty the bath, then get into it and sit, meditatively regarding the passers-by, and grumbling happily to himself. If it rained he would heave himself out of the bath, drag it up against the trunk of the tree, turn it bottom upwards, and then crouch on it with his face to the trunk and fore-paws over his ears to shelter them from the pattering raindrops, looking like a naughty child who has been put in the corner.

As Bhalu grew older he became more boisterous, though no less affectionate, and we children were warned not to allow him to play games with us for fear that he should try to hug us with possibly disastrous results. Poor Bhalu could not understand this ostracism, and would pursue us all over the garden, we shrieking with half-apprehensive laughter, and he grumbling and chuntering.

From *Quiet Skies in Salween* (Jonathan Cape, 1945)

M. R. G. Grylls (PPE), Lady Mander, was a writer and biographer, and Visiting Professor at Long Island. Her other biographies include *Mary Shelley*; *Clare Clairmont*; *William Godwin and his World*; *Mary Kingsley*, and *Elizabeth Barrett Browning*.

ROSALIE GLYN GRYLLS
LMH 1924

My family and other animals

ROSSETTI SET ABOUT FILLING Tudor House with the pieces of old furniture he enjoyed picking up. He had an eye for what was good as well as what was curious – genuine pieces as well as junk – and now could afford to back his fancy. He began to fill the large garden, too, with statuary and with the strange animals that became such a feature of the place: indeed, it was due to Rossetti that there remains a clause in the leases of the Cadogan estates forbidding tenants to keep peacocks.

Wombats were always favourites with him and one of them was the original of the dormouse in *Alice in Wonderland*. Its sudden decease much grieved him: 'I had gone to the expense of a magnificent glazed mansion for him, picked up at a broker's shop.' The characteristic mixture in Rossetti of a whimsical but practical affection for his pets comes out also in a later letter to Madame Bodichon:

'My joys here have been overshadowed at intervals by the sight of darling little moles lying murdered. I mean to get two and keep them in a large glass case, so as to see them sometimes.'

And referring to some dormice he had sent her for a child in London:

'They eat apples, nuts, corn, etc., and require no drink – indeed ought not to have water as a rule but may be allowed a little milksop which they like. Their bed should be of hay rather than of wool. Will you give the young lady my love with them?'

Ellen Terry had a story of Rossetti giving a party to celebrate the waking-up of some white dormice in the spring. 'They are awake now,' he said, 'but how quiet they are! How full of repose!'

One of the guests went to inspect the bodies and Rossetti followed. 'Wake up,' he said, prodding them.

'They'll never do that,' said the guest. 'They're dead. I believe they've been dead some days.' Do you think Rossetti gave up livestock after this? Not a bit of it; he tried armadillos and tortoises!

From *Portrait of Rossetti* (Macdonald, 1964)

E. M. R. Seton-Watson (Modern Languages) served in the Foreign Office in London and Moscow 1942–46, which led to her reading Russian at LMH. She worked for the BBC External Services 1949–82, and was Russian Programme Organiser from 1969.

MARY SETON-WATSON
LMH 1946

Dogs in Moscow

THE REALLY 'IN' HOBBY among the young professional Moscow élite in the late 1960s was to keep a large pedigree dog, according to the writer Ananiev. He gives a long description of a dog show held on the banks of the Moskva river on a summer Sunday, where the dog-owners range in occupation from ordinary workers to members of the Academy of Sciences. He tries to explain, with somewhat ponderous sarcasm, why these people have all been seized with such a passion for man's four-footed friends.

A large part of their lives is devoted to the animals, and they justify this to themselves on the grounds that they are nature-freaks. Keeping a large dog in a small Moscow flat (probably spending most of its time shut up in a stuffy room or kept out on a dusty balcony) means, so they maintain, that they have got regular contact with nature in the form of a living being sharing their home – and contact with nature, as is well known, renders the human heart better and nobler.

But is this really the reason for the craze for large dogs, Ananiev asks? In the opinion of some observers, all this love of nature conceals some quite different motives. Three times a day, winter and summer, the owners have to take their charges out for a walk to satisfy the needs of nature. And a man taking a well-groomed setter out on a lead resembles – even in the distance – a nobleman. And although the packs of hounds for hunting, and the kennels where the noblemen used to keep them and which are so vividly described in Russian literature, have long since ceased to exist; although these noblemen's apartments, where big English or German dogs wandered around or lay on sofas next to their masters and were looked after by the servants – although all that has gone, that way of life with plenty of beautiful objects and dogs still has a great attraction for many people. The animals complicate their lives enormously: but it is well worth it to them, for the sake of those few minutes every day when they can appear in public with their well-groomed dog, and can feel themselves to some small extent a part of that old, noble way of life.

A few years after the big-dog craze, yoga hit Moscow.

From *Scenes From Soviet Life* (Ariel Publications, BBC, 1986)

A. J. Davis (English), writer and poet, has worked for the British Council, been a medical literature researcher in Australia, and is currently organising the architectural archives of her father A. J. Davis for the University of Buckingham. She now lives in Somerville, Massachusetts. Her poems have been published in *Oxford Poetry*, *The Atlantic Monthly* and *Poetry Ireland*.

From *A Safe House* (Northlight Studio Press, 1996)

ANN THOMAS
LMH 1944

Lamentation for Shiraz

To the memory of Riya Israqi, Muna Muhmudnizad, Zarrin Muqimi, Shirin Dalvand, Akhtar Sabet, Simin Dabiri and Munshid Mirumand, of the Baha'i faith, hanged in Shiraz, 18 June 1983.

AT THE MOUTH of the bazaar
is a small mosque
tiled with pink roses
that waits like a child
for copper to cool,
for silks to fold up
as flowers in dusk gardens,
for the leper's bowl
to be somewhat replenished,
for barter to end.

But the way winding back there
will never be taken
past the revving of bikes
round the Courthouse of Fars,
past the crack of the gavel,
the thud of the scaffold,
where seven girls slowly wind
round and back in their nooses,
as in winter black pears
wheel on stalks in the wind.

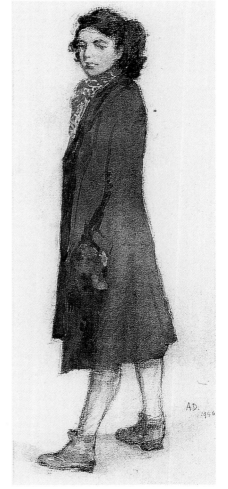

Ann Davis in 1946,
drawn by her father,
Arthur Davis, RA, FRIBA

ROBERT HOBHOUSE
LMH 1981
Levels' Tartan
oil on canvas

R. B. Hobhouse (English)
is a painter, writer and
landscape gardener,
and has taught English
in comprehensive schools
in Mosely, Romford and
Cheddar.

*Robert Hobhouse's painting forms the cover of his surreal novel T.I.L.T.
[Time Is Like Toffee] (Starhaven, 2000), in which he describes the living
nightmare of a patient held in sinister captivity, unable to tell if he is suffering from paranoia, schizophrenia, hallucination or the after-effects of
nuclear fallout.*

U. M. D. Orange (English) published six novels, among them *Portrait of Adrian* and *Have Our Cake*. She is the mother of novelist and historian Gillian Tindall (see p. 212).

URSULA ORANGE
LMH 1928

Plus ça change . . .

'WELL, I THINK,' SAID HENRIETTA, firmly closing the lid of her suitcase, 'that if you want to keep on any sort of terms with your family, you have to tell lies. But since you don't believe in telling lies,' she went on in a terrifyingly casual voice, 'I'm going away for the weekend – with John Fortescue.'

For a moment Sylvia was physically incapable of speech. Henrietta turned her back and began relocking the suitcase.

'If you mean Captain Fortescue,' said Sylvia at length in a strangled voice, 'I wish you wouldn't call him John. It makes me feel quite – sick.'

'Of course I mean Captain Fortescue,' said Henrietta tonelessly.

'You mean the man with the invalid wife,' said Sylvia brutally.

'I suppose,' she said at length, 'that he tells you that you've brought a new meaning into his life. When he's with you he realises what he's missed.'

'No, he doesn't,' said Henrietta, untruthfully.

'He's old enough to be your father.'

'He's forty-six. That's not old.'

'And you're eighteen. My God!'

'You've said yourself,' retorted Henrietta, repressed indignation struggling with attempted calm, 'that a man in his forties from the point of view of sex – '

'Don't talk nonsense,' interrupted Sylvia. 'A man with a past like his – '

'What do you know about his past? Anyway, I thought you believed in people having lots of experience.'

'I don't believe in a nasty old rip seducing a girl of eighteen.'

'He's not "seducing" me. I'm going away with him because I want to. I – I love him.'

'No, you don't. He flatters you. I know. He tells you you're the most beautiful girl he's ever seen and he's proud of your courage and spirit.'

For a horrid moment Henrietta wondered if Sylvia had by some extraordinary chance overheard some of their conversations.

'Anyway, what right have you got to criticise?' she cried, passionately. 'You've often said people must do as they like and experience is good for everyone.'

'I thought I was talking to someone who'd be sensible enough to realise that all old men who are unhappily married talk like that to pretty girls.'

'He's not old. And if he's unhappily married – it's not his fault. You've often said people shouldn't be tied by their mistakes.'

'I never said it was your job to console them.'

From *Begin Again* (Hamish Hamilton, 1936)

D. Athill (English) was a founder-director of the publishing house André Deutsch, and has been described as 'one of the most loved editors in publishing'. Her publications include a collection of short stories, *An Unavoidable Delay*; a novel, *Don't Look at Me Like That*, and her autobiography, *Stet*.

DIANA ATHILL
LMH 1936

Wear a wedding ring and no one will suspect a thing . . .

THE SQUARE, SCRUBBED WOMAN with cropped hair sat behind a desk on which was a vase of catkins. Her consulting room was decorated in cream and green, a combination I detest.

'Well, now,' she said in a voice intended to nip hysteria in the bud, 'it's not the end of the world.'

I had never thought it was. She saw, I supposed, a great many unmarried women who had become pregnant, so that she could hardly have avoided treating them according to formula, but I began at once to resent that she was applying her formula to me.

'In fact,' she went on, 'one might almost say that in wartime, when there is such a shortage of beds in the maternity wards and so on, it is simpler to have a baby when you are not married than when you are.'

'Oh?' I said.

'Yes, there is a lot of help available. I would strongly advise you to go on with it. It's your natural function and if you frustrate it you will find that a trauma results, a profound trauma. And it's quite simple when you have made up your mind to it – there are plenty of war widows about. You can change your job and wear a wedding ring and no one will suspect a thing.'

'But what about afterwards, when the baby is born?'

'That's the simplest part,' she said. 'I can put you in touch with organisations to look after that. There are three alternatives. One: you have the baby and its adoption is arranged beforehand. You won't even see it. The committee is extremely careful in its vetting of couples who want to adopt children – we make sure that they really want them, as well as that they are able to support them, and I can assure you that it is pure sentimentality to worry about the child in that case. It will probably be a good deal better off with its adopted parents than it would be with you.' She laughed as she spoke: little shocks of briskness were the thing.

'I don't see much point,' I said, 'in going through nine months of pregnancy and a birth, and not even seeing my child after all that.' I had a vivid mental picture of waking in a hospital bed to an emptiness through which I could never crawl.

'No. Well then, there's the second alternative: foster parents. We find a foster mother for it and you are free to see it whenever you like, and then, when you are in a better position to look after it, when you are making more money or have got married, you can take it back. You would be surprised at the number of men who can be made to accept such a situation.'

From *Instead of a Letter* (Chatto & Windus, 1963)
See also p. 229

What, I thought, if I never make any more money, or never get married, or can't make a husband accept the situation? And what of a child brought up by a woman who must seem to be its real mother, only to be snatched away by someone who has been no more than a visitor? It was less intolerable than the first prospect but not something I would risk. I nodded and looked expectant.

'The third solution,' she said, 'is to my mind much the best. You take your parents into your confidence straight away and get them to help you keep the child. What have you got against that?'

'My parents,' I said. 'They would be horrified.'

'Do them good, silly old things,' said the woman.

I looked at her in astonishment. Her high-handed dismissal of my parents as 'silly old things' was a piece of gross impertinence. I sat there thinking, 'What a frightful woman!' while she went on to explain that most families, once an illegitimate child becomes a *fait accompli*, adapt themselves to the situation after a time, however shocking they find it at first. 'You would probably find,' she said, 'that it would become your mother's favourite grandchild. I have seen that happen.'

My reason told me that she was right, but . . .

'No,' I said.

'Well,' said the woman, 'you will regret it terribly if you have an abortion. You're in perfect shape physically – I would say that yours is an ideal pregnancy, so far. You will suffer in every way if you terminate it.' She looked down at her hands, then reached out to straighten a folder on her desk. When she looked up, her eyes were sharp with calculation. 'It is, of course,' she went on slowly, 'entirely your own business. It is entirely up to you if you want' – she paused a moment to throw the verb into relief – 'if you want to murder your first child.'

'Yes, it is,' I said, getting up. Her look, the choice of verb, had clarified my mind in a flash. I knew, now, that I must get on with the job of finding an abortionist.

G. L. Bell (History; CBE) was a traveller, archaeologist and historian of Iraq and Syria. In 1909 she crossed the Euphrates to find Khedir; in 1913 she crossed the Desert of Nedj to Ha'il; in 1918 she won the Founder's Gold Medal of the Royal Geographical Society, and was four times mentioned in despatches between 1916 and 1918 for her intelligence and political work in the Near East. In Iraq, she was advisor to King Feisal and Director of Antiquities. She died in 1926.

GERTRUDE BELL
LMH 1886

An encounter

Gertrude Bell meets the Sheikh of Barah as she rides from Damascus to Aleppo.

'I ALWAYS GO TO ALEPPO when my sons are in prison there,' the Sheikh explained; 'sometimes the gaoler is soft-hearted and a little money will get them out.'

I edged away from what seemed to be delicate ground by asking how many sons he had.

'Eight, praise be to God! Each of my wives bore me four sons and two daughters.'

'Praise be to God,' said I.

'May God prolong your life!' he said. 'My second wife cost me a great deal of money,' he added.

'Yes?' said I.

'May God make it Yes upon you, Oh Lady. I took her from her husband and by God (may His name be praised and exalted) I had to pay two thousand piastres to the husband and three thousand to the judge.'

This was too much for my guide Haji Mahmud's sense of the proprieties.

'You took her from her husband?' said he. 'Wallah! That was the deed of a Nosairi or an Ismaili. Does a Moslem take away a man's wife? It is forbidden.'

'He was my enemy,' explained Yunis. 'By God and the Prophet of God, there was enmity between us even unto death.'

'Had she children?' enquired Mahmud.

'Ey wallah!' answered the Sheikh, a little put about by Mahmud's disapproval. 'But I paid two thousand piastres to the husband and three thousand –'

'By the Face of God!' exclaimed Mahmud, still more outraged, 'it was the deed of an infidel.'

And here I put an end to further discussion of the merits of the case by asking whether the woman had liked being carried off.

'Without doubt,' said Yunis. 'It was her wish.'

From *The Desert and the Sown* (Heinemann, 1907)
See also pp. 158–60

M. Peake (Modern
Languages; St Anthony's
College, 1974–78),
worked at the Monitoring
and External Services of
the BBC 1978–86. From
1986 she was a leader-
writer for *The Times*
on foreign affairs,
then became Moscow
correspondent.
She was Paris and
then Washington
correspondent for
The Independent, and is
now based in London.

MARY DEJEVSKY
LMH 1970

Brigitte Bardot: the triumph of hope over experience

BARDOT'S AUTOBIOGRAPHY has only added to her trials, because those
who have responded most strongly are blinded by greed, sententiousness
and old man's lust. In fact what she says is a revelation, but not the one you
would expect. France's animal welfare campaigner and eternal sex symbol,
Brigitte Bardot, will be in court today for another round of the public humil-
iation that the world seems to think she deserves in return for her life of free
living and loving.

Her second husband, Jacques Charrier, and her only child, 36-year-old
Nicolas, want almost one-quarter of her recently published autobiography
to be excised, claiming that its graphic details of marital discord and child
rejection constitute a violation of their privacy – a civil offence in France.

For Bardot, who is now 62 and – to judge by recent television appear-
ances – as magnetic a figure as ever, the lawsuit is just another twist of the
knife that was plunged into her still lithe body by the book's first reviewers.
The fifty- and sixty-something men who had drooled over her for decades
discovered in place of their goddess a feckless child who never made a
decent mistress, let alone a good wife and mother. The few women reviewers, French women of a certain age, are still jealous, and conventional.

But judgement on Bardot's long apologia cannot be left to this mostly
male or Gallic establishment. For what she has produced is an excruciat-
ingly honest account of a woman's place in an age and a society where the
position of women was very different from what it is in much of the Western
world today. The Sixties and Seventies were a social and biological water-
shed, but they came too late for Brigitte Bardot. She offers a sad and salu-
tary reminder of what it meant to be female, even a female of independent
means and considerable chutzpah, before the Pill, before legal abortion,
before divorce became acceptable, before respectably married women took
paid work and before the Catholic Church lost its role as moral arbiter.

Unfortunately for her own peace of mind, Bardot was not quite as free a
spirit as her behaviour suggested. She had been brought up to respect the
conventions, and half of her did, and still does. She says she would like to
have found 'the right man', 'settled down' and had a family. It just never
happened.

Even when she was earning sums that were fabulous by the standards of
her compatriots, she was as helpless as they were to avoid becoming pregnant. Like tens of millions of others, she was dependent on the 'rhythm
method' and was as desperately counting the days from her last period as
they were.

From 'Brigitte at War',
The Independent,
31 October 1996

When this primitive method failed, there was no legal remedy, in France or elsewhere in Europe. Money helped, but fame was a drawback. What doctor would dare perform an abortion on BB? She admits to two abortions: both were risky, and one almost fatal.

Bardot's marriages (at seven-year intervals) tell of the family expectations invested in wedlock – even into her thirties – and the sudden change in status that a wedding ring brought. When she first fell in love, with Roger Vadim, at the tender age of 15, her instincts were entirely conventional. She wanted to marry, but her parents refused.

By the time the marriage took place, three years afterwards, it was almost too late. Her career was taking off; she soon fell – as she was to do so often – for her leading man. Divorce followed, and her 'reputation' was lost.

Small wonder that she gradually descended into promiscuity. The greater wonder, perhaps, is that it took so long, and that she persisted in regarding marriage as 'for life'.

But she hesitated to marry again, all too aware of the limits a fifties marriage entailed. These dictated not only who she slept with, but also what films she appeared in, where she lived, whether she had a baby and what she did with her money. 'But it was my money, I earned it,' she says. She wanted

Brigitte Bardot in Et Dieu créa la femme *(1956)*

to manage her own career. Having discovered this liberty, she was loath to sacrifice it. She is proud to be famous in her maiden name.

Once remarried, Bardot found herself subject to demands that many a working wife today would find unacceptable. When her new husband, the actor Jacques Charrier, stopped her going to the hairdresser and invoked his legal rights, that marked the beginning of the end of their relationship.

Yet she had married him. Why? Because she was pregnant, because he wanted the child, because it was hard to get an abortion, but above all because she refused to be an 'unmarried mother'. The young woman whose image as the French 'sex kitten' was an open challenge to convention wanted her child to be legitimate. The mother whose behaviour already broke all manner of Church teachings had her son christened.

When French readers embarked on BB's autobiography they were looking for scandal, and they found it: in the fist fights she had with her husbands and lovers, in her brutal admission that she rejected her child, in her pithily dismissive comments on such cinematic luminaries as Alain Delon (as responsive as 'my Louis XVI dresser') and Catherine Deneuve ('cold').

In the end, though, she emerges not at all as a licentious, score-settling harpy, but as a spirited and wilful woman caught between what she wanted and what was permitted. The gap between the two would still exist today, but it would be far, far narrower. The impossibility of finding privacy and security in a world not yet equipped to protect a global superstar only compounded her problems.

M. A. Gove (English), Assistant Editor of *The Times*, has written on political and social matters for *The Times*, the *TLS* and *The Spectator*. His publications include a study of Edmund Burke, a biography of Michael Portillo, and *The Price of Peace*, a critical analysis of the Good Friday Agreement.

From *The Times*, 22 December 1998
See also p. 187

MICHAEL GOVE
LMH 1985

MONICA LEWINSKY
Got far too frisky
And discovered that DNA
Is a devil of a stain to wipe away

H. C. Pym (Classical Mods) was a producer for BBC Schools, translator of Greek songs and poetry, and joint editor of a biography of her sister, the novelist Barbara Pym, *A Very Private Eye*.

HILARY PYM
LMH 1934

Chios

A SHIP from Chios
with its two boats
went aground and anchored,
sat there and reckoned
the price of a kiss
in the West and in the East.
A married woman – four,
A widow – four plus ten,
A stolen kiss, one snatched unbidden – forty-four,
A virgin – say, a thousand Venetian crowns.

Translated from the Greek

From 'Songs of Greece', *The Sunday Times*, 24 December 1967

K. E. Kingshill (English) is a playwright, and granddaughter of Katharine Moore (see pp. 29, 30).

From 'The Golden Apple', part of *The Odyssey*, a community play staged at Shoreham in 1999

KATIE KINGSHILL
LMH 1973

Aphrodite

I AM LOVE'S own goddess,
Pure Mills & Boon,
The original ripped bodice.

SALLY ANNE PURCELL
LMH 1963

S. A. J. Purcell (Modern Languages) was a writer, translator and poet. Her publications include translations of the Provençal troubadors, *Dark of Day* and *Lake and Labyrinth*. 'What mattered to Sally was what was going on in (in a line from one of her own poems) the luminous abiding city of the mind' (Virginia Osborne, *The Brown Book* 1999). She died in 1998.

OUT FROM time's tumulus,
The black bonds laid on Cronos,
Our Lady comes walking
with a dish full of light,
light that flows through her fingers,
waves, ebbs and returns,
between wandering walls of shadow;
Maria, gateway to the great sea,
draws near
like a sound growing clearer,
bringing together at last
the holly-berry sun
and pearls of mistletoe.

From *Fossil Unicorn* (Anvil Press, 1997)

S. Bathurst (English; Dipl. Psychology, 1984) is a teacher and writer. Her publications include books on Chaucer, T. S. Eliot, Sterne and the Brontës.

SHEILA SULLIVAN
LMH 1946

A history of torment and enchantment

MANY MALE WRITERS LIKE TO THINK that the naked penis provokes excitement and awe in women; in the eighteenth century John Cleland's Fanny Hill describes 'the white veins, the supple softness of the shaft' . . . carrying 'a head of the liveliest vermillion . . . such a breadth of animated ivory!' Flaccid, D. H. Lawrence supposed the penis to be a source of tenderness, as Lady Chatterley describes it: '. . . when he's soft and little I feel my heart quite simply tied to him.' But Sullerot points out that a woman rarely, if ever, describes it as a wondrous love object, and Leroy argues that it is often a positive deterrent. Certainly Joyce's Molly had no time for it. For her the penis was 'that tremendous big red brute of a thing'; 'like iron or some kind of a thick crowbar'; 'sticking up at you like a hat-rack'. Lawrence did his best to solemnise the mystery of erection, as when Lady Chatterley decorates Mellors's penis with flowers – but it seems not all women think of the erect penis as a maypole to be decked. As a concept of masculinity and power, the significance of the phallus is immense, but its naked self – purple, one-eyed and absurdly hopeful – is not always a sexual thrill. And to women who have had alarming experiences in childhood, such as confrontation with a flasher, or worse, the erect penis can be a terrifying object.

From Falling in Love: A History of Torment and Enchantment (Macmillan, 1999)

BARBARA BOWEN
LMH 1955

B. C. Cannings (Modern Languages; Doctor of University of Paris, 1962; Professor of University of Illinois, Vanderbilt University). Her publications include Les Caractéristiques essentielles de la farce Française, and a comparison of P. G. Wodehouse and Rabelais.

A story from an anonymous collection of Florentine wit, the Bel Libretto, *or* Detti Piacevoli, *published in 1480. It is described as 'a ragbag of anecdotes about Lorenzo and Cosimo de' Medici, along with undatable witticisms, proverbs, maxims and riddles.'*

Grossi o Piccoli o Mezzani
Una donna dimandata qual fussero migliori bordoni [literally 'pilgrim's staffs'] per le donne, e grossi o piccoli o mezzani, rispose: E mezzani sono migliori. Dimandata perche, rispose: Perche de grossi non se ne trovano.

From One Hundred Renaissance Jokes (Summa Publications, Birmingham, Alabama, 1988)

A woman was asked what kind of penises women preferred, big or small or medium-sized. She answered: 'Medium-sized are best.' When asked the reason she replied: 'Because there aren't any big ones.'

CELIA BROWN
LMH 1973
Harlequin
with heart
acrylic on wood, 1997

A. C. Brown (Human
Sciences; Ph.D., 1982 LSE)
attended Frankfurt School
of Fine Art and now works
as an artist and sculptor
in Germany. Her many
exhibitions include
'Handmaidens of Venus'
at LMH in 1999.
See also p. 214

A Proposal

When Ella Sykes advertised for a post as a home-help (see p. 119), she received one reply.

DEAR MADAM, I see you're 'ad' in the Province. I have 100 and twenty acres of my home, it is all payed for I lost my wife 4 years ago I ham 36 years of age I have horses and cattle and a lot of chicken would you cair to go in Pardners with me as I want to settle down again. Pleas let me know by return mail.

The Hon. M. Lambert
(PPE; CMG, 1965; Ph.D)
was Assistant Editor of
British Foreign Policy
Documentation and worked
for the BBC European
Service 1940–45; was
Lecturer at Exeter and
St Andrew's universities, and
on the Council of the Royal
Institution of International
Affairs, 1959–65. Her
publications include *The Saar*
and *When Victoria Began to
Reign*. She died in 1995.

From *English Popular Art*
(with Enid Marx, Batsford
1951; Merlin Press, 1989)

MARGARET LAMBERT
LMH 1926

Valentines

PAPER VALENTINES, made by embellishing a set of verses with a picture, seem to have arrived at the end of the eighteenth century; by the early nineteenth they had become very popular amongst all classes of society; Pickwick fans will remember Sam Weller composing one, and no doubt the advent of the penny post in 1840 encouraged Valentines still more. The first ones were entirely amateur, and often show much skill and ingenuity; verses are composed and arranged to form patterns such as a heart and decorated with painted pictures, paper cut-outs or bits of silk and satin.

LUCY NEWLYN
LMH 1975

Geometry

WHEN YOU WERE ALIVE
and there were four of us
we made either a square
or a four-pointed star.

Red, fire, sun   green, air, sky
vision, action, communication   voice, music, laughter

blue, moon, water   brown, earth, rain
ideas, words, reflection   sensation, touch, sculpture.

But because two of us are twins
we saw ourselves more often
either as a triangle
(you . . . me . . . them)
or as two half-
squares, two
separate
pairs.

Red and blue   Earth and air
sun and moon   sky and rain
actions, words touch and music
fire and water sculpture, laughter.

Now you're dead, we lack an obvious pattern. But we're not a square
missing one corner, we're not a star without a point. We are a chaos of
shapes and forms, tendencies to formation and shape: blue-green air red
sensation watery earth fiery communication seeing words touching
actions music laughter vision sculpture in all kinds of combinations . . .

After
a while,
there will be
a new dimension.
We'll be more like
a pyramid. And in this
shape, every face will be
a triangle, every triangle a face:
sensation and music in words; words
and thought in action; action and laughter
in voice. Voice sensation words action laughter
music in communication. It's a figure I keep turning and
turning. And every way I turn it, you're the apex and the base.

K. C. Kellaway (English) is a critic and columnist for *The Observer*. She has taught English at a mission school in Zimbabwe, worked as an advertising copy-writer, been a publisher's fiction reader and Deputy Editor of *The Literary Review*. She contributes regularly to *The New Statesman*, television and BBC radio.

From *The Observer*, 16 November 1997

KATE KELLAWAY
LMH 1976

Seeing double

CYRIL CONNOLLY DESCRIBED THE PRAM in the hall as the enemy of promise. What, I wonder, would he have said about the double buggy? I was 38 when I conceived twins. I discovered the truth at a 12-week scan. I knew something out of the ordinary must have happened when the scanner suddenly went quiet. I feared the baby must be malformed or dead. Then she said: 'There are two of them.' Two of what?

When she pulled the screen back to show me the two babies, what I saw was beyond anything I felt. In two separate caves, they danced, an amazing double act. One had his tongue out and was waving like a football supporter, the other was dancing in a more decorous style. My partner said it was like finding a surprise party going on in your house, without your permission.

It often happens in life that when you become interested in a subject, it starts to take a keen interest in you. Suddenly, I was seeing double. The window cleaner turned up with his unprepossessing brother who was revealed to be a twin. More startlingly, my father told me he had been born a twin. I forgot the first person singular, I was a walking crowd. Twins made their presence felt in literature, too (Tweedledum, Tweedledee, Castor, Pollux, not to mention Shakespeare's own children Hamnet and Judith). Even Hercules emerged as a twin with a weedy, non-identical brother, Iphicles. As babies, they slept in a shield together.

I had my twins at 40 weeks. The first night in hospital, I needed a shield. The babies, non-identical boys, bellowed. I was never good at sport and this was like some game in which you had to catch two balls at once. They and I were panicking. I was in despair. I described them, in my diary, at four days old: 'Bernie weighs seven pounds, one ounce. His hair is the colour of a cygnet. His skin, where unbruised, is palest alabaster. He looks as though he is trying to play a musical instrument, the name of which, to judge by his expression, he has forgotten but is trying to recall. Os weighs six pounds, two ounces. His head is a beautiful shape and squirrelly red. He seems less scathed than his brother, though less able to cope now that he is here. He needs private tuition with breast feeding, prefers to sip water from a dainty china cup.'

Those early weeks pass slowly – but they pass. Now, I am tired of hearing, when I say I have twins: 'Double trouble' or 'You've got your hands full'. The double trouble is also double joy. It is not bad luck (the Japanese believe that twins are lucky). Although my hands are full, my heart is too.

L. A. Newlyn (English; D.Phil., 1983; Fellow of St Edmund's Hall, 1986) was born in Uganda and is the daughter of D. Harrington (LMH 1942). Her publications include *Coleridge, Wordsworth and the Language of Illusion* and *Reading, Writing and Romanticism*, which won the Rose Mary Crawshay Prize for the British Academy in 2001. Four of her poems are included in *The Oxford Poets Anthology*.

Poplars, nightingales, snapdragon, grey walls, loosestrife and meadowsweet by the river, the blush of virginia creeper on grey walls, or of the bells across the meadows which are the spirit of Oxford made audible . . . – Winifred Peck, diary, Trinity Term 1904

G. E. EDWARDS
LMH 1886
**The Gardens,
Cape Town**
watercolour

G. E. Edwards (English) became a headmistress in Bloemfontein and taught at Rhodes University, Grahamstown. She died in 1955.

C. E. Edwards . 1925.

Illustrations by G. E. Edwards, *Cape Town: Treasures of the Mother City*, with Cecil Lewis (The Speciality Press of South Africa, 1927)

The Gardens in Cape Town were originally planned to provide fresh vegetables for the Dutch East India Company's ships when they anchored in the Bay. In those days, as at present, the order not to pick flowers was often circumvented. But flower thieves were properly punished by our ancestors, for anyone who damaged shrubs or picked flowers might be sentenced to one hundred lashes and a year's hard labour, or even two years in chains.

L. S. Sutherland (CBE, 1947; DBE, 1969; FRSA, 1950; FBA, 1954; Hon. DCL, 1972; Pro-Vice Chancellor, Hebdomadal Council, Oxford, 1960–69; Hon. Litt.D./D.Litt. Cambridge, Glasgow, Kent, Keele, Belfast and Smith Academy of Arts and Science, USA) was Fellow and Tutor of Somerville College, 1928–45, with war service spent at the Board of Trade. Her publications include *A London Merchant*; *The East India Company in Eighteenth-Century Politics*, and *The History of Oxford University* (vol. V). She died in 1980.

From *The Brown Book* 1970

LUCY S. SUTHERLAND
LMH Principal 1945–71

Maria Edgeworth's tree paeony in the LMH garden

THERE WAS A FINE TREE PAEONY (*P. sufruticosa*) at 14 Norham Gardens, the direct descendant of a tree paeony planted by Maria Edgeworth in 1826. Tree paeonies were still a considerable novelty in England at that date, and were considered difficult to rear. They had been bred and cultivated in China and Japan for 1,500 years, and a specimen was presented to Kew Gardens in 1789 by Sir Joseph Banks where it flourished until 1842.

Miss Edgeworth's plant was a gift from her old friend the second Lord Oriel of Cullum, Co. Louth, who had set up the first nurseries for seedlings in Ireland. She recounts his advice about its treatment and that of other rarities in his collection.

He said that he has succeeded in naturalising what are thought tender shrubs and plants by not taking too much care. 'Give them good mould, that is the first and greatest point – Never cover till you see the plant is touched by frost. In frost or bleak winds I cover them with branches of fir leaving an opening at top for the air to get in and for the damp to get out – But I never put on their fir caps even till I see they want them – I shall not cover mine till the frosts or winds of March. The peony tree I sent you which is a year-old plant will require only to be covered with fir branches. But remember, you will kill it if you forget to leave an opening at top of the fir cap for the damp to escape. More plants are killed by damp than anything else.'

In 1967 a portion of the original plant was transplanted to LMH gardens. Though it was an old plant to move, Frank Britnall, our then head gardener, carried out the operation successfully. The main plant was put in the bed in front of 'red' Old Hall, and a small part of it was detached and planted to the west of Deneke East in a very sheltered position. This small plant has flowered twice abundantly with the clear pink double flowers and brilliant gold stamens characteristic of its variety – rather like big pink cabbage roses.

B. J. Scott (English) was
called to the Bar, then
studied at the Courtauld
Institute; she writes on
art and art history for
Country Life, Apollo and
The Collectors' Guide.

BARBARA SCOTT
LMH 1956

'A garden composed like a painting'

BAGATELLE IN THE BOIS DE BOULOGNE is the most famous of the small
parks on the outskirts of Paris. The Pavilion, which has been restored by the
City of Paris, was built for Louis XVI's younger brother by the architect
François-Joseph Bélanger in 1777, and the gardens were laid out in 1778–
80. His idea of the Anglo-Chinese garden was essentially Picturesque,
conceived as a miniature landscape in the fashionable Anglo-Chinese taste,
with winding paths, artificial rivers, small lake, rocks and cascades. He was
influenced by the gardens he had seen in England and set out some of his
ideas in a letter to one of his clients, Mme Joly:

> I must point out that since a garden is a large version of a landscape
> painting, it must contain objects that will enhance the perspective. Every
> garden needs a touch of poetry and without wishing to erect too many
> small buildings, it cannot be designed as a simple, geographical plan but
> must be composed like a painting with the sky for a background.

Bélanger invited Thomas Blaikie to help him with the laying out of the
park and overseeing the planting of the trees. The Comte's Scottish gardener
became something of a celebrity. Born just outside Edinburgh in 1760, the
son of a crofter, he was well educated and kept a diary during the years he
spent in France. He had a boundless curiosity and, like Boswell, a gift for
seeing everything and meeting the right people.

Blaikie's diary records the progress of the work. In December 1779, he
brought honeysuckles and other shrubs to Paris and began the plantation
along the side of the road. To make the lawns, cartloads of sand were
brought up from the River Seine. He employed between 30 and 60
workmen and was assisted by two tree specialists. A year later he sowed the
first melon bed and, as an experiment, seven varieties of cucumbers. When,
however, he triumphantly presented the first 'brace of cucumbers', he was
disappointed to find out that, in France, 'they were not much fond of green
cucumbers, as they only use them for stewing'. But the melons were a great
success, Queen Marie-Antoinette declaring that they were the best she had
ever tasted.

Blaikie also sowed many seeds from England, including several sent by
Sir Joseph Banks and obtained by Captain Cook on his last voyage to
Hawaii. The gardens were maintained by 20 gardeners, three pruners, two
mole-catchers and a man to look after the pump which brought water from
the Seine to feed the artificial lake and streams.

From 'Bagatelle – an
Anglo-Chinese Garden',
Country Life, 12 August
1993

DEBORAH KELLAWAY
LMH 1946

On hellebores

THE CHRISTMAS ROSE is a paradoxical flower: it is white yet it is called black – *Helleborus niger*, the black hellebore – because its rhizomatous rootstock is encased in a blackish-brown skin. The flower is cool and pure, the root deadly poisonous; both men and beasts are said to have died of it, though it was used medicinally for centuries. Gerard prescribed it as a purgative for 'mad and furious men'. Gilbert White of Selborne reported that its powdered leaves could be given to children 'troubled with worms'. It heralds the spring, but there is nothing spring-like about it; the whole plant is leathery, sculptured, timeless. The Elizabethan poet Spenser listed it ominously among the flowers growing in the unearthly garden of Proserpina. In the nineteenth century it inspired one German romantic poet, Eduard Mörike, to write sepulchral verse (later set to music by Hugo Wolf). He first encountered it in a churchyard. It made a dramatic impact on him; he hymned it as a strange flower of the moon, not the sun, of coldness, not warmth. He detected a barely perceptible fragrance in its heart; it filled him with yearning and, as well as turning it into a mystical poetic symbol, he dug it up and took it home and planted it in his window-box. Thence it was blown away in a high wind.

D. V. Newton (English) taught at Melbourne University and then Camden School for Girls; her two daughters also went to LMH. She has written four books on gardening, including *Favourite Flowers* and *The Making of an English Country Garden*; edited *The Virago Book of Women Gardeners*, and is now gardening correspondent of *The Oldie*.

But it would not have lived, anyway. If Mörike could have read Brian Mathew's Alpine Garden Society monograph, *Hellebores*, he would have learnt that it is inadvisable to dig up whole clumps of *Helleborus niger* and transplant them intact. The best you can do is break them up into small divisions, each with its own leaf-shoot, and plant these divisions in wide holes filled deep with compost and leaf-soil. Gertrude Jekyll used to do this, digging up her Christmas roses in spring, 'washing out' the clumps and then performing delicate surgery with a sharp knife at what she called the 'points of attachment'. But herbaceous hellebores are long-lived, if undisturbed; I am well content to leave mine where they are, feeding them with a general fertiliser and mulching them generously in spring, then watching them slowly thicken and prosper. By February the cloches are off and the white flowers are coming thick and fast and more and more and more, like Lewis Carroll's oysters scuttling up the beach. If you cut one stem it makes more room for another.

From *Clematis and the Ranunculae* (Pavilion, 1994)

M. Keswick (English) went on to study at the Architectural Association, and drew on her upbringing in Shanghai and Hong Kong to write about Chinese gardens. Her publications include *The Chinese Garden: Art, History and Architecture*, and *The Thistle and the Jade*. She died in 1995.

MAGGIE KESWICK
LMH 1959

The making of a Chinese garden

FOR THE GARDEN-MAKER this is a task that requires not only individual skill and imagination but serious consideration of feng shui principles, and a tradition that supports the suspension of disbelief. 'The question of reality will not bother the visitor', says the modern historian Chuin Tung, 'as long as he ceases to be in the garden and begins to live in the painting.' Just as the connoisseur of painting unwinds a landscape scroll from right to left, and sees the hills and valleys rise and fall around the little human figures travelling through it, so a gardener should unfold a series of linked views around the visitor as he strolls along its three-dimensional paths. But the scrolls are linear and the gardens enclosed, and to make the most of each successive vista the garden-maker creates a labyrinth, in which available space is layered by gateways and subdivided by walls that wind among the trees and rocks with the regular undulations of sea snakes or dragons. Each garden is a composition of courtyards, some large, some small, some disappearing round corners, some open-ended, some cul-de-sacs, some fitted together like pieces of a puzzle. And the visitor is led on through them, not only by pebble-patterned pathways and open doorways, but by the constant suggestion of something new and delightful half revealed through the latticed windows or above the walls of the next enclosure.

Rocks and water form the structure of these gardens, then architecture, and only then trees, shrubs and flowers; for the Chinese word for landscape (*shanshui*) means 'hills and waters' and, while in English we speak of 'planting' a garden, a common phrase for garden-making in China translates literally as 'piling rocks and digging ponds'. The two elements are inseparable. Rocks are not only built up into 'false mountains' or used singly, like pieces of sculpture in the garden, but also represent 'the bony structure of the earth'; as the 'masculine' (*yang*) element – hard, rough and unmoving – they must, in the Chinese phrase, 'harmonise' with the soft, reflective *yin* of water. *Yin* and *yang*, the two elemental forces which the Chinese see lying behind all creation, are also quite consciously balanced out in the garden as high places lead to low, open to closed, shady to sunny, and wide to narrow, in a finely tuned patterning of opposites. In practice the effect can be almost magical. By leading him on through twisting galleries or over bridges, by allowing the glimpse of a distant roof, or an end vista, by turning him back or suggesting a momentary pause, or by 'borrowing a view' beyond the garden wall, the Chinese designer manages so to confuse the visitor that the space of his little garden seems to extend indefinitely.

From *The Oxford Companion to Gardens* (Oxford University Press, 2001)

Planting increases this layering of space. Obviously there are great regional differences between, for example, plants in a Beijing garden with its dry climate and extreme variations of temperature, and those of the subtropical south, but no garden is complete without the 'Three Friends of Winter' – pine, plum and bamboo. All old and especially twisted trees, like the junipers, are valued for their age and dignity as are fruit trees – crabapples, persimmon and peach in Beijing, loquat and kumquat as well as flowering cherries further south. A great many plants, especially *Wistaria sinensis*, lilacs and all the languorous frangipanis of the south are chosen for their scent, but few for their horticultural novelty.

In fact, though China has one of the richest natural floras in the world, the Chinese do not appreciate plants for their rarity but rather for their accumulated symbolic and literary associations. Among others the lotus, which in summer makes a new, swaying, blue-green surface some 1.2 metres above the level of garden pools, symbolises the Buddhist soul rising, 'without contamination from the mud, reposing modestly above the clear water, hollow inside and straight without'. Bamboo, which bends with the wind but does not break, suggests an honourable man, and the orchid a true gentleman because it scents a room so subtly nobody notices it until he leaves. The peach, hallowed by centuries of cultivation, lore and legend, still promises fecundity and immortality; the peony wealth and elegance. Peony growing became almost a national obsession, with Luoyang the greatest centre. Today they are mostly grown in raised beds to make a short but dazzling seasonal display. Chrysanthemums, the symbol of autumn, and probably the oldest cultivated flower in China, are grown in pots and set along the garden *lang* (twisted galleries) or formally on the terraces of grander halls, while the Chinese bonsai, tended in special courtyards of their own within the garden, are brought into halls and pavilions to decorate stands and tables, often silhouetted in open window frames.

All the arts come together in the garden – which not only needs a painter to design it, but to appreciate it too, a poet to immortalise it, and a calligrapher to write it down. As far as possible, all these accomplishments were combined in each garden visitor, who, using the nom de plume that absolved him from the formalities of life outside, would write poetry with the aid of a little yellow wine, in pleasant competition with his friends or family. These poems, engraved on stone tablets and let into the garden walls, record –

from perhaps 50 or 100 years ago – the same sights and sounds that still surround a visitor today. Thus, a Chinese garden gradually acquires an extra dimension over time, while the names of halls and the couplets chosen for tablets on each side of pavilions – names drawn from earlier poems or literary works known to everyone in that highly cultivated society – make another link with great men of the past.

Chinese gardens were not, however, the holy places of hushed reverence this might suggest. Though the intellectual pleasures they offered might seem austere – and the formally arranged furniture of garden pavilions, though elegant, was, in modern terms, decidedly uncomfortable – unlike the gardens of Japan, they can accommodate without a violation a wide variety of human activities, from family festivals to amorous assignations. The Chinese garden is above all a sensuous delight, and full of joy and laughter as well as peaceful contemplation.

JENNY PERY
Chinese garden
wood engraving, 2001

The Hon. P. M. Curzon (English) is a writer, journalist and garden designer. She wrote for eight years on gardening for *The Evening Standard*, six years for *The Independent*, and now writes for *The Daily Telegraph*. She designed the gardens for the new opera house at Glyndebourne, and her publications include *Creating a Garden* (1996).

MARY KEEN
LMH 1959

Auriculas

ONCE I MET A MAN WHO WAS, I knew a distinguished grower of rhododendrons on the grand scale. Never having gardened acres of acid soil, I was nervous of drawing him out on his favourite topic. Instead, I said, 'Did you see the auriculas at the show last week? Weren't they wonderful?' The Distinguished Grower put down his knife and fork and stared into the space beyond his plate. 'One man's meat', he said, 'is another man's poison.' If you gloat over the ample blowsiness of rhododendrons, the chances are you may not admire auriculas. But if, like me, you find rhododendrons overwhelming, rather like fat women dressed to kill, the bright and tidy auricula, like a child with a clean face, may capture your horticultural heart.

Primula auricula was an alpine flower known to the Romans. The common form has egg-yolk petals and a white eye with a golden pupil at its centre. Unlike its retiring relation, the primrose, it looks such an intelligent flower, with its lively and open face, that you might pass the time of day with it.

Early European growers were besotted with the plants that they bred from this alpine. Lacemakers and silk-weavers in the northern counties of England traditionally collected and created auriculas in colours that never grew in the Alps, and watched over their progeny with the sort of care that others reserve for their children. Although auriculas can manage frozen winters, they cannot abide the wet, so shelters were arranged to keep them dry and shaded from the sun, as though the brightly painted colours might run or fade if exposed to the elements. The eighteenth-century weavers would leave their looms several times a day to adjust the position of their pets, whenever the sun or rain threatened. . . .

Getting almost a hundred auriculas through their infant diseases and problems is nerve-racking. Opening and shutting the windows overhead; watering very carefully and only occasionally, with a teapot, so that no water touches any leaf; turning the pots; picking off the dead leaves (with tweezers, the books say), and waiting for the flowers makes winter fly. . . .

From *My Favourite Plant* ed. Jamaica Kincaid (Farrar, Straus & Giroux, 1998)

If you grow auriculas, nothing is too good for them. Societies exist for the exchange of information on how best to cosset and pamper them and the Fellowship of Fanciers is another good reason for becoming addicted.

R. S. Padel (Classical Mods; D.Phil., 1977) is a lecturer, poet and literary critic, with a weekly poetry column in *The Observer*. Her publications include *Alibi* and *Summer Snow*. This poem won the 1997 National Poetry Competition.

RUTH PADEL
LMH 1965

Icicles round a tree in Dumfriesshire

WE'RE TALKING different kinds of vulnerability here.
These icicles aren't going to last for ever
Suspended in the ultra violet rays of a Dumfries sun.
But here they hang, a frozen whirligig of lightning,
And the famous American sculptor
Who scrambles the world with his tripod
For strangeness au naturel, got sunset to fill them.
It's not comfortable, a double helix of opalescent fire

Wrapping round you, swishing your bark
Down cotton you can't see,
On which a sculptor planned his icicles,
Working all day for that Mesopotamian magic
Of last light before the dark
In a suspended helter-skelter, lit
By almost horizontal rays:
Making a mist-carousel from the House of Diamond,

A spiral of Pepsodent darkening to the shadowfrost
Of cedars at the Great Gate of Kiev.
Why it makes me think of opening the door to you
I can't imagine. No one could be less
Of an icicle. But there it is –
Having put me down in felt-tip
In the mystical appointment book,
You shoot that quick

Inquiry-glance, head tilted, when I open up,
Like coming in's another country,
A country you want but have to get used to, hot
From your bal masqué, making sure
That what you found before's
Still here: a spiral of touch and go,
Lightning licking a tree
Imagining itself Aretha Franklin

continued . . .

From *Rembrandt Would Have Loved You* (Chatto & Windus, 1997)
See also p. 106

Singing 'You make me feel like a natural woman'
In basso profondo,
Firing the bark with its otherworld ice
The way you fire, lifting me
Off my own floor, legs furled
Round your trunk as that tree goes up
At an angle inside the lightning, roots in
The orange and silver of Dumfries.

Now I'm the lightning now you, you are,
As you pour yourself round me
Entirely. No who's doing what and to who,
Just a tangle of spiral and tree.
You might wonder about sculptors who come all this way
To make a mad thing that won't last.
You know how it is: you spend a day, a whole life.
Then the light's gone, you walk away

To the Galloway Paradise Hotel. Pine-logs,
Cutlery, champagne – OK,
But the important thing was making it.
Hours, and you don't know how it'll be.
Then something like light
Arrives last moment, at speed reckoned
Only by horizons: completing, surprising
With its three hundred thousand

Kilometres per second.
Still, even lightning has its moments of panic.
You don't get icicles catching the midwinter sun
In a perfect double helix in Dumfriesshire everyday.
And can they be good for each other,
Lightning and tree? It'd make anyone,
Wouldn't it, afraid? That rowan would adore
To sleep and wake up in your arms

But scared of getting burnt.
And the lightning might ask, touching wood,
'What do you want of me, now we're in the same
Atomic chain?' What can the tree say?
'Being the centre of all that you are to yourself –
That'd be OK. Being my own body's fine
But it needs yours to stay that way.'
No one could live for ever in

A suspended gleam-on-the-edge,
As if sky might tear any minute.
Or not for ever for long. Those icicles
Won't be surprise any more.
The little snapped threads
Blew away. Glamour left that hill in Dumfries.
The sculptor went off with his black equipment.
Adzes, twine, leather gloves.

What's left is a photo
Of a completely solitary sight
In a book anyone can open.
But whether our touch at the door gets forgotten
Or turned into other sights, light, form,
I hope you'll be truthful
To me. At least as truthful as lightning,
Skinning a tree.

K. E. M. Thicknesse
(History) worked at the
LMH Settlement
1899–1911, returning
as Warden in 1915, after
four years as a house
mistress at Godolphin
School. She died in 1957.

KATHARINE THICKNESSE
LMH 1895

Life in Lambeth

The LMH Settlement was established in Lambeth in 1897.

ONE OF THE CROWDED airless courts of Lambeth was called Providence Place, and the family I used to visit, to inquire after a delicate child, Rebecca, had lost eight babies under a year old. In 1899 the Lambeth children looked incredibly old, wizened and listless, and it was the sight of them more than anything else which made Waterloo station a temptation to me. There one could have got into a train and run away.

There was little done for cripples except Christmas hampers. I once persuaded a mother to take her small boy to hospital, for he had talipes and was hobbling about with both feet turned inwards. He was taken in for operation and when I went to see him on his return home I found him running merrily about the little court, but his scowling mother said, 'I'd never 'ave let 'im go if I'd known what they'd do. Why, 'e runs abaht like any other child. There won't be no 'ampers nor nothin' for us at Christmas.'

From *The Brown Book*
1953

*From the 'Flu Album',
1919 (see also pp. 28,
29, 39)*

M. E. Benson (Modern Languages), elder daughter of the Archbishop of Canterbury, cut short her studies at Oxford to take up domestic duties at Lambeth Palace. Her book on social work in Lambeth was published after she died of diphtheria, contracted from her work, in 1890.

NELLIE BENSON
LMH 1881

A drunken mother

AGAIN SHE PROMISED ME most solemnly that she would go to an Inebriate Home. But the next thing that was heard was a telegram to say that she had arrived there drunk and quarrelsome, and had insisted on going home again.

Her husband was so angry and sick at heart that when he went to meet her he only took the child silently from her and left her to follow. She was insolent now.

'Ah, you thought you'd got rid of me, didn't you?' she said, taunting him as she walked behind him. 'You thought wrong – Here I am – Oh yes, here I am.'

Two days passed before anything could be done. She drank on openly, evading him when he tried to watch her; rushing out at the side door, and sitting drinking in the public with worthless women.

Coming up on the third day, with a promise from the Inebriate Home to take her back, I found him standing in the shop, the picture of haggard misery.

'She's going on worse than ever,' he said. 'It'll kill me, if this goes on. She is quieter this morning, crying and going on, but she ain't sober. She's there in the parlour, and a terrible sight too.'

It was a terrible sight. There she lay anyhow on the shabby sofa; dressed in a dirty draggled ulster, her torn stockings and boots hanging down helplessly. Her face was dirty and smeared with tears, her hair lustreless and hanging over it, her eyes red and swollen, her mouth ceaselessly moving and twitching, and her hands clenched. She was moaning and crying. 'Oh, there you are, are you,' she said, 'Ah! go away, go away; I might have got better, but I've done for myself now. I'm past forgiveness now; let me go to hell. Go away, don't come.'

Her eldest girl was standing by; and if ever shocked loathing was written on a young face it was on hers. My only hope seemed to be to speak decidedly.

'Mrs Ballard, stop talking and listen to me. You have failed; you've given way again. Now you must keep your promise. I shall come back in half an hour, and then I must find you tidy and clean, and your things put together, and I shall take you to the Home I spoke of. You will stay there till you have got rid of this horrible habit, and learnt to be a respectable woman again.'

From *Streets and Lanes of the City* (privately published, 1890)

Eglantyne Jebb's draft
of the Declaration
followed 'the natural,
imprescriptible and
inalienable' rights of
man, as proclaimed by
the National Assembly
of France in 1789

THE DECLARATION
of the RIGHTS of the CHILD

The basis of the work of

**THE SAVE THE CHILDREN FUND and the Charter of
THE INTERNATIONAL UNION FOR CHILD WELFARE**

*Drafted in 1923 by Eglantyne Jebb (1876-1928).
Revised in 1948.*

BY the present Declaration of the Rights of the Child, commonly known as the Declaration of Geneva, men and women of all nations, recognising that Mankind owes to the Child the best that it has to give, declare and accept it as their duty to meet this obligation in all respects:

I.　THE CHILD must be protected beyond and above all considerations of race, nationality, or creed.

II.　THE CHILD must be cared for with due respect for the family as an entity.

III.　THE CHILD must be given the means requisite for its normal development, materially, morally and spiritually.

IV.　THE CHILD that is hungry must be fed, the child that is sick must be nursed, the child that is physically or mentally handicapped must be helped, the maladjusted child must be re-educated, the orphan and the waif must be sheltered and succoured.

V.　THE CHILD must be the first to receive relief in times of distress.

VI.　THE CHILD must enjoy the full benefits provided by social welfare and social security schemes, must receive a training which will enable it, at the right time, to earn a livelihood, and must be protected against every form of exploitation.

VII.　THE CHILD must be brought up in the consciousness that its talents must be devoted to the service of its fellow men.

*　　*　　*

*A pocket edition of the Declaration, printed on stiff paper, may be had
for a 2½d. stamp from the Public Relations Department,
Save the Children Fund, 12 Upper Belgrave St.,
London, S.W.1*

EGLANTYNE JEBB
LMH 1895

Saving the children

HISTORY AS WE TEACH IT to our children today is a mass of fables. Unconsciously we have mirrored our egotism in our painting of the past – polishing up what flattered us, obscuring and effacing that which humiliated. But were it possible for us to reconstruct from our incomplete and distorted records, as a scientist reconstructs an antediluvian monster from the study of a single recovered bone, a world history cast into some correspondence with actuality, should we have the courage to contemplate it?

In the year 1789 the 'natural, imprescriptible and inalienable' rights of man were proclaimed by the National Assembly of France in the famous Declaration of the Rights of Man and of the Citizen, and, after this verbal expression of the spreading consciousness of human rights, its recognition through legislative action followed apace.

The year 1924, on the other hand, witnessed the promulgation of a second charter of human rights, the Declaration of Geneva. It remains to be seen whether the awakening of the world's conscience which is shown by its adoption as a World Charter of the Child will also lead to vigorous action and legislative reform.

We are in truth living under a Despot – Ignorance with a capital I, and its inseparable ally, Prejudice

B. Kendall (Modern
Languages; Harkness
Fellow, Harvard; did
postgraduate studies in
Russian at St Anthony's
College; MBE, 1994)
joined the BBC in 1983,
working on *Newsnight*
and *24 Hours* before
moving to Moscow in
1989. She was the first
woman to win the James
Cameron Award for
Distinguished Journalism
in 1992, and also won
the Bronze Sony Award
for Reporter of the
Year. She became
BBC Diplomatic
Correspondent in 1998,
and is on the Board of
a Russian project at
the Royal Institute for
International Affairs.

BRIDGET KENDALL
LMH 1974

The railway children of Moscow, 1993

In 1993, Bridget Kendall reported on the crisis of homelessness that was beginning to hit Russia. Not for the first time, Moscow stations had become a refuge for destitute adults and homeless children – repeating a problem common in the years of turmoil that followed the Bolshevik revolution of 1917 and the Second World War. The new Russia, with its uncertain reforms and collapsing economy, found itself unable to cope with its mounting welfare problems.

I WANTED TO MEET the railway children, the bands of Oliver Twist kids that skidded past the grown-ups, bypassing gypsy families camped in corners, living their own secret station life.

For that I needed a guide – Yasha, a fourteen-year-old who looked about ten. After two years dossing in Moscow stations he'd been picked up by Russian charity workers who persuaded him to swap his hideaway under the station stairs for a bed in a children's sanctuary. He was small and wiry, with a big grin and quick eyes. The kindly women who ran the charity home asked us to keep an eye on purses and other valuables: Yasha, it seems, is an experienced pickpocket. As we wandered past the fruit machines, Yasha explained how he'd ended up living rough. He'd run away, he said, from a mother who used to beat him and a father who was always drunk. There were hundreds and hundreds of kids at the stations, he said. They lived by stealing and selling ice cream.

At that point sixteen-year-old Andrei strolled up. If Yasha looked like Oliver Twist, then sturdy Andrei was the Artful Dodger, with a big grin and jacket too big for him. His pockets were weighed down with books – an English–Russian phrase book on one side, and science fiction on the other.

Andrei proudly told us about his station life. This, he said, was his home. He'd negotiated a comfortable corner as a permanent bedroom, he had several lucrative jobs. 'Excuse me,' he said politely, 'but I must be off now, or I'll be late for work.' Work, it turned out, was running a newspaper stall in the bustling, filthy, underground passage near the railway tracks. As weary travellers learned their train was late again, there was Andrei smiling from ear to ear, waiting to sell them a magazine or book to pass the time.

Round the next corner we stumbled upon Garik, a small stern boy of about ten, sitting on his holdall munching sunflower seeds. He had just smuggled his way up from Armenia. He was sixteen, he lied boldly, and looking for a job. 'It's bad back there in Armenia,' he announced in his high-pitched childish voice, 'They've cut down the trees, there's nothing to eat.'

From 'Homeless in
Russia', BBC broadcast,
24 June 1993

Garik was clearly streetwise. He pulled out a jack knife and two guns to impress us, letting his sleeve fall open to reveal several electronic watches wound around his arm like silver bangles. If the Moscow police catch a boy like Garik, they take him to the police detention centre for homeless children. It's hated by the station gangs. And I could see why. I had been there the day before. It's surrounded by high concrete walls, and barbed wire. Most of the staff wear police uniform. Children with fleas and lice and worse – young girls with venereal disease – are instantly put into quarantine.

A policewoman in uniform unlocked the door to the girls' section to let us in, and then locked the door again. Thin obedient girls shuffled up in a crocodile and chanted hello. Half had been deloused, their heads shaven.

The chief warder pushed forward ten-year-old Katya to be interviewed. She looked like an angelic six-year-old, dressed in a clean red dress a little too big for her. Katya perched on a chair, dangled her feet and confessed her sins. 'I'm here for the fourth time,' she whispered, 'I was living at Kursk and Leningrad stations, but the police picked me up. Me and my friends we were just having a look round. It's nice at the station,' she added wistfully, staring at the floor. 'We sleep in the trains, the police don't find us there. We buy things to eat and have a good time.'

She did smoke, whispered Katya, she'd begun when she was seven.

The warder interrupted. In a loud disapproving voice, she explained that Katya had run away from her children's home so often, no orphanage would take her any more. Her mother was an alcoholic, a degenerate.

'No, she's not,' objected Katya.

'Katya's the worst child in the orphanage,' said the warder. By law, she could stay in the detention centre no longer than a month. After that, wherever they sent her, she'd steal away to rejoin her station friends.

Back at Kursk station, young Garik twisted his knife thoughtfully. 'It's not good here at night,' he volunteered. 'People get beaten up. You wake up in the morning and you've lost your cap and your knife. They steal everything.' 'Come back with us,' our guide Yasha suggested suddenly, 'Come to the children's charity refuge. It's not the police and they don't lock you up. You can have supper, sleep and leave tomorrow if you want.'

Garik looked doubtful. But then the Artful Dodger, Andrei, appeared. 'You should go,' he said paternally to the younger boy. 'You'll be all right there.' But Andrei shook his head in amusement when we suggested he come too. He had work to do, he said.

At the station entrance he waved goodbye proudly, standing in the doorway in his dirty baggy jacket, like the lord of a stately home.

In the car, Garik was having second thoughts. 'I'm not coming if I have to give up my weapons,' he warned. Yasha reassured him he'd be all right and begged one of his many watches as a gift.

ELEANOR C. LODGE
LMH 1890

Work with the Croix Rouge: refugees in 1918

TRAIN AFTER TRAIN – they were very tiny with open trucks – seemed to be coming along the line, looking strangely and unusually black; and presently a little black line began to form itself from the station towards our camp. We rushed out and our hearts fell. It was the first contingent of the refugees. They were women and children for the most part, with a few old men, dragging with them what household goods they eould carry, weary and sad at heart. The Germans were advancing in overwhelming numbers. They had gassed Fîmes and the shells were falling; the inhabitants could do nothing but fly.

All night they came; the trains ceased to run as the line was destroyed and many of them had walked all through the darkness, some little children dragging on their poor tired feet, others carried by their still more tired mothers. The soldiers who were in the camp were splendid. They gave up their own beds at once, and they set to work to collect rugs or anything they could lay hands on, that the refugees might rest.

From *Terms and Vacations* (Oxford University Press, 1938) See also pp. 42, 56

Every war, just or unjust,
successful or disastrous,
is a war against the child –
Eglantyne Jebb

B. M. Margolis (PPE) became a radical barrister, then entered politics 'to combat anti-Semitism': her parents are in part Spanish, Portuguese, Polish and Russian. She was elected Labour MP for Hornsey and Wood Green in 1992, became Minister of State at the Home Office in 1999, and Minister of State in the Cabinet Office in 2001.

From a speech to the Institute for Public Policy Research, 1999

BARBARA ROCHE
LMH 1972

Migration in a global economy

BRITAIN HAS ALWAYS BEEN a nation of migrants. There were in practice almost no immigration controls prior to the beginning of the twentieth century. The 1905 Aliens Act was a direct response to Jewish immigration and it is difficult to deny that it was motivated in part by anti-Semitism. Major Evans Gordon, an MP, speaking in support of the legislation, said: 'It is the poorest and least fit of these people who move, and it is the residuum of these again who come to and are let in this country. Hon. Members opposite do not live in daily terror of being turned into the street to make room for an unsavoury Pole.' He would be spinning in his grave if he knew that one of their descendants would not only be the Immigration Minister, but would be standing before you today making this speech.

By 1998 the Labour Force Survey estimated that there were well over a million foreign nationals working legally in the UK, of whom 454,000 were EU nationals and 63,000 were from the USA. This is one of the strengths of the financial services sector here in the City. One in seven City workers was born outside the UK, in countries such as India, Japan, Kenya, Jamaica, the USA, Australia and New Zealand. Nearly a third of doctors nationally are non-UK born, and nearly a third of all nurses in inner London are non-UK trained. The evidence is that economically driven migration can bring substantial overall benefits both for growth and the economy.

T. M. Hayter (History) is a writer on development issues who worked at the Overseas Development Institute. Her publications include *Hayter of the Bourgeoisie* and (with A. Moyes) *World III: A Handbook on Developing Countries*.

From *Open Borders*, (Pluto, 2000)

TERESA HAYTER
LMH 1958

Immigration controls and human rights

IMMIGRATION CONTROLS TEAR FAMILIES apart and prevent parents and children visiting each other, they force both migrants and refugees into the hands of often unscrupulous agents, they subject them to long periods of arbitrary detention and expose them to destitution, isolation and racial harassment. Refugees and asylum seekers in particular are punished not for anything which they themselves have done, but in a vain attempt to deter others. The detention centres are reminiscent of concentration camps. Governments try to cut the numbers of applications for asylum, through the ever harsher application of extremely repressive controls. Such cruelty is incompatible with the hard-fought-for gains of liberal democratic societies.

GERTRUDE BELL
LMH 1886

Gertrude Bell arrives at Oxford

Gertrude Bell was a traveller, archaeologist, historian, and finally creator and administrator of Iraq. In 1906 she travelled alone into the heart of the Druze country; in 1909 she crossed the Euphrates to find Kheidir, and in 1913 she crossed the desert of Nedj to Ha'il. She won the Founder's Gold Medal of the Royal Geographical Society.

I THINK SHE WAS THE MOST BRILLIANT creature who ever came amongst us, the most alive at every point, with her tireless energy, her splendid vitality, her unlimited capacity for work, for talk, for play. She was always an odd mixture of maturity and childishness, grown-up in her judgements of men and affairs, childlike in her certainties, and most engaging in her entire belief in her father and the vivid intellectual world in which she had been brought up. She was only seventeen, half-child, half-woman, rather untidy, with vivid auburn hair, greenish eyes, a brilliant complexion, a curiously long pointed nose and a most confiding assurance of being welcome in our society. And from the first we took her to our hearts. She came up in the April term (1886), which was unusual; but she wanted a preliminary look round, before she settled down to her history work. She had it all mapped out in her mind and I remember her chagrin when she found she must take some preliminary examination, especially when Bodley's Librarian refused a ticket for the Radcliffe on the ground that she was not yet an Honours student. She never could pass him in the street without wanting to shake her fist at him.

From the obituary in *The Brown Book* 1927 by Janet Courtney (LMH 1885; see also pp. 25, 70, 90)

Into the heart of the Druze, 1906

MY CAMP WAS PITCHED IN A FIELD outside the town at the eastern foot of the castle hill. The slopes to the north were deep in snow up to the ruined walls of the fortress, and even where we lay there were a few detached snowdrifts glittering under the full moon. I had just finished dinner, and was debating whether it were too cold to write my diary, when a sound of savage singing broke upon the night, and from the topmost walls of the castle a great flame leapt up into the sky. It was a beacon kindled to tell the news of the coming raid to the many Druze villages scattered over the plain below, and the song was a call to arms. There was a Druze zaptich sitting by my camp fire; he jumped up and gazed first at me and then at the red blaze above us.

From *The Desert and the Sown* (Heinemann, 1907) See also p. 129

I said: 'Is there permission to my going up?'

He answered: 'There is no refusal. Honour us.'

We climbed together over the half-frozen mud, and by the snowy northern side of the volcano, edged our way in the darkness round the castle walls where the lava ashes gave beneath our feet, and came out into the full moonlight upon the wildest scene that eyes could see. A crowd of Druzes, young men and boys, stood at the edge of the moat on a narrow shoulder of the hill. They were all armed with swords and knives and they were shouting phrase by phrase a terrible song. Each line of it was repeated twenty times or more until it seemed to the listener that it had been bitten, as an acid bites the brass, on to the intimate recesses of the mind.

> Upon them, upon them! oh Lord our God!
> that the foe may fall in swathes before our swords!
> Upon them, upon them! that our spears may drink at their hearts
> Let the babe leave his mother's breast
> Let the young man arise and be gone!
> Upon them, upon them! oh Lord our God!
> that our swords may drink at their hearts . . .

So they sang, and it was as though the fury of their anger would never end, as though the castle walls would never cease from echoing their interminable rage and the night never again know silence, when suddenly the chant stopped and the singers drew apart and formed themselves into a circle, every man holding his neighbours by the hand. Into the circle stepped three young Druzes with bare swords, and strode round the ring of eager boys that enclosed them. Before each in turn they stopped and shook their swords and cried:

'Are you a good man? Are you a true man?'

And each one answered with a shout:

'Ha! ha!'

The moonlight fell on the dark faces and glittered on the quivering blades, the thrill of martial ardour passed from hand to clasped hand, and earth cried to heaven: War! red war!

And then one of the three saw me standing in the circle, and strode up and raised his sword above his head, as though nation saluted nation.

'Lady!' he said, 'the English and the Druze are one.'

I said: 'Thank God! we, too, are a fighting race.'

Indeed, at that moment there seemed no finer thing than to go out and kill your enemy.

And when this swearing in of warriors was over, we ran down the hill under the moon, still holding hands, and I, seeing that some were only children not yet full grown, said to the companion whose hand chance had put in mine:

'Do all these go out with you?'

Below: from the Oxford Dictionary of Twentieth-Century Quotations

He answered: 'By God! not all. The ungrown boys must stay at home and pray to God that their day may soon come.'

I feel at times like the Creator about the middle of the week. He must have wondered what it was going to be like, as I do – Gertrude Bell on the creation of Iraq, Cairo Conference, 1921

S. J. Leviton (Natural Sciences), Medical Physicist at St Mary's Paddington, is also the biographer of Marie Stopes, and author of the Oxford Children's Pocket Book of Living Things.

A cure for heartache, 1914

Before her lonely journey to Ha'il in January 1914, Gertrude Bell wrote to her friend Domnul of her resolve to overcome the heartbreak of an impossible love for a married man.

I WANT TO CUT ALL LINKS with the world, and that is the best and wisest thing to do. The road and the dawn, the sun, the wind and the rain, the camp fire under the stars, and sleep, and the road again – we'll see what they can do. If they don't cure, then I know of nothing that can. And I have begun to look forward to it, so don't think I'm going off on a wild and desperate adventure in the hope that it may be desperate. It is quite reasonable for an adventure, and yet exciting enough to divert me. Oh, Domnul, if you knew the way I have paced backwards and forwards along the floor of hell for the last few months, you would think me right to try for any way out. I don't know that it is an ultimate way out, but it's worth trying. As I have told you before, it is mostly my fault, but that does not prevent it from being an irretrievable misfortune for both of us. But I am turning away from it now, and time deadens even the keenest things.

From Susan Goodman, Gertrude Bell (Berg Publishers, 1985)

MAGGIE BENSON
LMH 1883

Excavation in Luxor

From earliest days, LMH graduates seemed drawn to the East. Maggie Benson was the first: in 1895, she went to Luxor, where she supervised excavations 'from her seat on a white donkey, fly whisk in hand'.

JANUARY 2nd 1896

The excavation is allowed. It's lovely – though the Museum claims everything is found. I am already in treaty for a tent. I find that I am beginning to be considered in the light of an Egyptologist. The difference in feeling is so enormous now one begins to get better. Instead of idling as a pursuit, one had pursuits, and idles for pleasure – and it is so much easier to do that in this climate.

Feb 9 1896

We found a rose-granite Osiride sitting statue of Rameses II yesterday. Not a portrait statue probably, but very nice; the bottom part was completely rotted, so that it broke in half, and the knees and one shoulder were broken off, but the top part and the face are very good. Also we have got the largest cat – in pieces – that I have ever seen; the head is perfect, disk half broken, but uraeus perfect, it belongs to the colossal feet. We have now got down to the corner-stone, and are going to dig under it tomorrow.

The Duke of Cambridge has just gone – taking all our butter with him – none for tea, but there remain an Austrian Archduke and at least five Countesses, one Viscountess, and a few earls and some lesser lights.

From A. C. Benson,
The Life and Letters of Maggie Benson (John Murray, 1917)
See also p. 14

SAM KILEY
LMH 1984

Valley of death

ISRAEL IS BEING POISONED — by the very people who have fought to keep it.

It took the Chosen People 2,000 years to end their exile and return to the Promised Land. It has taken them only 52 years to turn the land of milk and honey into a country of foaming rivers, carcinogenic water and dying fish.

Surrounded by enemies, Israel has become aggressively self-sufficient, greening its deserts and increasing industrialisation. But in doing so, it has poisoned its own land so badly that, if Christ were born today, his first miracle would be to survive his own baptism. In fact the holy River Jordan, where Jesus was baptised, is officially an 'effluent channel' — or stinking ditch — by the time it reaches the lower Jordan Valley.

It seems extraordinary that the Israelis, who have fought so long and so passionately for their land, could have polluted it so completely in such a short time. But it was their determination to turn this desert into a habitable land that is killing their life source. The fact that Israel not only has no water conservation policy but no environmental policy to speak of has been a significant contributor to its downfall.

In the Negev Desert kibbutzim and Bedouin tribes (often sworn enemies) have been brought together in protest at a toxic waste incinerator at Ramat Hovav, near Beer Sheva. The plant burns polychlorinated biphenyl (PCB), obsolete pesticides such as 245T and DDT, and waste contaminated with heavy metals. The smoke billows into the desert sky, and the ash is dumped in landfills which, environmentalists claim, also threaten the water table.

Most of the rivers in Israel are now so badly polluted that fish can live in them for minutes only, and the fishermen's flesh is rotting. Already, admits Dalia Itzik, the country's Environment Minister, 40 per cent of water piped to Israeli and Palestinian homes is 'undrinkable'. Some scientists have already warned that carcinogens are turning up in tap water. 'The situation is catastrophic,' says Itzik. 'We simply do not have enough water to meet the needs of the population.'

The Kishon's toxicity was shown in a test performed by an Israeli TV station. A jam jar of the river's water was mixed with three litres of fresh water. Three varieties of fish were then put into the jar; every one of them died in less than three minutes. According to Greenpeace and the University of Exeter, the Kishon is a poisonous brew of heavy metals and other carcinogens. One environmental campaigner recently joked that there were no biological dangers from human waste, such as dysentery, typhoid or cholera, because 'not even bacteria can live in the Kishon'. A fall into the

From 'Valley of Death',
The Times, 4 July 2000
See also p. 100

Yarkon, the river which runs through Tel Aviv, can be fatal. The Alexander River and the holy River Jordan are not much cleaner.

Charlie Beitom, a former Navy commando who has been a fisherman for forty years, stood on the quayside of Kishon harbour and shrugged when the swirl of a fish was pointed out just as he was in full flow on the subject of the river's 'fizzy' water. 'It'll be dead in a couple of minutes,' he muttered. Sure enough, less than two minutes later a fish floated to the surface, rolled on to its back and shivered its last in water that resembled oxtail soup, smelt like an Elsan toilet and was, indeed, fizzy.

Israel and the Occupied Territories are suffering from a drought. Pumping from the Sea of Galilee, which supplies a third of the water for both communities, has been stopped. The coastal aquifer, an underground lake, is dropping by 70cm a year and is in imminent danger of sucking in salt from the Mediterranean. It is already badly polluted.

The level of the mountain aquifer, which is mostly under the occupied West Bank and thus will one day be at least partly controlled by Palestinians, is also dropping fast. Ordinary Israelis use 79 per cent of the mountain aquifer, leaving the rest to the Palestinians. They consume five times as much water as the Palestinians, unless they live in one of the Jewish settlements on the West Bank or in Gaza, in which case the figure is seven times as much.

The Israeli human rights organisation Btselem says that 215,000 Palestinians in 150 villages on the West Bank rely on rain as their principal source of water. When this runs out they collect what they can from springs or buy black-market water from Israeli farmers and their middlemen. Israeli settlers enjoy the lowest water tariffs, their Palestinian neighbours pay the highest price – the opportunities for profit are obvious. Ordinary farmers who grow thirsty crops such as oranges – which means they export Israel's water – also enjoy a huge subsidy. So, the Finance Ministry says, the water system will not receive the $100 million filter it needs to clean it up until the farmers agree to give up their subsidy and grow something that will not suck the country dry. And there will be no long-term peace between Israelis and Palestinians until they resolve how to share the mountain aquifer.

S. C. J. Campbell
(Classical Mods, PPE)
is a writer and poet. Her
publications include an
edition of Shakespeare's
sonnets, *Only Begotten
Sonnets*, and a novel,
Conquest of Angels.

CLARE CAMPBELL
LMH 1938

Shore scene with plastic cup

LITTLE DEFILEMENT
Where only wildness was,
You pop up crackling and grinning
Your split lip no improvement,
A cloud the size of a man's hand,
Whose predatory talons
Grasp at the sky.

I bend to pick the yellow sea poppy –
Oil-stained gash bleeds back
From glass not grass;
I plunge for refuge into the bracken,
Blue plastic fertiliser sacks
Deputise for the harebells
Indestructible, dead blue all seasons.

Homo sapiens deposits
Not animal dropping, that
The shore could use –
Excrement of the soul,
In idiot vanity declaring
Let all things vanish except me and mine
I am the only life worth having.

One day creation
Will take him at his dreadful word:
The sun fume-sickened flee
The sea boil tar-bubbles
The trees collapse like packs of cards
The billion genera and species
One by one lose heart –

Man's last temptation
To make a poem of an eyesore,
Forgetting sore eyes close;
Content to label
The obscene scrapyard
Neatly
'Police aware'.

From *Poems Formal
and Informal* (2000)

B. Bhutto (PPE) was the first woman president of the Oxford Union, 1977; Prime Minister of Pakistan 1988–90; Honorary Fellow, 1989. Leader of the Pakistan People's Party, she has been in political exile but hopes to return to her country and to political life.

BENAZIR BHUTTO
LMH 1973

A woman's place was in the house and behind the veil

FROM HARVARD I WENT TO OXFORD, where I became the first foreign woman to be elected as President of the Oxford Union. It was my first election, my first victory. I had been told that as a foreigner, I could not win and should not run. I had been told that as a woman, I could not win, and should not run. But I did run and I did win. And I learned a valuable lesson: never acquiesce to obstacles, especially those that are constructed of bigotry, intolerance and blind, inflexible tradition. I also learned another critical lesson in life – to follow my own political instincts.

I returned to Pakistan in 1977, hoping to pursue a career in the Foreign Service. But circumstances soon unfolded that would dictate the path of the rest of my life and change the direction of the future of my country. Within one week of my return from Oxford, a military coup toppled the elected democratic government of my father. Our house was surrounded by tanks. We did not know if we would live or die, if we would survive to see the dawn of the next day's sun. My father was arrested, released, re-arrested and finally hanged.

I was catapulted into politics by the force of circumstance. When my father was executed, I was called upon by a people in despair to take charge and pursue his mission for freedom and constitutional rule.

As the daughter of the martyred, I had a special position in the hearts and minds of the people I led. I was their leader, but also their sister – one of the larger family that sticks together no matter how strong the political strain, no matter how grave the adversity.

I am proud that the Pakistan People's Party provided me, a woman, with the opportunity to lead a nation with deeply rooted tribal values and a hierarchical order based on social division. This was not an easy task at a time when the military dictatorship insisted that a woman's place was in the house and behind the veil.

Many believe that the women leaders of South Asia have inherited leadership through assassination of loved ones in the family. But that is to forget that each of us had to win our badges of honour by paying a political price. I paid that political price, spending nearly six years in one form of imprisonment or another, mostly in solitary confinement, in an all-pervasive climate of fear and dread.

From a speech given in the USA, 14 March 2001 See also pp. 51, 166

Benazir Bhutto
(continued)

Punished for what I do

How I have grown to hate the ring of the phone in the night, it invariably brings bad news. Two weeks ago I was woken by a midnight call and told that my husband Asif had been kidnapped from his prison hospital bed in Islamabad where he was kept in solitary confinement.

My heart sank. Three hours earlier an interview I had given to the BBC had been broadcast in Pakistan. I knew that the Generals who seized power two years ago would dislike what I had to say. But I also knew that my democratic principles called upon me to speak out.

As has happened so often, the regime had reacted by venting their anger on my husband . . . My husband is blamed for permitting me to walk and work outside the four walls of the house and the four confines of the *chador*, the full-length cloth with which women cover themselves. According to extremists, he is to be punished for what I do.

From *The Sunday Telegraph*, 22 July 2001

R. V. Schofield (History) is a broadcaster with the BBC World Service, and writes for *The Financial Times* and *The Independent*. Her publications include *The Bhutto Trial and Execution*, and *Every Rock, Every Hill: The North-West Frontier and Afghanistan*.

VICTORIA SCHOFIELD
LMH 1974

Kashmir in conflict

In 1989 a significant number of the Muslim inhabitants of the valley began a movement of protest, which was both an armed struggle and a political rejection of their continuing allegiance to the Indian Union, but the Kashmiri activists lacked any obvious unanimity of objective in their movement. Some were still fighting for the plebiscite to be held so that the valley could join Pakistan; others wanted a plebiscite which would include a 'third option' – independence of the entire state. The Buddhist Ladakhis and the Shia Muslims of the Karqil area did not support the movement of protest. The Hindus and Sikhs of the Jammu region resented the dominant will of the numerically superior Muslims of the valley.

Spanning the history of the past fifty years are the lives, and sadly often violent deaths, of innocent men, women and children who have been caught up in a war which seems unending. After half a century, the conflict remains both a struggle for land as well as about the rights of people to determine their future. As I was often told during my research on Kashmir, 'You cannot talk about Kashmir as a dispute between two nations. It is a conflict because we – the Kashmiris – are in the middle.'

From *Kashmir In Conflict* (I. B. Tauris, 2000)

CHARIS WADDY
LMH 1927

Caricatures of Islam

Benazir Bhutto at the award of her honorary fellowship in 1989, in conversation with Dr Charis Waddy

C. Waddy (Oriental Languages; Ph.D., SOAS, 1934; Visiting Professor at Cairo University, 1977; awarded Pakistan Star of Excellence by the then Prime Minister Benazir Bhutto, 1990) was the first woman to be awarded the Bryce and Oxford University Senior Studentships in oriental languages, in 1932. Her publications include *Women in Muslim History*.

From *The Muslim Mind* (Longman, 1976)

I FOUND MYSELF TRYING TO DEAL with the caricatures of the Muslim and the Arab so deeply engraved in the Western mind. Few cared to ask what Islam looked like to those who practised it. But this was a question I was equipped to ask. I offered a platform on which Muslims could say what they themselves wanted to say about their own beliefs.

At the United Nations or at any world conference today almost a quarter of the delegates are likely to have a background of the Muslim faith. It is a matter of some importance to understand the values and beliefs of so large and influential a segment of the human race.

The chequered history of the past does not make it easy to understand the Muslim mind. There are bloodstained pages on both sides of the record, and old wounds still fester. But even at the times when confrontation has been most bitter, there have been voices in both Islam and Christendom giving a truer interpretation of the spirit of both religions.

The simplistic view of the *Chanson de Roland* – 'Chretiens ont droit, paiens ont tort' – has never been the limit of Western thought. At the height of the period of crusading fervour, Peter the Venerable commissioned a translation of the Qur'an in Latin. When Europe was threatened by the Ottoman invasions, the Swiss scholar Bibliander made sure that the new invention of printing should bring the Qur'an to the attention of scholars and statesmen. His edition, first published in 1543, is still to be found on the shelves of the great libraries of Europe. His comment was, 'The beginning of all these wars, captivities and plagues may be clearly perceived to be in ourselves which are Christian men by name only, not in deeds and living. The same ungracious deeds which we abhor in others, yea or greater mischiefs, are done amongst Christians. Neither would Mahumet seem at any hand to be Christ's enemy.'

Western attitudes towards Islam have often been shaped by some dim and biased memory of the Crusades, or by headlines of political or military activities in Muslim countries. It would hardly be fair to judge the merit of Christian faith by IRA or extreme Protestant action in Ireland, yet that is how Islam is often viewed. Western statesmen have failed to grasp the fundamental opposition between dialectical materialism and Islam. They have also failed to assess the determination in the Muslim world to provide an alternative to the materialism of both the capitalist and the communist systems.

N. M. Abu-Zahra
(Anthropology; B.Litt.,
1964; D.Phil. 1968;
Lecturer at Kuwait
University 1977–78).
Her publications include
*The Pure and the
Powerful: Studies in
Contemporary Muslim
Society.*

NADIA ABU-ZAHRA
LMH 1960

Tunisian villages

FAMILY CONNECTIONS ARE STRONG. All the inhabitants of a village quarter are the descendants of one ancestor, or so they claim. All families are at some point connected by marriage. Tunisians value highly these ties of kinship and marriage. Above all they value their ancestors and their parents. If a man wants to thank a person for rendering him a service and show the utmost respect he would say to his benefactor: 'May God have mercy on your parents.' He means ancestors as well.

Tunisians hate to leave their birthplace. If they have to work in another town they do not live there but ride miles back at the end of the day on their bicycles, motorcycles, cars or buses. People are surprised if a person leaves his place of origin and moves to live in another village. They usually think he has disgraced himself, for why else would he leave his home and family and live where nobody knows him, where he has no connections and where he is ignorant of the innermost values of the community? They have little respect for outsiders.

These values, in which the family is held in such importance, conflict with harsh economic conditions caused by the droughts and floods as well as the fact that the land cannot support the increasing population. Better medical care has decreased the rate of infant mortality, but in spite of the government encouragement to diversify their economy some Tunisians are forced to leave their villages and emigrate to France, West Germany and Libya. They always try to return for holidays, bringing with them the latest European fashions. They come back to fulfil the vows they may have made to the patron saint of their village. As custom demands, they do this by slaughtering an animal and inviting the villagers to participate in a feast for the saint. They then sing the usual mystic hymns in praise of the prophet and the saint; reflecting on the events of their life, they say: 'Between sweetness and bitterness our lives are spent.'

From *Peoples of the
World*, ed. Dr Ahmed
Al-Shahi (Danbury Press/
Europa Verlag/Grolier
Enterprises, 1982)

R. J. Hendry (Social Anthropology; D.Phil., 1979; FRAI; Professor of Social Anthropology, Oxford Brookes University) has published extensively on Japanense society and was given the Japanese Festival Award for the promotion of Anglo-Japanese understanding. Her publications include *The Orient Strikes Back*.

From *Wrapping Culture: Politeness, Presentation and Power in Japan* (Clarendon Press, 1993)

JOY HENDRY
LMH 1971

Japanese wrapping – 500 ways to fold paper

FOR MOST EXCHANGES OF GIFTS in Japan, as elsewhere, there are customary ways of wrapping and presenting the article in question. There are also occasions when it is appropriate to present gifts, and there are commodities which are thought suitable to be presented at those times. Books of etiquette advise about details of wrapping practice, but in modern Japan it is often possible to have a gift wrapped in the appropriate way at the point of purchase, and most stores will include the price of the wrapping paper and any decoration in the cost of the gift.

Some stores will offer a range of wrapping materials from which a choice may be made, others will charge extra for coverings which differ from the regular wrap they provide. One specialist shop in Tokyo has even gone to the trouble of publishing its own hardback manual, with English versions of the explanations. The custom of wrapping gifts purchased in a store was probably imported from America, and a decorative bow of the same origin is often used for gifts made on imported occasions such as birthdays and Christmas, but indigenous occasions have more complicated rules.

First of all, there is a clear division into two types amongst gifts made in the more traditional Japanese order, these being gifts for happy or auspicious occasions associated with celebrations of life, and gifts for memorials for the dead.

The paper used for auspicious events is decorated with an emblem known as a *noshi*, properly a small piece of abalone wrapped in a hexagonally shaped open envelope, but often simply printed on the paper itself. This piece of shellfish officially indicates to the recipient that the donor of the gift is free from the pollution associated with death, when it would be prohibited to use meat of any kind, although it has recently simply become a customary symbol of a gift. Paper for memorial gifts is decorated with a suitable motif such as lotus flowers.

Further distinctions are made in the way of folding the paper, a more ancient indicator of meaning with up to some 500 possibilities, and if the gifts are to be tied up, the strings are in different colours and may indicate further divisions in types of gifts.

N. F. Khan (English; OBE, 1999, for services to cultural diversity) was a columnist on *The Guardian*, the *Evening Standard* and the *New Statesman*, and theatre editor of *Time Out*. She is Co-Director of the Academy of Indian Dance, and adviser to the Arts Council on Cultural Diversity. Her publications include *The Arts Britain Ignores*, a study of ethnic minority arts.

NASEEM KHAN
LMH 1958

Svetlana's place: a gift from Stalin's daughter

KALAKANKAR IS A SMALL OVER-COOKED in-turning Indian village, marooned somewhere miles from the metalled road, on the edge of the River Ganges. Dusty-coloured, yellow, white, it is indistinguishable from the baked hot land around it, and little different from the thousands of other villages that go to make up India's 85 per cent rural poor. It has, however, one claim to distinction. Stalin's desperate daughter, Svetlana, stopped here briefly to visit the home of her new Indian husband, Brijesh Singh.

Kalakankar became a symbol of refuge for her. Instead of seeing poverty and struggle, she noticed the calm rhythm of life, the importance of a spiritual dimension, the grave magnificent colouring of the soil, the sandbank and the waters of the Ganges. Her stay was brief, ending in conspicuous defection from her father's Russia to the West, but she did not forget the place. When Brijesh died, she presented it with an extraordinary gift, a 41-bed hospital – an act that raised doubts over its appropriateness.

'We suggested to her, why don't you give scholarships for some deserving students?' said her sister-in-law Prakashvati gently, who, with her husband, Suresh, cares meticulously for Svetlana's love-child. But no, only a hospital would satisfy Svetlana.

The checks have been – as they suspected – enormous. First of all, no contractors would bid for the job at all, so far from anywhere, and with only bricks and sand available locally. Doctors and nurses were averse to burying themselves in the sticks. And the building has not helped. The designer omitted to consider the force and direction of the sun. As a result, the male ward was unusable when I visited five months after the grand opening, and I could not help noticing that the legs of the operating table were propped up with bricks.

There are hurdles to overcome. Blood takes twenty-four hours to travel there from the nearest city. No local woman had, when I visited, consented to give birth in the hospital. But, imperfect as it is, the Brijesh Singh Memorial Hospital has left its mark – 3,000 villagers had travelled up to forty miles to its Out-patients Department in the first six months: no mean tally. It would seem the hospital shares Svetlana's qualities – stubbornness, contrariness, but an engaging and effective generosity.

From 'Svetlana Station', *The Guardian*, 21 August 1970

C. Anson (Modern
Languages, 1917;
Emeritus Fellow 1926;
Librarian 1930–47)
was compiler of the
LMH Registers for 1923,
1925, 1928 and 1947,
and editor of *The Brown
Book* from 1957 to 1971.
She died in 1991.

*Christine Anson's
passport, cancelled
as she travelled in
Germany at the
outbreak of war
in 1914*

N. L. Beloff (History)
spent World War II in
the French section of
the Political Intelligence
Department, and in 1945
began writing for Reuters.
She was the first woman
political correspondent
on a national newspaper;
and the first woman
correspondent in
Washington (for *The
Observer*). In 1979 she
was arrested on the
borders of the USSR
and Hungary and accused
of 'spreading hostile
propaganda'; she was
expelled from Yugoslavia
in 1984. Her publications
include *The General Says
No*; *Tito's Flawed Legacy*,
and *Yugoslavia – An
Avoidable War*, the last
published after her death
in 1997.

NORA BELOFF
LMH 1937

No travel like Russian travel

BEING DRIVEN THROUGH THE CENTRE of Tbilisi by a young Georgian, son of a senior police officer and therefore able to travel without registration plates, was one of the most alarming experiences of my life. He not only ignored the lights. He also broke the speed limit, went the wrong way along one-way streets and ignored even the normal dictates of self-preservation.

Georgians are the Cavaliers to the Russian Roundheads. They retain an unshakeable belief in their superiority over every other group, the Russians included. Racialism is endemic: ruthless economic and social discrimination is practised, particularly against the Asian minorities. The chief victims are the Kurds. Tbilisi is probably the richest city in the Soviet Union, but there were more beggars – mainly of Kurdish origin – than in any of the other cities we visited. Despite Moscow rule, Georgians do not feel the same animosity towards the Russians as, for example, the Irish towards the English. For Georgia has a far longer experience of being repressed by Mongols or Muslims than by Russians. By far the most destructive of the many invasions was by Genghis Khan in the thirteenth century. Fortunately, despite Hitler's exhortations, the German armies never managed to cross the Caucasus. The dread of Asia is still strong. The 'yellow peril' and the danger of an invasion by China is just as frightening to the Georgians as to the Russians.

Our next destination was Ordzhonikidze, just across the Russian–Georgian border, and we travelled over the famous military highway. According to Baedeker, the building of the road took 53 years from 1811 to 1864; it proceeded at the same time as the fighting. Baedeker describes the highway as 'one of the most beautiful mountain roads in the world'. It was certainly the most beautiful I had ever seen. The peaks are always snow-covered, the rock is shiny black or rich brown, the trees and grass, in many shades of green, suggest the texture of soft velvet. We saw hardly any people except the occasional shepherd (one asked to buy cigarettes) but any number of animals. There were spotted pigs, mountaineering sheep, goats with corkscrew horns and thin cows clambering up slopes where, I thought, goats would fear to tread. Perched on the hills were numerous monasteries and villages, built by independent craftsmen and each different from the rest in shape and colour.

From *No Travel Like
Russian Travel* (Allen and
Unwin, 1979)
See also pp. 78, 95

T. E. Whitehouse (PPE) worked, after graduating, as an actor for the Renaissance and Hull Truck theatre companies, among others. He turned to journalism in 1991, reporting from Prague for the BBC World Service and *The Scotsman* before moving to Moscow in 1995 to become *The Guardian*'s correspondent there. He now lives in London and works as an energy analyst specialising in eastern Europe and the former Soviet Union.

TOM WHITEHOUSE
LMH 1983

Expect nothing and forget about tomorrow

YURA PLOTNIKOV, aged 39 and a seller of second-hand bicycle parts, avoids despair by refusing to think about the future in any detail. But unlike many of his neighbouring traders on the fringes of Volgograd's open-air flea market, his equanimity is not supported by bootleg vodka. 'I'm fine. I don't need to drink. I earn about 100 roubles (£4) a day,' he says. 'It's a lot better than working in a dead factory and not being paid at all.'

Mr Plotnikov is not fine. Few Russians are. His wife, two teenage sons and retired parents live in dilapidated concrete housing blocks on porridge, potatoes, cabbage and tea. They are all gaunt and grey. The children are doing well enough at school to qualify for university, but unless he can find £625 a year for fees their education will soon finish. Mr Plotnikov says he is saving 'bit by bit'. Demand for bicycle parts has fallen with the onset of winter, so he has had to diversify. Laid out on a sheet in the snow next to a bicycle pump are three heaters, several door-knobs and transformers, bought from friends who steal them in lieu of wages from the

factories where they work. He wants 45 roubles for a round metal clock which began life in a military helicopter dashboard. Unless trade picks up miraculously, his sons will not be going to university.

'I will try to earn more money,' he says, knowing this is nearly impossible.

So why does he say and mean it? He is not a shoulder-shrugging optimist and is certainly not indifferent to his children's future. But without refusing to acknowledge that they face a hand-to-mouth existence like his own, he could not maintain his dignity. His wife, a nurse, finds the best way to control her anger is to keep busy at work and at home, and to talk rarely.

'I have not been paid in three months. We live wonderfully,' she says abruptly.

The Plotnikovs have so far resisted the lure of crime and alcoholism – two common Russian responses to the disappearance of jobs. Instead they appeal to the mutual support of family and friends. As the post-Soviet state undergoes involuntary privatisation, pre-Soviet traditions of collective self-help are revived. Next to Mr Plotnikov's parents' television are three sacks of potatoes harvested from his sister's dacha garden. Fruit for the jam that

From 'A Russian Family's Values', *The Guardian*, 18 November 1998

adds flavour and sweetness to their monotonous diet also comes from the intensively cultivated country allotment about three hours' bike ride from the city. At the end of the summer neighbours brought the potatoes back in their car. They were given some potatoes in thanks. Mr Plotnikov's 20-year-old Soviet racing bike is a crucial lifeline. To save money on bus fares he cycles to and from work through the ice and snow. It takes 20 minutes to pile his market goods on panniers at the front and back.

'More reliable than a Russian car,' the bike is washed and oiled in the hall every evening. Dinners are small, quiet and brief. His two sons then do their homework or go to visit their grandparents' nearby flat with their mother. Here only the fridge's death-rattle drowns out game shows and Soviet-era cartoons on the black and white television which is rarely turned off. Since his retirement from a local metal factory 10 years ago, Grandfather Plotnikov, aged 71, has seen his pension dwindle in value to the point where it is almost worthless.

His son has stayed home for some solitude. He listens to 1980s Soviet pop in the kitchen on an old ghetto-blaster which needs regular repair. It reminds him of more hopeful times. 'Back then, when Gorbachev came to power, it looked like things might change. But nothing came of it.' He answers questions curtly but not rudely. 'If I was unable to work because of illness I would borrow money from friends. My cigarettes cost 2 roubles a packet (8p). I smoke a packet a day. We call them contraceptives because they're probably bad enough to stop you having children.'

His flat was given to him by the factory where he worked five years ago. He pays no rent. Unlimited gas and electricity cost 200 roubles (about £8) a month – the last vestige of the once all-providing Soviet state. In remoter regions even these are being withdrawn.

A sort of urban survivalist, Mr Plotnikov lives outside the state, not in rural isolation but in the heart of the city. The government has not paid his parents' pensions, wife's wages or children's benefits for months. In return he pays no taxes. Utterly uninterested in politics, he has not voted in the last two elections and did not know that Yevgeny Primakov, the former Foreign Minister, had been appointed Prime Minister.

In developed countries not knowing who is Prime Minister is regarded by psychologists as prima facie evidence of insanity. Mr Plotnikov smiles at the thought.

SALLY CHILVER
Principal 1971–79

Colonial conference

OPPOSITION OF PAPER faces across tables,
Paper-clips shaped like foibles,
Lip lapse of peardrop-smelling clerical errors
In the hall of dirty mirrors,
Indomitable bluebottle life of old jokes
Among ashtrays and headaches,
And fixed for ever on a page with wide margins
The small griefs of virgins.

Ah, but somewhere, while a furtive rifle speaks
Among the elephant grass, a cross-eyed child
Is given his liberty with spectacles, and looks
Impertinently at his father; and undefiled,
However, and nevertheless, the moon asserts
Her queendom over deserts.

OLIVE LODGE
LMH 1905

Bosnian song

IF IN THY GARDEN the sweet stocks grow
Ask of my father, O love, my hand.

If in thy garden the scented geraniums grow
Ask of my brother, O love, my hand.

If in thy garden the sweet basil grows
Barefoot, my love, after thee I will go.

If in thy garden yellow marigolds grow
I shall fade away, O my love, from thee.

Allo ti nikne albabar,
Isti me, dragi, od babe.

Allo ti nikne malvata,
Isti me, dragi, od brata.

Allo ti nikne basiok,
Bosa cú, dragi, sa to bom.

Allo ti nikne zute neven,
Venucu, dragi, sa to bom.

Translation from *Peasant Life in Jugoslavia* (Seeley, Service & Co., 1941)
See also pp. 116, 118, 176

L. P. Neville-Jones
(History; DBE; CMG,
1987) was Deputy
Secretary of the Cabinet,
and Political Director
at the Foreign and
Commonwealth Office.
In 1994–95 she led the
UK Delegation at Peace
Negotiations for Bosnia
in Dayton, Ohio.

From *Survival: the
International Institute for
Strategic Studies* (Oxford
University Press, Winter
1996)

PAULINE NEVILLE-JONES
LMH 1958

Negotiating peace

WHILE THE GENERAL FRAMEWORK AGREEMENT on Peace for Bosnia (at Dayton) and the Peace Implementation Force in Bosnia (IFOR) are not necessarily models for the future, they do carry some important lessons to be learned, and point to specific errors to avoid.

If there is to be an intervention, do not leave it until there is a war; go in with a capability more than adequate to meet the situation on the ground; and above all, agree on and stick to attainable political goals.

A clear mandate, unity of command in theatre, and balanced deployment on the ground among the intervening powers are all essential.

Do not try to be too ambitious politically.

O. C. Lodge (Natural
Sciences) did relief work
1918–22 and scientific
research on behalf of the
Zoological Society 'in
devising means to
combat the menace of
flies to troops in the field'.
She travelled extensively
in Yugoslavia, collecting
family histories. She
broadcast in Serbo-Croat,
became an advisor to the
Yugoslav government in
World War II, and did
further relief work with
UNRRA in the Middle
East. She died in 1953.

OLIVE LODGE
LMH 1905

TITO: four giant letters

Olive Lodge travelled regularly to Yugoslavia between the wars. In 1952 she retraced her footsteps.

I SOON DISCOVERED that in the Yugoslavia of 1952 you could not long escape from politics. There was not so much downright political discussion on the pros and cons of Communist rule – for criticism of the Party is not encouraged, and some kinds not permitted at all, although more freedom of speech, so everyone told me, is now allowed than in the days before the break with the Cominform in June 1948. Yet people still keep looking over their shoulders as they talk. You cannot escape the effect that present-day politics have on the economic and social life of the people, the way they penetrate and affect its every aspect. Regulations and restrictions, 'musts' and 'don'ts' invade the home, the school, the shops; you find them both in the towns and in the villages. Then propaganda, oral and visual, is everywhere, pervading everything, in loudspeakers, compulsory flags on every house, photographs of Tito in every shop window, often four giant letters – TITO – shining electrically from ancient fort or tall modern building, slogans marked in paint or whitewash on walls and roofs, guarding everywhere, so it seems, against the possibility of any forgetfulness that Yugoslavia is now a Communist state and Tito its ruler.

From *The Brown Book*
1952
See also pp. 116, 118,
175

J. V. Brown (English) has lived in Croatia for over twenty years, where she has taught at the SUVAG Institute of Zagreb.

JANET V. BERKOVIĆ
LMH 1975

Croatia, August 1992

IN MY HEART OF HEARTS, it seems so random. I am the lucky one. My close friend, also British, also married to a Croat, last heard of her in-laws last November; they lived in Vukovar. A neighbour, whose son is in my daughter's class at school, was called up and stood on a mine ten days later; he lost a leg and a living. Other friends escaped from Sarajevo in August, having spent three months underground with their two-year-old son. These are people I know well. Our church has been a channel of humanitarian aid and through that work we have come into contact with hundreds of people with personal tragedies.

It has been distressing to watch the slow response of the outside world. It has been frustrating to be on the receiving end of EC and UN even-handedness, in a situation so blatantly uneven. No one underestimates the difficulties ahead politically. While the heads talk, we focus on the suffering. As I write, selected information about conditions in concentration camps/ detention centres is filtering out, ghosts of a previous holocaust and victims of another 'ethnic cleansing' rise up to challenge the world to action.

From *The Brown Book* 1992

L. M. Jones (Human Science; MRC Psych., 1989) was made OBE in 2001 for services to child psychology and mental health in war-affected areas.

LYNNE MASTNAK
LMH 1970

An extract from one day of Lynne Mastnak's Drenica diary: part of the daily round during the bombing in Kosovo on Monday 12 January 1999.

ILLIR'S SISTER LAURA EXPLAINED that their father and two sisters, aged eight and one, were killed by shells as he tried to load them all on to a tractor. She herself was wounded and watched her little sister die, asking for water, as they were taken to the doctor. Illir was too badly injured to know what was happening. Now he is very angry. When I asked if he wanted to explain what happened to him, he started to cry and an uncle rushed across and begged him to stop – so I gently suggested perhaps it would be good if he could cry for a bit and then he started to rage – not so much about his dead father but about how dangerous everything was now, how hundreds and thousands had been made homeless and how many had been killed. 'And they will lay mines and they will shell us again and they will kill old ladies and children and they do not care, and who will look after us now? There is no one and we will never be safe.'

From 'Why are you leaving?', *The Psychotherapy Review*, vol. 2, January 2000

J. C. Cavendish (English) eloped to South Africa with her first husband, and was imprisoned during the apartheid era. Caroline Cavendish (Lassalle) became an advertising copywriter and founding editor of Picador Books. She writes detective novels under the name of Emma Cave, and now lives in Cyprus. Her publications include *The Inferno Corridor.*

CAROLINE LASSALLE
LMH 1951

Breaking the rules

This autobiographical novel describes Caroline Lassalle's own experience in a South African jail.

IT WAS VERY HOT during her first eighteen days in the Female Prison. She walked up and down her cell; it was the condemned cell. A white prisoner with an Eton crop (she was in for theft; the only other white prisoner was a brothel-keeper) had muttered this information through the spyhole.

The spyhole had no cover, and its glass was missing, too. This made it easier to talk to passing prisoners. It also meant that Ida had to give away most of the small loaf of coarse brown bread – baked in the prison, and issued at breakfast – which was the only food that tasted clean. African women prisoners, who received no bread, just porridge and beans, would come to the spyhole asking for it, and Ida would break off pieces and push them through. She passed cigarettes to the two white prisoners. She was allowed to smoke, but they were not. She did not know how they lit the cigarettes she gave them. She could get a light only when a wardress came round, and this made her chainsmoke.

In the morning, African women prisoners cleaned her cell and polished the floor while a wardress stood in the doorway with a leather switch in her hand. The wardress never used this switch in front of Ida, but sometimes, when the door was closed, she heard the sound of it striking against flesh.

As well as cleaning the prison, the African women did the laundry of members of the government. Ida, during her exercise hour, walked up and down between the lines of clothes. Once she saw the name of the Minister of Justice on a pair of sagging underpants.

In the yard was a big wash-house with six bathrooms in it, but only one bath plug, which seemed to be in a different bathroom each day. During her first week in the prison Ida used each bathroom in turn. Later she always (after she had found the plug) used the same one. This made her feel safer.

At meal times, the wardress opened her door and put her food down on the floor, just inside, but, after a day or two, Ida waited by the door when she heard the food-trolley coming, so that the wardress had to hand her her plate and mug. The greyish-brown stew had a wrinkled skin on top, and she could not bring herself to taste it. She still had a small piece of bread and she ate that.

From *Breaking the Rules* (Hamish Hamilton, 1986; Penguin, 1987) See also p. 45

D. C. Elliot (English; DBE; Hon. Doctorate from Bradford University) was, with her husband Canon John Collins, co-founder of the Campaign for Nuclear Disarmament.

DIANA COLLINS
LMH 1937

Partners in protest

THE ANC TOGETHER with the Indian National Congress had decided upon a campaign of non-violent resistance to unjust laws – the Group Areas Act, by which Africans were being forced out of areas where many had lived for generations, and the hated Pass Laws. An African had to carry on him seventeen documents; failure to produce one meant immediate arrest, a fine or, more often, imprisonment. These laws were now to be extended to women. The ANC put out an appeal: 'With clear consciences and the knowledge that we are armed with lofty humanitarian principles common to all the great philosophies and religions of the world, we appeal for that moral and practical support which will enable us to enter into the liberty and dignity which is the birthright of all men everywhere.' . . .

John accepted the challenge immediately. He preached sermons, wrote letters to the press, spoke at meetings and drafted appeals. His return to the anti-apartheid scene produced a predictable new crop of hate mail and of worse. As well as in South Africa, there was unrest in the three provinces of the Central African Federation, and one morning our daily help arrived on the doorstep in tears.

'Whatever is the matter, Mrs Welch?' I asked.

'They want to hang Canon Collins,' she sobbed. 'It says so outside'.

And sure enough, our old enemies the League of Empire Loyalists had been at work in the night, and had painted slogans in large white lettering along the respectable wall of Amen Court: HANG CANON COLLINS – BANDA'S REBEL HEADQUARTERS.

They had used indelible paint, so there the slogans had to remain, somewhat to the embarrassment of our ecclesiastical neighbours. Later we had bricks through a downstairs window, car tyres slashed, and threatening telephone calls. 'I wonder', wrote Trevor Huddleston, 'whether at any time in its history that quiet and lovely Wren house had dreamed of being such a revolutionary place!'

From *Partners in Protest* (Victor Gollancz, 1992)

ANNE STEVENSON
LMH Research Fellow 1975

Terrorist

ONE MORNING I despaired of writing more,
    never any more,
when a swallow swooped in, around and out
    the open door,
then in again and batlike to the window,
    against which
beating himself, a suicide in jail,
    he now and then collapsed into
his midnight iridescent combat suit,
    beautiful white markings on the tail.

Inside his balaclava, all he knew
    was something light and airy he had come from
flattened into something hard and blue.
    Thank God for all those drafts I used to
scoop, shove or shovel him to the transom,
    open just enough to let him through.

Off he flew, writing his easy looped
    imaginary line.
No sign of his adventure left behind
    but my surprise
and his – not fright, though he had
    frightened me, those two
bright high-tech bullets called his eyes.
    What they said was
'Fight and fight and fight. No compromise.'

From *Collected Poems* (Oxford University Press, 1996; Bloodaxe Books, 2000)
See also p. 97

C. R. W. Nevinson, 'On seeing the swallow for the first time in summer',
oil on canvas. Collection of Lynda Grier

*Meredith Hooper on pack ice
in Prydz Bay, Antarctica, with
an Emperor Penguin*

M. J. Rooney (History;
B.Phil., Nuffield; Visiting
Fellow at the Royal
Institution, London)
is a writer of over 50
books on science,
aviation, Antarctic
exploration and the
history of Australia. She
worked in the Antarctic
with the Australian
Antarctic Division in
1994, 1998 and 1999,
and won the US Congress
Antarctica Service Medal
in 2000.

MEREDITH HOOPER
LMH 1961

Antarctica? Is that the North Pole . . . ?

SOMETIMES PEOPLE'S EYEBROWS KNIT. 'Antarctica? Is that the North Pole . . . ?' and I think of the bumpy line running along the bottom of our maps. Impenetrable. Meaningless. Bearing no relation to the magnificent continent sprawled across the bottom of our world.

The North Pole is in the ocean, but in the south the Pole is on a massive continent which is one tenth of all the world's land mass. The stripy pole that marks the position of the south pole is hammered into a mighty slab of ice 2,740 metres thick. A hundred metres below the surface is snow that fell with William the Conqueror. Each year the stripy pole moves 10 metres as the great ice sheet it stands on grinds slowly towards the Southern Ocean.

Every winter the surface of the Southern Ocean freezes, until the sea ice surrounding Antarctica covers 20 million square kilometres. The sea ice stretches in vast deserts, with tumbled piles like quarried rock, or narrow ribbed ridges like the beach when the tide goes out; in flat thick floes, and tilted, broken floes, and patches of inky-blue open ocean where penguins dive.

On Magnetic Island I saw 20,000 Adélie penguins nesting, and dead chicks lay on the cold ground like flat grey glove puppets. Dead perhaps twelve years, or two. Who knew? The cold preserves. The largest plants growing on land in Antarctica are finger-high. The biggest permanent land animals are one to two millimetres long. But all around the edges where opportunities exist, in the brief crowded months of spring and summer, are animals that live from the ocean's resources, breeding, feeding, resting.

From *LMH News* 2000

M. J. Miller (English) was a scriptwriter for BBC Schools Broadcasting and Associated Screen News films in Montreal. Her publications include *The Queen's Music*.

From *Amundsen: First to the South Pole* (Hodder & Stoughton, 1981)

MARGARET JESSY MILLER
LMH 1930

Antarctica: 'an awful place', wrote Scott in his diary

AMUNDSEN HAD STUDIED THE WORKS of earlier explorers and had noticed that in one particular place, at the Bay of Whales, there had been no change in the glacier's shore-line since its first discovery by Sir James Clark Ross in 1841. Amundsen came to the conclusion that in this place the giant glacier was firmly grounded on solid rock. That was where he would make his camp. He was doing a daring thing. 'It must be remembered that no one had yet wintered on the Barrier,' he wrote, 'so we had to be prepared for anything.' If his gamble of camping on the Ice Barrier worked, he would have an additional advantage – he would be sixty miles nearer to the Pole than Scott.

JO ANDREWS
LMH 1974

Captain Scott's base camp

J. H. Andrews (PPE) is ITN's Senior Political Correspondent, now based at Westminster after reporting on Kosovo and the Washington 'Zippergate' scandal. She runs her own news agency covering the Antarctic region.

ON ROSS ISLAND, on the edge of the vast Antarctic continent, lies the loneliest house in the world. It was Captain Scott's base camp for his ill-fated journey to the South Pole in 1912. It has been empty now for more than eighty years, but it remains almost exactly the way it was when it was abandoned by the British expedition after the grim discovery that Captain Scott and his companions had perished on their return journey.

The little house at Cape Evans is almost untouched by time. Entering it is as close as anyone can come to turning back the clock. Inside it looks as though Scott and his men have gone out briefly and will shortly be back through the wooden door, stamping their feet with cold. Their boots still lie at the ends of their bunks. On Scott's bed, his caribou fur sleeping bag is rumpled as though he has just got up from it. Above the bed hangs his hot water bottle and his green woollen socks with holes at the heels. The *Illustrated London News* lies on the bedside table.

In the kitchen the stores are neatly stacked on shelves or still in their original boxes. There is mustard, syrup, tomato ketchup, cocoa, biscuits and a host of other provisions all perfectly preserved down the years. Most of these supplies are still fresh and perfectly edible.

At the central table there is a chair for each member of the expedition. Captain Scott's is at the top, close to the heavy iron radiator. Beside the table is Edward Wilson's little laboratory; an experiment sits by the window half

From 'Scott Base Antarctica', *The Times / Los Angeles Times* January 1995

Jo Andrews' camp near Cape Evans, Antarctica, on sea ice beside an iceberg

finished. And outside, by the stables, bales of hay for Captain Oates's beloved ponies are still stacked in perfect condition. The hut has endured for more than 80 years some of the harshest conditions the planet has to offer. At Cape Evans the winds can howl off Mount Erebus behind at anything up to 120 miles per hour. And in winter temperatures can dip below minus 50°C. In effect, the hut and its contents have been in the deep freeze for more than three-quarters of a century. There are no insects, mice or rats, and very little dust. It is too cold for anything to moulder here. In these conditions nothing can deteriorate.

But recently that has begun to change. Antarctica's climate has started to warm up very slightly. That means that in January, the Antarctic summer, the temperature inside the hut is no longer reliably below freezing. About a thousand people a year visit the hut, and when they breathe they create condensation. There is enough water around for the metal items to rust and the fabrics to rot. The springs on the men's bunks have begun to give way, the old iron stove and the kettle on top are starting to decay, and so are the metal items in the old laboratory and the photographic darkroom.

D. M. Emmet (Classical
Mods; Professor of
Philosophy, Manchester
University 1946–66;
President, Aristotelian
Society) gave WEA
classes on Plato after
being inspired by a
speech at the General
Strike in 1926 by the
socialist historian Tawney.
Her publications include
*Function, Purpose and
Power: Rules, Roles and
Relations*, and memoirs,
Philosophers and Friends.
She died in 2000.

From *Outward Forms,
Inner Springs* (Macmillan,
1998)

DOROTHY EMMET
LMH 1923

Philosopher among the politicians

THE FIRST POINT THAT I TAKE from Plato's *Republic*, read as a moral critique of politics, is that one should not trust a politician who is purely a politician. It may be overstating the case to say, as Plato does, that no one should hold office willingly, since here, as in other things, one probably does a job better if one enjoys it. But the politician should know in his bones that politics is not the whole of life; indeed that there is 'a life better than politics', and he must be able to turn contemplatively to this in whatever form it may take for him: doing philosophy and mathematics (as Plato would have him), or going on a religious retreat, or painting pictures, or all of these.

The Hon. S. E. M. Boyd-
Carpenter (PPE), now
Baroness Hogg, is an
economist and journalist.
She has worked for *The
Economist*, *The Sunday
Times*, *The Daily
Telegraph* and *The
Independent*; was a
presenter for Channel 4
News from 1982, and
Head of the Downing
Street Policy Unit from
1990. She is a Governor
of the BBC, director of
the National Theatre
and of the Institute of
Development Studies.
She is the first woman to
be Chair of a FTSE 100
Company.

From *Prospect*, October
1995

SARAH HOGG
LMH 1964

Politics: a rough old business

JUST WHEN WESTERN DEMOCRACY has resoundingly defeated communism in the great global battle of ideas, democratic politics and politicians everywhere in the west are sinking lower and lower in public esteem.

It took someone from Chicago to cut the hand-wringing short. Politics, he reminded us, is bound to be a rough old business. 'Look,' he said briskly, 'if all the airlines competed for business by telling you that the others were flown by incompetent drunks who couldn't read a dial straight, pretty soon the airports would be empty.'

As one member of the present British cabinet likes to say, you shouldn't expect a pay cheque and a round of applause too. Government is, has been, and always will be a difficult and thankless trade. But hasn't it got more difficult? And more thankless? Asked how our arrangements measure up against the yardsticks of 'dignity' and 'efficiency' identified by Walter Bagehot in the nineteenth century, most people's instinctive reply would be: badly.

Disillusion seems to be affecting not only the public but even the politicians themselves, to judge by the number packing their House of Commons bags in preparation for exit at the next election. Some point the finger at an increasingly aggressive media and the over-inflated expectations of voters for making political life less and less worth living Others blame the system.

A. N. Widdecombe (PPE) was secretary and treasurer of the Oxford Union, then a Senior Administrator at London University, 1975–87. In 1987 she was elected Conservative MP for Maidstone and became Minister of State at the Home Office in 1995, with responsibility for immigration and prisons. In opposition, she has been Shadow Home Secretary and has written two novels, *The Clematis Tree* and *An Act of Treachery*.

ANN WIDDECOMBE
LMH 1969

Scrutiny is our duty

As shadow Home Secretary, Ann Widdecombe describes life on the Opposition benches, as she faced House of Commons censure after trying to disrupt committee sessions on a guillotined bill.

THERE WAS OF COURSE an early indication of this government's contempt of parliament itself when the Prime Minister decided to come and answer questions in the House only once a week instead of the time-honoured twice, without even so much as consulting the Speaker, and ministers announced new policy to the press rather than parliament.

Then along came the criminal justice and police bill, including provisions to retain the DNA of unconvicted people, to widen the ability of the police to inspect individuals' tax records and to impose fixed penalty fines for criminal behaviour. We did not oppose the bill but we did want to alter parts of it. Despite our helpful attitude, a government guillotine meant we arrived at the last day of committee with 56 clauses, six schedules, 42 opposition amendments and 10 government ones still to be debated and only a few hours left.

There had been no filibustering. At one point a Labour minister accused us of stringing out proceedings on Clause Seven. The chairman himself stamped on that, by saying that in his view there had been no untoward or overlengthy debate and that the committee was dealing with intricate issues. His Labour co-chairman agreed. Now Labour has decided to drop Clause Seven altogether as it was too 'confusing'. Suppose we had never debated it? Suppose we had only done so briefly? Suppose we had failed to produce the arguments which so wearied the Minister and his colleagues? The result would have been confusing legislation. Scrutiny is our solemn duty.

There is a great deal of law to which we have not been allowed to apply that duty. So we decided quite simply that the committee would not finish at seven o'clock on Thursday with so much undiscussed and therefore we used the only technique available to make sure it did not finish. At ten to seven I and three whips entered the committee room and quietly sat in the seats reserved for committee members. Parliamentary procedure and precedent specify that this puts the committee out of order and does not allow it to proceed. That should have meant the committee would have to meet again on another day and we had hoped it might then have been granted a few more hours of debate.

We should have known better. The government instead tabled a motion 'deeming' the committee to have completed its passage. I mock you not. That is what they are doing – without so much as a blush.

From *The Guardian*, 14 March 2001

*He has something of
the night in him –
Ann Widdecombe
on Home Secretary
Michael Howard,
11 May 1997*

MICHAEL GOVE
LMH 1985

SADDAM HUSSEIN
May be a pain.
But could we be told what this war
Was for?

RON DAVIES
Should have been christened Mavis.
Then no one would have thought him a wrong 'un
For chatting up strangers on Clapham Common.

ROBIN COOK
Should have thought before he took
A mistress called Gaynor
Who, compared to his wife, is considerably plainer.

From *The Times*,
22 December 1998
See also p. 132

C. L. Churchill (English), has been writer-in-residence and experimental dramatist at the Royal Court Theatre from 1972. Her work is translated and performed all over the world; *Top Girls* (1982) and *Serious Money* (1987) transferred to New York. *Serious Money* won the Olivier Award for Best Play, the Evening Standard Award for Best Comedy, and the Plays and Players award for Best Play.

CARYL CHURCHILL
LMH 1957

Serious Money

The play, which a long and successful run in London and on Broadway, deals with the new financial climate of the 1980s, when the City was altered for ever by the Big Bang. A cartel led by CORMAN *plots to take over unsuspecting Albion, but* JAKE, *one of the team, is shot and the Department of Trade and Industry starts to investigate.*

CORMAN, ZAC, ETHERINGTON *and others of* CORMAN's *team.*

CORMAN
Right, you all know the position,
Biddulph's stepped in as a white knight to stop us making the acquisition.
Don't worry, she hasn't a chance, it's just a try on.
We've 15% of Albion stock plus 20% fan club holdings whose votes we
    can rely on.
Two aims:
One. Boost our own share price by getting anyone at all to buy Corman
    stock to increase the value of our offer. Two. Get anyone at all who'll
    vote for us to buy up Albion shares.
So in a word, get anyone you can by any means you can to buy both our
    stock and theirs
From today we're coming to the crunch.
Nobody's going out any more to lunch.
(You can cancel dinner too.)
From today, we're going for the gold.
Put your family life and your sex life on hold.
A deal like this, at the start you gently woo it.
There comes a time when you get in there and screw it.
So you get the stock. And I don't care how you do it.

ETHERINGTON
My reputation for integrity Compels me to suggest you should take care.
    No point succeeding if that same success Destroys you and your
    company forever. Remember Guinness.

CORMAN
Thank you, Etherington. Some of us have work to do here.

ZAC
There's no question there are thin lines and this is definitely a grey area.
And since Guinness it's a whole lot scarier.

From *Serious Money*, Royal Court Theatre (Methuen, 1987)

You can't play ball if you keep off the grass.
So promise whatever you have to. Peddle your ass.
Let's give it all we've got and worry later.

CORMAN (*to* ETHERINGTON)
Are you standing there as some kind of arbitrator?
You can piss off, I'll get another broker.
The last thing I need in my pack is some tight-arsed joker.
(I thought you were good at this.)

ETHERINGTON
My duty has been done in speaking out.
And now I'll help in every way I can.
My reputation for integrity
Will reassure our colleagues of their safety
In making any purchase we advise.

CORMAN
Then let's get on / with it.

ZAC
Let's get on with it, guys.

OTHERS *on phones*
This works as a round, i. e., each starts at slash in previous speech and continues with speeches as long as required. At end of each speech, each shouts out the amount of stock the person at the other end of the phone has agreed to buy, e.g., twenty thousand, a hundred thousand.

1. If you were interested in acquiring some Corman stock / there is a considerable sum on deposit with Klein Merrick so / in the event of any subsequent fall in the share price you would be guaranteed against loss – 20,000

2. If you were interested in buying some Albion stock / there would be no question of being unable to dispose of them at a price at least equal to what you gave – 100,000

3. If you were able to see your way to supporting the bid / the new Albion under Corman management would naturally look favourably at any tenders for office cleaning that compared favourably with our present arrangements –

4. If you should be interested in following our recommendation to acquire Corman stock, an interest-free loan could be arranged at once with which the purchase could be made –

Meanwhile ZAC *(on phone)*
Remember me to Vanessa and the boys.
Listen. Corman, this may just be a rumour.
But if it's true it doesn't appeal to my sense of humour.
I've just had a word with a colleague in Atlanta & Gulf.
Marylou's been dealing with Biddulph.
I think it's time you spoke to her yourself.

CORMAN
Dealing with Biddulph? I just sent her some flowers.
What the fuck does she think – ? She's meant to be one of ours.
I tried to call her this morning but I got the machine.
Leave a message after the tone? I'll leave something obscene.

CORMAN *phones* MARYLOU

CORMAN
Marylou? You got the flowers? A tragic bereavement.

MARYLOU
Yes, TK made a real pretty arrangement.

CORMAN
And our pretty arrangement's still OK?

MARYLOU
I did dispose of a large holding today.

CORMAN
You what? Disposed? A large Albion holding?
I gave you that on the clear understanding –

MARYLOU
No, Corman, don't pursue it.
Anything I do I just happen to do because I want to do it.

CORMAN
You owe me, Marylou.

MARYLOU
I owe you?
I'm not even certain that I know you.

Unnoticed by CORMAN *or* ZAC, SCILLA *arrives, explaining herself quietly to one of* CORMAN's *team.*

SCILLA
Kissogram for Mr Corman from Marylou Baines.

Meanwhile CORMAN *and* MARYLOU *continue:*

CORMAN
How much Albion did you have?

MARYLOU
15%.

CORMAN
Can I just ask you where the hell it went?

MARYLOU
Don't be slow, Bill. That's quite upsetting
I like to think I'm dealing with an equal.

CORMAN
Marylou, it's not that I'm not smart.
It's just hard to believe you'd break my heart.
Biddulph? Biddulph? what? you knew you were getting
Information from me via / Zackerman via Jake Todd.

MARYLOU
You can't predict the sequel.

CORMAN
But you knew Jake Todd was one of mine.

MARYLOU
You are slow, / Bill.

CORMAN
Because he's dead? you didn't want to be connected
With Jake now he's dead in case someone suspected – /
So that's why you sold to Biddulph.

MARYLOU
I hope these phones are adequately scrambled.

CORMAN
I don't give a fuck who else is on the line.
You cheated me. / I hate you. I'll fucking annihilate you.

MARYLOU
Corman, you'll get rumbled If you don't keep your temper. Be glad you're
    alive,
(as my very irritating old aunty used to say.)
Don't worry about it. What's 15%? Get after the other 85. . . .

CORMAN
Can you see your way to going back into Albion?
Will you buy Corman and support our price?
Smashing Biddulph would be very nice / If you've anything –

MARYLOU
Bill I'd be glad to do something for you / but

CORMAN
I understand your problem, how can I reassure you?

MARYLOU
I'm playing with about a billion
But most of that's occupied over here.
If I had another hundred million
In my investment fund,
Then I guess / I'd have a freer hand.

CORMAN
I think I can probably see my way clear.
This is hardly the moment with so much else on our minds.
But I had been meaning for some time to approach you with a view to
    becoming a contributor to your investment fund because I have of
    course the greatest admiration / for your wide experience and market
    timing

MARYLOU
I could have my people send you some documentation.

MARYLOU *hangs up.*
SCILLA *approaches* CORMAN *and sings.*

SCILLA
Happy takeover day.
Take Albion away.
Happy takeover, Corman.
Happy takeover day.

CORMAN
What the hell?

SCILLA
Kissogram from Marylou Baines.

CORMAN
From Marylou Baines? I'll kill her.

SCILLA
I'm not really. I'm Jake Todd's sister, Scilla.

ZAC
What the –

CORMAN
What?

SCILLA
Jake Todd's sister.

CORMAN
Is this a terrorist a- / ttack?

SCILLA
I heard you. 'Jake Todd was one of mine.'
Tell me what it's all about. / Did someone kill Jake?

CORMAN
Will someone please get this lunatic out?

ZAC
Hold it, hold it, everything's fine.
I know her, it's O K, she's not insane, she won't be armed, don't press
The security button, we'll be held up for hours with water sprinklers and
    the S A S . / (Let's get on with the job here.)

SCILLA
You killed my brother . . . / Now will you explain
What 'one of mine' means. One of your what?
He did something illegal. You were frightened of what he'd say
To the D T I and you wanted him out of the way.
Tell me what's going on or I'll tell the press
My brother was acting for you the night he was shot.
Did you kill him yourself or get your broker to pull the trigger?

CORMAN
After the deal, after the deal I'll confess
To murdering anyone just let me get on with the deal.

SCILLA
You and Zac got Jake into some mess.
He did little fiddles but this must have been much bigger.
You and Zac got him involved in some corrupt / ring

CORMAN

Suppose I had killed Jake, his ghost would have had more sense than walk in here today and interrupt. /

ZAC

Can you spare me for five minutes?

CORMAN

He got on because he knew what was a priority / and he'd have reckoned

SCILLA

He got on. Doing what exactly?

CORMAN

That matters of life and death came a poor second.

MARY WARNOCK
LMH 1942, Fellow 1972

Save and prosper

PERHAPS OF ALL THE LEGACIES of Margaret Thatcher the most pervasive was the assumption that nothing matters except the non-squandering of money, and that no positive value exists except to save and prosper. Thatcherism increasingly, as the 1980s went on, became associated with the yuppie culture, the admiration for the upwardly mobile. But 'upwards' meant 'richer'. Increasingly, people talked about 'offers they could not refuse'. And these, of course, were offers they could have refused, but did not want to, because they were offers that would enrich them. In such a culture it becomes increasingly easy to cross the line between honest and dishonest means of becoming rich. If personal wealth is generally seen as the highest value, then the means to attain it may gradually become a matter of indifference. The erosion of moral standards in the City and the Stock Market illustrates what may come to seem inevitable. And once such a scale of values is adopted within a society, it is very difficult to see how to change track. The idea of the common good, which genuinely lay behind the welfarism of the 1940s and 1950s, has simply got lost.

I certainly would not condemn all that Margaret Thatcher did. I don't think anyone could. Nor would I deny that her brisk insistence on good-housekeeperly virtues such as thrift and individual self-reliance was timely and bracing. Yet out of her character and her tastes arose a kind of generalised selfishness hard to reconcile with the qualities of a truly civilised society; and since Thatcherism is by no means dead, even under a Labour government, the damage is widespread indeed.

H. M. Wilson (Classical Mods; FCP, DBE, 1984; Honorary Fellow, 1984; life peerage as Baroness Warnock of Weeke, 1985) is a teacher, philosopher and writer. She was Headmistress of Oxford High School, 1966–72, and Mistress of Girton College, Cambridge, 1985–92. She has chaired government inquiries into environmental pollution; special education; animal experimentation; human fertilisation, and teaching quality. Her publications include *Ethics Since 1900*; *Imagination*; *Schools of Thought*, and *Education, A Way Forward*.

From *A Memoir* (Duckworth, 2000) See also pp. 13, 94

V. Bennett (Modern Languages) is Reuters correspondent in Paris, London, Cambodia and South Africa; correspondent for *The Independent* in Chechnya, and for *The Times*. Her publications include *Crying Wolf: The Return of War to Chechnya*.

VANORA BENNETT
LMH 1981

Unlamented

THE OLD EAST END was buried with Reggie Kray – and about time too.

All human life is here, innit? The gangland characters paying their last respects to Reggie Kray on the Bethnal Green Road yesterday clearly thought so, anyway. Limo after darkened stretch limo crawled through the East End, in chilly sunlight, towards the cemetery in Chingford where the first two Krays to die are buried.

On top of each car were heaps of expensive wreaths and flower messages in foot-high letters, and inside, in the dozens of cars behind, were gangsters from the dreams of Guy Ritchie or Quentin Tarantino: big pasty faces, hair razored down to a threatening fuzz, lashings of gold at neck and wrist, shades, cigarette smoke, tattoos and mobile phones. More burly men in black paced along beside the cars, haughtily ignoring a hushed, respectful crowd. Most importantly of all, from behind red postboxes and double-decker buses, the cameras rolled.

This peacock display of traditional East End mourning might have been more impressive if it hadn't seemed so stagey and hammed up. For, however modish it has become to glamorise old-style London baddies, and however powerful the Kray brothers' bizarre grip on the popular imagination, the East End just isn't like that any more.

It is years since the real Cockney gangsters moved families and swag out to huge new homes in the suburbs of Essex or beyond. Any criminal old enough to remember the glory days of Kray-era badness will by now be drawing a pension. The fierce young men swaggering self-consciously through Bethnal Green almost certainly learnt all they know about gangland from watching TV.

It is a long time, too, since the down-at-heel streets leading from the City of London out to Essex have been a backdrop for such an all-white event. Reggie Kray's funeral briefly revived a fantasy construct of pearly kings, rhyming slang, caffs selling jellied eels or pie'n'mash with green parsley sauce and a nice cup of bright orange tea with three sugars, and urchins with pale pinched faces and muddy knees.

While the faces in yesterday's procession were mainly white, the shop-keepers and stallholders watching them from the pavement were mostly black or Bengali, and probably moved into the London Borough of Tower Hamlets after the Krays were banged up for murder more than three decades ago. There are a few old-fashioned shops in Bethnal Green Road, the kind of bakery that still sells cakes with cherries on top, and the funeral directors, W. English, doing the honours for Reggie Kray. But times are

From 'The Funeral of Reggie Kray', *The Times*, 12 October 2000

changing even here. No. 332, Pellicci's café, where locals say Charlie Kray used to eat every day, is closed for a revamp. And 'the Firm's' one-time home street, Vallance Road, is now full of sights, sounds and smells that the brothers might have trouble recognising as home: Bengali lettering echoing English-language street names, a modern row of houses named Fakruddin Street, the Osmani Primary School and the Picklish rice'n'curry café.

The arrival in East London of another group of newcomers might have puzzled the Krays still more. The narrow Georgian houses of the East End now command exorbitant prices. Gentrification is in full swing. Middle-class City types live in Bow and Bethnal Green. Teachers and social workers have been priced out of Hackney. Clerkenwell is trendy loft land and, in Spitalfields, seventeenth-century Huguenot houses jostle Internet cafés. The mean streets of yesteryear are filling up with wheat-grass health bars.

The paradoxes of the occasion, the clash of past and present, were not lost on yesterday's audience. On closer inspection, bystanders at the funeral turned out to be more bemused than respectful. Given that 100,000 enthusiastic Kray fans had been expected, the few thousand who did show up were strangely reticent about why they had bothered. Most 'just happened to be passing'. Kray's solicitor may genuinely believe that his client was 'an icon of the twentieth century'. But there was no support on the street for this easy sentimentality. Most of the people who turned out for a look at the big cars, big flowers and molls with big hair were, it emerged, there out of nothing more than curiosity about a vanished past of which they had no personal experience – a kind of historical film-set. If Reggie Kray's passing also marked the end of an old, bad, poor, violent era in the East End, it went unlamented.

M. S. Starkey (Modern Languages), spent time as a journalist and press officer before being ordained; he is now Vicar of Holy Trinity, Twickenham Green, and is also a poet. This sermon takes a humorous angle on the morning of Christmas; it reached the finals in *The Times'* Preacher of the Year Competition, and is published in the fifth *Times Book of Best Sermons*. His publications include *Frogs and Princes* (poems); *Born to Shop*, on the 'loadsamoney' culture; *Restoring the Wonder*; and *What's Wrong: Understanding Sin Today*.

From 'King Herod and Anarchist Football', *The Times Book of Best Sermons* (Cassell, 1999)

MIKE STARKEY
LMH 1981

Christmas, King Herod and Anarchist Football

This extract from Rev. Mike Starkey's Christmas sermon was delivered at St John's, Finsbury Park, on 20 December 1998.

ONE OF MY FAVOURITE STORIES from the *Hackney Gazette* this past year was their report on the annual Anarchists' Five-a-Side Football Tournament. Every year our local Anarchist community celebrates Hackney Anarchy Week. And the centrepiece of the week is a grand picnic in the park and football tournament.

Now, you might think the idea of Anarchist football is a contradiction in terms. After all, anarchy means the absence of order or rules. And all my fears were confirmed when I read the *Gazette*'s account of the games. During the football matches, said the reporter, anarchy prevailed. It all came to a great climax as the matches ended with the goalposts being symbolically ripped down, presumably by way of protest against people dictating to them where they ought to be kicking, or drawing oppressive distinctions between real goals and missed goals.

I enjoyed the report. This was partly due to some unintentional irony. The Anarchists wore bright Mohican hairstyles and trademark safety pins. Now, I find it oddly heartwarming to think of Anarchists having a rigid dress code, or trademark anything. But there was a deeper irony afoot. Before the event, posters went up around Hackney promoting it as A Celebration of Subversion in east London.

But to most of today's young adults, the ideas behind Anarchism – that authority is oppressive, that there are no absolutes, that the only morality is what we concoct for ourselves – are not subversive. This is what practically all my contemporaries were brought up to believe. It's what many academics in our universities believe. It's what most of our media promotes. So the Hackney Anarchists seem rather safe and predictable. They've chosen to make a political ideology of something most of my contemporaries believe anyway.

Let me suggest what a real celebration of subversion in east London might look like. How about this: an event held in honour of a great King, who has supreme authority. An event which announces uncompromisingly that he alone is Lord, and that to him every knee should bow in service. It would be an event which tells us the only sure path to freedom is complete submission, putting yourself out of the picture and putting others first. And of course, such an event does exist. It's called Christmas.

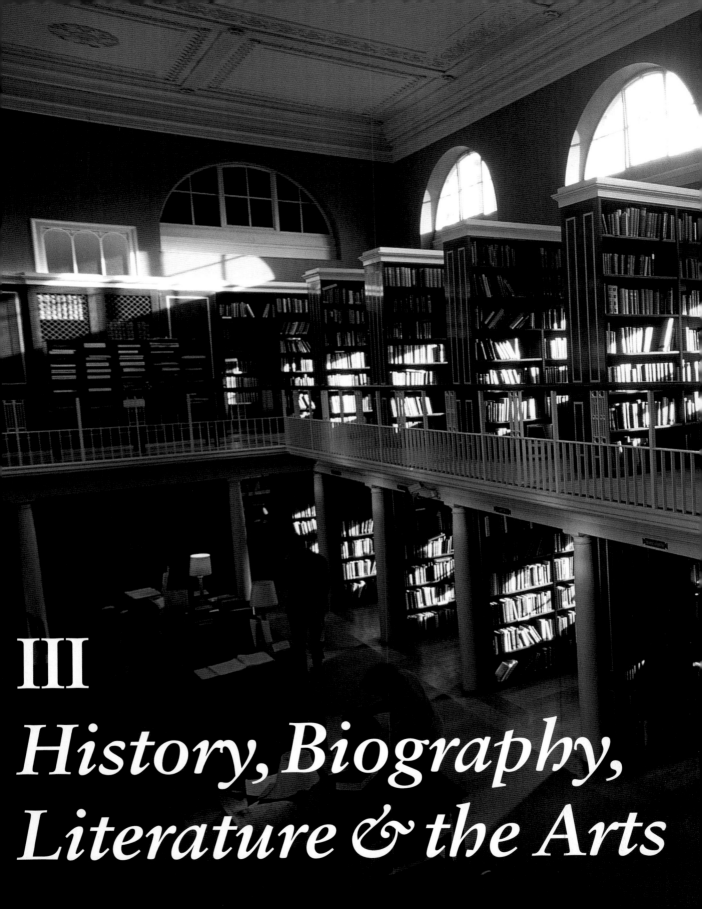

III

History, Biography, Literature & the Arts

I never somehow pictured to myself such a blissful paradise of books, books, books. Only one never gets enough of it –
Eglantyne Jebb

HELEN WADDELL
LMH 1923

The departing of my books

The Wandering Scholar laments the loss of his 'clergie', his library, at dice.

EACH MAN ASKS and each will speir
What is come of all my gear,
And how I be so desperate
To have neither cloak nor hat,
Coat ne surcote ne good tabard –
All is done and lost at hazard !
Game of hazard confoundeth me,
All is lost by mine own folie.
Dice hath cost me all my lere,
Dice hath cost me all my gear,
Turned my revel into woe.
Never a town in France, I know,
Never a chateau I call to mind,
Where I have not left some book behind!
At Gandalus above La Ferté,
There left I my A B C,
My Paternoster at Soissons,
And my Credo at Monleon,
My Seven Psalms are at Tournai,
My Fifteen Psalms are at Cambrai,
My Psalter is at Besançon,
And my Calendar at Dijon.
Back I came through Pontarlie
And there I sold my Litany.
And at the town of the great salt mine
I drank my Missal down in wine.
At the spicer's in Montpellier
Left I my Antiphonary.
My Legends and my Holy Grail
Left I at Dun, in the castel.

My body of Divinity
Left I at Paris, in the city.
And all my Arts and all my Physic
And all my canticles and music.
The greater part of all my authors
Left I at St Martin at Tours.
Donatus is at Orleans,
And my Chansons at Amiens.
At Chartres I left Theodulus,
At Rouen my Avianus.
Ovid abideth at Namur,
Philosophy is at Saumur,
At Bouvines above Dinant
There lost I Ovid le grant.
My Regimen is at Bruyères,
And my Glosses at Mezières.
My Lucan and my Juvenal
I clean forgot at Bonival.
Statius the great and eke Virgile
I lost at dice in Abbeville.
My Alexander is at Guerre,
And my Graecismus at Auxerre.
Tobit lieth in Compeigne,
 – Never handle him again –
My Doctrinale is at Sens,
And my most wit with it gone.
Gone is thus my whole clergie,
Even thus as I do tell ye,
Lost in all these divers ways,
All my books for all my days,
Never to be bought again.

From *The Wandering Scholars* (Constable, 1927)
See also p. 207

M. L. Jacobus (English;
D.Phil.; Professor at
Cornell; Professor of
English at Cambridge,
2000). Her publications
include *Body/Politics:
Women and the
Discourses of Science*.

MARY JACOBUS
LMH 1962, Fellow 1971–80

Two readers at a table

MATISSE'S PAINTING, *The Silence Living in Houses* (1947; in French, more ambiguously, *Le Silence habité des maisons*, the inhabited silence of houses), is an image of interior space inhabited not only by silence, but by a reading couple and a book. An abstract, minimally perspectival representation of domestic space opens via a window on to a fluid natural landscape of tree, sky and cloud. The flatness of the black interior background contrasts with the airily brushed vista outside. In this still life with figures, lines divide the window, frame it with curtains, scratch rudimentary building blocks on the walls, and compose the group itself: two readers at a table, with an open book in front of them and a vase of flowers to one side. But the book remains an empty space, a blank – for light to fall on, and for the viewer to fill with imaginary text or images; perhaps it is one of Matisse's own illustrated books, which he made by a process he considered analogous to that of painting. The cool blue of the figures, the vase and the table, outlined with light against the sombre ballast of their background, provides both a tranquil focus and a visual connection with the distant blue of the sky. The non-visual (the book as more-than-object) is coded as the colour of intimacy, relationship and silence, with a bit of distance thrown in. But the overlapping pose of the two human figures (two girls? a mother and child?) conveys as much about the mental activity of reading as the darkened interior. The painting constitutes a meditation on the relation of pictorial elements (volume, mass, perspective, depth, colour) to the mental representations that inhabit them. How effortlessly we 'read' this as an interior that leads the eye from the book to an inviting glimpse of a summer landscape seen through the window; and how easily, too, we understand its flat blackness and light-filled recession, not just as the contrast between darkness inside and the brightness of a summer day, but as a visual allusion to the peculiar mental absorption involved in the activity called 'reading'.

From *Psychoanalysis and
the Scene of Reading,
The Clarendon Lectures
1997* (Oxford University
Press, 1999)

From *The Brown Book*
1926
See also pp. 33, 112

K. M. LEA
LMH 1921, Fellow 1936, Vice-Principal 1947

Closing time in the libraries of Italy

LIBRARIES IN ROME I found for the most part clockless and the processes of ejection were varied and amusing. From the Casanatense one is shut out with a clang; by the Corsini, remote and peaceful under the Janiculum, there is a monastery with a tinkle of a bell at 4 p.m.; only the librarian hears it sound, and then he coughs. The Vittorio Emanuele has a screaming electric arrangement exactly suiting a malevolent porter whose cat has an equally terrific sneeze. There is a clock and a sober bell in the Vatican, where everything is orderly and discreet, even to the fountain that hops on one leg in the inner courtyard. But for all its punctuality its students forget time and when I signed my name in the readers' book the entry above was dated 'Gennaio 1, 1296' by some absorbed medievalist. In Naples they close the shutters and in darkness whisper 'Chiuso'. In Venice, to the joy of the custodian, I was invariably shot out of my seat by the noon-gun which goes off under the window of the Museo Correr.

K. M. Lea by John Ward, RA, watercolour, May 1971

C. V. WEDGWOOD
LMH 1928

Velvet studies

The title for Veronica Wedgwood's inspirational description of becoming an historian comes from a quotation from Thomas Fuller's 'Holy Warre': 'If you fear to hurt your tender hands with thornie school-questions there is no danger in meddling with history which is a velvet study and recreation work.'

IF I WAS NOT BORN A HISTORIAN I was an aspirant at six and a practitioner at twelve. Nothing that was paper could escape me even though the physical labour of writing opposed a frustrating barrier between me and my goal, and the mind had five acts complete before the pencil (blunt at one end and chewed at the other) had got further than Dramatis Personae copied from the front of a Temple Shakespeare.

Dramatis Personae or, as I learnt to put later, Characters in order of appearance – the first inspiration was evidently dramatic though the taste for history had come earlier. It began presumably with the shiny picture on rollers like a map which, in the echoing playroom at my grandmother's house, presented to my unrecognising eye Caradoc before Caesar, captive but unbowed. Not until my first history lesson was the remembered picture suddenly clothed with meaning. I was six; a world of inexhaustible possibilities opened before me – real people, real things that had really happened to them. Britons, Romans, an invasion, people with the most complicated names. I remembered them all; as soon have forgotten the names of my neighbours in class. The walk home that afternoon, up the tree-lined Kensington streets, was too short. With difficulty I compressed into it for my companion's benefit the substance of Caradoc's interesting fate, 'So he said to Caesar: Why did you want to invade us? and Caesar said . . .'

But the Yale key was already in the lock and upstairs in the nursery tea was on the table and it was 'Run along and wash your hands.' Only some weeks later when I instituted a brief oral examination of the term's work did I find to my dismay that I had been talking all the while to unlistening ears. It was an early lesson in the difficulty of imparting even the most interesting information.

Writing did not come until a year or two later, and then for a time the spell of imaginary characters was greater than that of real ones. There was my first theatre: the tiered immense semi-circle of darkness, the sudden, noiseless lifting of the curtain, and there against a mist-blue distance, lovelier than anything eye had seen or heart imagined, was a beautiful and evidently shipwrecked lady asking a group of pirates – but perhaps they weren't pirates – 'What should I do in Illyria?' From that charmed frame of light wherein they moved, the starry language flowed over me, meaningless as stars and as beautiful. It seemed reasonable on getting home to start in at once, between cocoa and bedtime, to write like Shakespeare.

In the end only the stage directions were like Shakespeare. I copied them faithfully. The failure did not greatly disconcert me. Shakespeare was acknowledged to be without an equal and I was young. Double figures lay all ahead. Meanwhile there were other impressions cramming and tumbling into my mind: Shelley and Herrick and Coleridge, *The Little Duke*, *The Pilgrim's Progress* and *Pinocchio*, and with these, unsorted and unclassified, from sources of every kind, a heroic multitude from epic and saga and ballad, fairy-tale and folk-lore: Roland and Achilles, Guy of Warwick and Lohengrin, Galahad and the Red Cross Knight, Beowulf, Theseus, and the Thrice-wise Helena, the Percy and the Douglas (and, like Sir Philip Sidney, I too found my heart moved more than with a trumpet). There were handsome books with gilded tops and coloured plates, there were squat little books 'told to the children', forbidding books of unrelieved print and wonderful French picture-books, Job's Napoleon on the bridge at Lodi and Boutet de Monvel's pale Joan of Arc.

Looking back now it is possible to analyse the peculiar dualism of childhood. One part of the mind stored these over-violent impressions to release them suddenly in fiery inspiration or panic fear. Yet alongside these moments of dazzling and fearful imagination, there were the agitated sortings and classifyings of a painfully industrious mind. And since the fears and the imaginings were less evident than the albums of Old Masters and the charts of dates it was as an unimaginative child with a memory for facts that my elders saw me. Certainly there were long periods, as I grew older, during which the strain of classifying, dating and placing the artist, the school, the style of poem or picture prevented all spontaneous enjoyment. Yet though the arts came thus, for some years, to be drained of pleasure, the past never lost its enchantment. A cross, difficult, lumpish child, I felt more at home in it than in the present. Among the friendly dead, being bad at games did not seem to matter.

New shapes and patterns gradually emerged. The disjointed procession of kings and statesmen spaced along the years assumed in perspective interesting formations. They were linked in chains of progress or movement, fascinating to follow as the pencil line which on the puzzle page of *The Rainbow* (my secret vice) could be drawn from dot No. 1 to dot No. 56 until there, complete, was a duck or a rabbit. Behind these emerging arabesques of development the jumbled backgrounds fell into place, poetry, pictures and cathedrals, and more remotely conceived, but quite clear even to me, an enormous population of nameless human beings.

The perception of form in history gave me I suppose the first discoverer's excitement, with the parallel recognition that truth has more than one face. Three things after that: all together, or at least so close as to make their chronology too hard to disentangle: my father's sobering advice on writing, my discovery of documentary evidence and *The Decline and Fall of the Roman Empire*.

By the time I was twelve my writing had grown dangerously swift. There was a special kind of writing pad called 'The Mammoth': two hundred pages, quarto, ruled feint; under my now practised pencil Mammoths disappeared in a twinkling. 'You should write history,' my father said, hoping to put on a brake. 'Even a bad writer may be a useful historian.' It was damping, but it was sense. It was, after all, unlikely that I would ever be Shakespeare.

Soon after came the electrifying discovery of the document. My temperament being neither scientific nor inquiring I had not given much thought to the sources of the historical information which I acquired. One day at school our teacher read us letters to illustrate a lesson, and a fragment of a diary. The immense revelation dazzled me. Here was direct knowledge for the asking. Immediate contact could be made with these dead, so distant yet to me so tantalisingly near. After that, certain of my goal but uninstructed how to reach it, I breathed for hours on the show cases of the British Museum copying out all the documents on view. I ransacked the historical tomes of my father's library for anything between inverted commas. I found Pepys of course and was puzzled and rather shocked, Clarendon and was swept out of my depth, the Verney papers and regained my footing.

There was at this time a more subtle influence at work of which the documents were but one outward sign. Certainly I could name the hour and the place of my starting-point on the long road I have followed since: it was a small classroom on the topmost floor of a majestic stuccoed house in Kensington. Out of the windows, far below, the traffic passed up and down the tree-lined street like clockwork. It must have been summer, for the trees were in leaf and the sun was shining. The classroom was painted dark green and white; at one end there was a picture of William III landing at Torbay and at the other of Wolfe scaling the Heights of Abraham. It was here that I found, in the witty, determined grey-haired lady who dominated the scene from 'behind a very large desk on a very small rectangular platform', the teacher who knew how to unlock the sluice gates between the arid flats of my intellect and the flood-waters of my imagination. The desert burgeoned; the Mammoth pads flowered into an enormous History of England.

I found the teacher who knew how to unlock the sluice gates between the arid flats of my intellect and the flood-waters of my imagination

Almost immediately afterwards came Gibbon, an imposing birthday present, half a challenge. I got down to it at once, ostentatiously out of bravado, but went on out of insistent passion, evening after evening, in the yellow nursery light. 'Understandest thou what thou readest?' my grandfather mocked. I understood this much: that here was a master, here was material shaped and subdued, men and centuries brought into order, a whole world frozen in the sharp, dispassionate light of a single mind. Before this immense achievement I stood amazed, almost, for the first time, humbled. But certain: this was the star for my wagon.

At twelve I had no theory of history. Since then I have had many, even for some years the theory that in the interests of scholarship it is wrong to write history comprehensible to the ordinary reader, since all history so written must necessarily be modified and therefore incorrect. This was I think always too much against my nature to have held me long.

Acquaintance with the work of foreign historians sharpened my consciousness of the different angles from which the same events may be viewed. The associations of places, the evidence of ballad and tradition, the 'accepted' errors revealed to me little by little the delicate embroidery which can be wrought by legend on fact, embroidery which may have value as well as beauty, since it may reveal a significance in the fact not apparent from the fact itself. My own varying estimates of the facts themselves, as the years passed, showed me too clearly how much of history must always rest in the eye of the beholder; our deductions are so often different it is impossible they should always be right.

Reading Bacon's *Novum Organum* I recognise in middle life how much I am a Platonist, how given up to the doctrine of acatalepsy. For the whole value of the study of history is for me its delightful undermining of certainty, its cumulative insistence of the differences of point of view. But Lytton Strachey has said that to write history three things are necessary: 'a capacity for absorbing facts, a capacity for stating them, and a point of view'. But what point of view can emerge from the deliberate multiplication of points of view? It is therefore in search of an ultimate point of view that I am now pursuing my velvet study back to its source.

H. J. Waddell (Susette
Taylor Fellow, 1923–25)
was a medievalist, writer
and translator whose
work includes a narrative
poem, *New York*; *Lyrics
from the Chinese*;
Medieval Latin Lyrics;
The Wandering Scholars;
and a novel, *Peter
Abelard*. She died in
1965.

From *The Wandering
Scholars* (Constable,
1927)
See also p. 200

HELEN WADDELL
LMH 1923

Popes as wanton as may-flies

THE TENTH CENTURY has a bad name; but good things came out of it. It saw a succession of Popes as short-lived and wanton as may-flies. It is true that thanks to the dangers and squalors of the century, invasion, rebellion and faction, there was no longer an educated society. The scholars of the century can almost be counted on the fingers of one hand; so can the lyrics. But they include the first aubade and the first love song; and in the manuscripts that contain them the lost tunes of the Middle Ages are for the first time caught and held.

From it, too, dates the beginning of modern music, ultra-modern even, for Hucbald of St Amand began that quest for the 'perfect fourth' which Holst, unmoved by discord, still continues.

Vidi
Viridi
Phyllidem sub tilia

A Wandering Scholar's rendering of the whistle of the blackbird

*Illustration
from Margaret
Lambert's*
English Popular Art

*Helen Waddell stood
out for the grace of her
learning, her love of fine
literature, and her poet's
gift of translation – from*
The Times *obituary,
6 March 1965*

P. M. Sanderson (Modern Languages; Doctor of the University of Paris) is also the translator of *Aucassin and Nicolette* and *The Redemption of Chivalry*.

PAULINE MATARASSO
LMH 1947

Court romance

THE QUEST OF THE HOLY GRAIL, despite its Arthurian setting, is not a romance, it is a spiritual fable. It forms part of a vast compilation known as the Prose Lancelot, which might justifiably be called the romance to end romances, but it is the product of a period when things were rarely quite what they seemed, when the outward appearance was merely a garment in which to dress some inward truth, when the material world was but a veil through which the immutable could be sporadically glimpsed and perpetually reinterpreted.

Most medieval literature can be read on more than one level, that of the story proper, and that of the meaning it served to illustrate, the famous combination of 'sens' and 'matière'. The author of the Quest was not therefore doing anything exceptional in using his story to clothe and exemplify a meaning that transcended it; he merely did it with greater single-mindedness and took it to more logical conclusions. One can fairly say that he did not write a single paragraph for the pleasure of story-telling.

The Quest of the Holy Grail has a place in the canon of spiritual literature, not among the theological treatises, but on the shelves reserved for works of popular appeal. This is a guide to the spiritual life aimed at the court rather than the cloister, and translated into what was then the most popular currency.

From *The Quest of the Holy Grail* (Penguin, 1969)

ANNE HUDSON
LMH Fellow 1961

From *Heresy and Literacy 1000–1393*, ed. with Peter Biller (Cambridge University Press, 1994) See also p. 69

THE ADVANTAGES OF BOOK LEARNING were plain to the early university-trained dissidents – the written word could stay when the persecuted preacher could not; a book is more easily hidden than a man; the text is constant, if not permanent, where the spoken word is fleeting.

P. Hodgson (English; D.Phil., 1936; Lecturer, Reader and then Professor of English at Bedford College, 1942–72; Chair of Board of Studies, London University; British Academy Prize, 1971) also published *The Cloud of Unknowing*, *The Orchard of Syon*, and editions of Chaucer's *Franklin's Tale* and *Prologue*. She died in 2000.

From *Three Fourteenth-Century English Mystics* (British Council/National Book League/Longmans Green, 1967)

PHYLLIS HODGSON
LMH 1932

OF ALL THE FOURTEENTH-CENTURY mystical writings, the Introduction to *The Cloud of Unknowing* makes the most emphatic distinction between the physical and the spiritual.

It was in the thick cloud at the summit, when Moses could see nothing, that God spoke. When further progress is impossible to the human intelligence, the contemplative must be prepared to plunge into that cloud. To eliminate all the distractions that play upon the mind in order to concentrate solely on the goal, this is to enter the cloud, or darkness, of unknowing. God will sometimes, perhaps, send out a shaft of spiritual light, piercing this cloud of unknowing that is between you and Him, and reveal something of His mystery to you, of which a mortal may not, or cannot, speak.

Perfect oneness with God, which is the aim of the contemplative, is to know God, not objectively as a being to be analysed and understood in all His parts, but subjectively, as a divine force working in and through the soul, the soul moving only in God.

S. M. G. Reynolds (History; F.R.Hist.S.) is an Oxford University Lecturer and Visiting Professor, Dartmouth College, New Hampshire. Her publications include *Kingdoms and Communities in Western Europe*.

From *Ideas and Solidarities of the Medieval Laity* (Variorum, 1995)

SUSAN REYNOLDS
LMH 1947, Fellow 1964

THERE WERE SUBURBS outside the defences – whether walls or banks and ditches – that by the twelfth century surrounded many towns. A good many towns may by then have been as big as they would be until the coming of the railway. Suburbs were not in general favoured, as they would be later, by wealthy people wanting space for their houses and gardens. The rich more often had their houses on the market square or main streets. While many smaller and poorer houses would be squashed into lanes and courts behind them, others would be put up in suburbs, particularly if the suburbs were outside the jurisdiction of the town authorities.

The siting of religious houses founded in the twelfth century and later, notably those of the friars, and of late medieval hospitals is often an indication of the extent of the built-up area at the time they were established: spacious new churches and cloisters were perforce built on the periphery of towns that were already crowded with housing. After the Black Death, when houses fell vacant and the property market was depressed, more space became available, so that the founders of colleges at Oxford and Cambridge were able to buy land that had once been inhabited and cover it with quadrangles or courts.

H. F. M. Prescott (History;
F.R.S.Litt.; Honorary
D.Litt., Durham, 1957)
was Vice-Principal of
Durham University from
1943 to 1948, when her
historical novels had
become so acclaimed
that she then made
writing her career. Her
biography of Mary Tudor
won the 1941 James
Tait Black Prize. Her
publications include
The Hurrying Chase; *The
Lost Fight*, and the much-
acclaimed *The Man on
a Donkey*. She died in
1972.

H. F. M. PRESCOTT
LMH 1914

Flamenca is a romantic narrative that rolls along like a medieval soap opera.

GUILLAUME RANG THE MASS BELL LUSTILY, and everyone came in as usual to Mass.

First of all the great crowd came, and after, last of all, Archambaut; if he could have had his choice there would not have been any Sundays or holidays. His head was like those shaggy heads of devils that the painters draw, and it was no wonder that Flamenca made no pretence of rejoicing in his love, for a lady has every right to be very much upset when the devil appears to her ...

So Guillaume stood before his lady, and when she kissed the psalter, he said very softly:

'Alas!' only he did not speak so low but that she heard it very well.

'Ah! How little worth is my comfort. It is worth nothing at all, for ill-fortune always catches up a man before long. They say, "Who loves much, fears much," and for that very reason I, who love so deeply, fear as greatly. There is no true joy for me but in my lady, and she can fill me with joy by a single word. There is no escape from this care-ful heaviness, from this sorrow, desire and bitterness.'

And that is how all lovers are; they willingly bear a hundred crosses for one good thing.

From *Flamenca*
(Constable, 1930)

HILDA PRESCOTT WAS ANOTHER FRIEND who idled with me on the river. She was a senior student of LMH who had returned to work at the book which afterwards became *The Spanish Tudor*. We referred to it, less felicitously, as Bloody Mary.

Lying back among the cushions of a punt Hilda, with her tall person, her distinguished narrow face, her marked features, her dark complexion, her dark straight hair cut in a bang, her eyes with their secret fires, her strong religious sense and fanatical spirit, looked more like a Norman lady than any actual Norman lady ever probably looked. She had strayed out of time and could, as she talked, draw her friends back with her into imagined epochs which she peopled with creatures partly of her own fashioning and partly historical.

Anne Treneer, *Cornish
Years* (Jonathan Cape,
1949)
See also pp. 10, 34, 35

The Hon. M. E. Bridges
(History; D.Phil., 1962;
FRHS; FSA; Lecturer at
St Anne's College and
Queen's University,
Belfast). Her publications
include *England's
Iconoclasts*.

From *The King's Bedpost*
(Cambridge University
Press, 1993)

MARGARET ASTON
LMH 1951

Elizabeth and Iconoclasm

THERE WAS NOTHING REMOTE about Rome, idols and idolatry, when Elizabeth I came to the throne in November 1558. Her sister Mary had seen to that. The re-establishment of papal authority had been accompanied by determined efforts to put imagery back in churches, and if some of the Queen's subjects were happy to be able to bring hoarded objects out of their hiding-places, others were indignant at the mushrooming of old idols and the 'cock-sure' reaffirmation of huge new-made roods. The new Queen was looked to by a number of influential advisers to undo the work of the previous five years, and to banish, along with the Pope, all the imagery that the 'Jezebel' Mary had either restored or helped to keep in place.

Much was achieved during the early months of Elizabeth's reign. Many church images, including the rood carvings on which Mary had concentrated attention, were destroyed and burned in London and elsewhere as the royal visitation, carrying the revival of reform into all parts of the country, took effect in the late summer and early autumn of 1559.

The Queen, however, did not see eye to eye with ardent iconoclasts. Arguments about ecclesiastical imagery were by no means over when the royal visitors finished their work, and the topic became delicate, not to say embarrassing, in view of the Queen's personal judgement and some of her own furnishings. She continued to keep a cross or (which was worse) a crucifix in a central position in her royal chapel. To some worthy purists that seemed an intolerable flouting of the law, tantamount indeed to flaunting an idol.

G. E. Tindall (English; FRSL; FRSA; Inner London JP) is a novelist and urban historian who won the Somerset Maugham Award in 1972 for her novel *Fly Away Home*. Her biographies include George Gissing and Rosamund Lehmann. Her historical study of French life, *Celestine*, won the 1995 Enid McLeod Prize. Her mother, Ursula Orange (LMH 1928) was also a novelist (see p. 126).

GILLIAN TINDALL
LMH 1956

'Un mari qui te soit toujours fidèle'

ONE AUTUMN DAY in the 1970s an old man left his small house in a village near the geographical heart of France and caught the weekly bus into the nearby market town. He was not a Frenchman; he had come to France as a soldier in 1916. The next war found him in Paris, where, no longer young, he encountered Zenaïde, a secretary of charm and intelligence who was not young either. In due course she took him back to the house she had inherited from her parents and introduced him to the covertly amused but respectful neighbours she had known since childhood.

Summers together continued for ten years, till she died, leaving him the house and its contents for his lifetime. A handyman, he had embellished the classic French exterior with a verandah and a blue-painted trellis, so that it now resembled an English cottage orné of the Edwardian era. He converted the grain loft into bedrooms, reached by an inside boxed ladder, and built on a kitchen and bathroom in a lean-to, with a soakaway to a covered pit beyond the apple trees. The two main rooms, however, were left as they always had been. He went on spending months at a time in the decor of past lives he had never known. The padded *prie dieu* stood where it always had, and so did the wood-burning stove. So did the footstool with the *gros point* cat upon it, worn now but still as lifelike as when it was worked long ago by Zenaïde's grandmother, when she was still a pretty girl, before her own life became harder and sadder.

Leaving the house, the old man secured the shutters and turned the heavy key, locking up all those things again in timeless suspension. The bed in his attic room was left made up, there were packets and tins in the kitchen cupboards; a carton with a little milk in it stood overlooked by the stove. He meant to return within two or three weeks. He never did.

The following summer the house was at last cleared by Zenaïde's distant cousins. They took most of the contents, except for a few things that were given away. They left behind, on a corner of the mantelshelf in the darkened, empty main room behind the shutters, a small case meant to contain those cards that are distributed in pious families to commemorate baptisms, first communions and Masses said for the dead. They were perhaps inhibited by respect or superstition from putting it on the great garden bonfire, which had already consumed so many long-paid bills, mildewed cushions, wormy chairs, quilts sticky with moths' eggs and mouse-wrecked packets of sugar.

Had they looked, as I did when I came to the house to collect the cat footstool which had been promised to me, they would have found the case

From *Celestine: Voices from a French Village* (Sinclair Stevenson, 1995; Minerva, 1996)

packed tight with seven letters. Two of them were in their small envelopes, the other showed traces of having been simply folded and sealed. The copybook handwritings varied; the ink was faded, and even a cursory glance through the soft wads of paper that was delicate as old skin showed that some of the French was very odd.

The Celestine to whom they were all written I knew to be Zenaïde's grandmother. From the way they were addressed – variations on 'Mademoiselle Celestine Chaumette, in her father's house, the Auberge at Chassignolles' – I saw that she had been the innkeeper's daughter. They were all from suitors except one from a soldier brother, and all, except that last letter, dated from the early 1860s. One was from a local schoolmaster, another from a salesman travelling for a wine merchant. Others came from a bakery, from a village where rural iron founaries then were, and from another known for its annual cattle fair.

Some sentences sprang fresh as flowers from the pages; others seemed for the moment impenetrable. Each letter was in a different hand except for two that were from the same young man, writing first in hope and then in disappointment. Even so, he was not bitter at Celestine: she seems to have had the gift of inspiring respect and affection: '. . . I havent put myself about to talk to your parents because it wouldnt be any use I wanted to know what you thought first of all tho' I do think they wouldnt a been averse . . . All I can say is, I wish you from the bottom of my heart a husband who will always be faithful to you for you dont deserve to be Cheated on' [je te soahaite du plus profond de moncoeur un marie qui te soie tonjours fidelle car tu merite pas detre Trompe].

I returned to my own cottage on the other side of the village. I took with me her letters. Once ephemeral as butterflies, they had been cherished and kept for reasons of obscure pride, comfort or regret; messages from a life already past to Celestine. They had undergone a long hibernation, and now were transformed into messages of another kind; to be cherished for new reasons. Now, when Celestine herself, all her correspondents, every single person they knew and most of those they were ever going to know had vanished as if they had never been, I would bring them to life again.

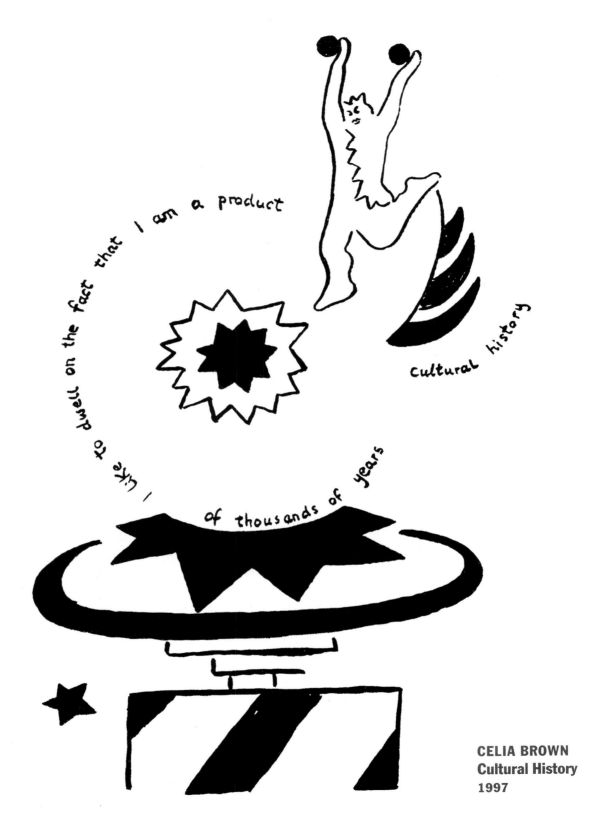

I like to dwell on the fact that I am a product

cultural history

of thousands of years

CELIA BROWN
Cultural History
1997

A. Foreman (History,
Henrietta Jex Blake
Scholar; D.Phil. 1998),
won the 1998 Whitbread
Prize for Biography for
*Georgiana, Duchess of
Devonshire.*

AMANDA FOREMAN
LMH 1994

Biographers are notorious

BIOGRAPHERS ARE NOTORIOUS for falling in love with their subjects. It is the literary equivalent of the 'Stockholm Syndrome', the phenomenon which leads hostages to feel sympathetic towards their captors. The biographer is, in a sense, a willing hostage, held captive for so long that he becomes hopelessly enthralled.

There are obvious, intellectual motives which drive a writer to spend years, and sometimes decades, researching the life of a person long vanished, but they often mask a less clear although equally powerful compulsion. Most biographers identify with their subjects. It can be unconscious and no more substantial than a shadow flitting across the page. At other times identification plays so central a role that the work becomes part autobiography.

In either case, once he commits himself to the task, the writer embarks on a journey that has no obvious route for a destination that is only partly known. He immerses himself in his subject's life. The recorded impressions of contemporaries are read and re-read; letters, diaries, hastily scribbled notes, even discarded fragments are scrutinised for clues; and yet the truth remains maddeningly elusive. The subject's own self-deception, mistaken recollections, and the hidden motives of witnesses conspire to make a complete picture impossible to assemble. Finally, it is intuition and a sympathy with the past which supply the last missing pieces. It is no wonder that biographers often confess to dreaming about their subjects. I remember the first time Georgiana appeared to me: I dreamt I switched on the radio and heard her reciting one of her poems. That was the closest she ever came to me; in later dreams she was always a vanishing figure, present but beyond my reach.

Such profound bonds have obvious dangers, not least in the disruption they can inflict upon a biographer's life. Sometimes the work suffers; its integrity becomes jeopardised when, without realising it, a biographer mistakes his own feelings for the subject's, ascribing characteristics that did not exist and motives that were never there. In his life of Charles James Fox, the Victorian historian George Trevelyan insisted that Fox held to a strict code of morality regarding the sexual conquest of aristocratic women; he only seduced courtesans. Trevelyan, perhaps, had such a code, but Fox did not. There is ample evidence to suggest that the Whig politician had several affairs with married women of quality, including Mrs Crewe and possibly Georgiana, Duchess of Devonshire. Her first biographer, Iris Palmer, was similarly wishful in her description of Georgiana as a 'simple woman'

From *Georgiana,
Duchess of Devonshire*
(HarperCollins, 1998)

without ambition except in her desire to help others. Palmer also claimed, in the face of contrary evidence, that Georgiana was only unfaithful to her husband with one man, Charles Grey. Both biographers illustrate how easy it is to fall prey to the temptation to suppress or ignore unwelcome evidence.

Fortunately, the emotional distance required to construct a narrative from an incoherent collection of facts and suppositions provides a powerful counterbalance. By deciding which pieces of the puzzle are the most significant – not always an easy task – and thereby asserting their own interpretation, the biographer achieves a measure of separation. The demands of writing, of style, pace and clarity, also force a writer to be more objective. Numerous decisions have to be made about conflicting evidence, or where to place the correct emphasis between certain events. Having previously dominated the biographer's waking and sleeping life, the subject gradually diminishes until he or she is contained on the page.

I discovered Georgiana in 1993, while researching a doctoral dissertation on English attitudes to race and colour in the late eighteenth century. I was reading a biography of Charles Grey, later Earl Grey, by E. A. Smith, and came across one of her letters. I was already familiar with Georgiana's career as a political hostess and as the duchess who once campaigned for Charles James Fox, but I had never read any of her writing, and knew little of her character. I was struck by her voice, it was so strong, so clear, honest and open, that she made everything I subsequently read seem dull by comparison. I lost interest in my doctorate, and after six months I had read just one book on eighteenth-century racial attitudes. Whenever I did go to the library it was to look for biographies of Georgiana.

There have been three previous biographies about her: a novelisation, and two that concentrate on her early life, both probably influenced by the edited selection of Georgiana's letters, *Georgiana, Duchess of Devonshire*, published by the Earl of Bessborough in 1955. (It was only much later that I discovered the extent of Lord Bessborough's editing for myself.) None of the books, not even the Bessborough edition of her letters, portrayed the Georgiana whose voice I felt I had heard. Eventually I realised I would never be satisfied until I had followed the trail to its source. Oxford accepted my explanation and graciously allowed me to start again and begin a new D.Phil. on Georgiana's life and times. A short while later I decided to write her biography in addition to the doctorate.

By the time I had consigned Georgiana to the page a different picture of her had emerged. Previous accounts portrayed her as a charismatic but flighty woman; I see her as courageous and vulnerable. Georgiana indeed suffered from the instability which often accompanies intelligent and sensitive characters. She was thrust into public life at the age of sixteen, unprepared for the pressures that quickly followed and unsupported in a cold and loveless marriage. Though most of her contemporaries adored her because she seemed so natural and vibrant, only a few knew how tormented she was by self-doubt and loneliness. Georgiana was not content to lead the fashionable set nor merely to host soirées for the Whig party; instead she became an adept political campaigner and negotiator, respected by the Whigs and feared by her adversaries. She was the first woman to conduct a modern electoral campaign, going out into the streets to persuade ordinary people to vote for the Whigs. She took advantage of the country's rapidly expanding newspaper trade to increase the popularity of the Whig party and succeeded in turning herself into a national celebrity. Georgiana was a patron of the arts, a novelist and writer, an amateur scientist and a musician. It was her tragedy that these successes were overshadowed by private and public misfortune. Ambitious for herself and her party, Georgiana was continually frustrated by restrictions imposed on eighteenth-century women. She was also a woman who needed to be loved, but the two people whom she loved most – Charles Grey and the Duke of Devonshire's mistress Lady Elizabeth Foster – proved incapable of reciprocating her feelings in full measure. Georgiana's unhappiness expressed itself destructively in her addiction to gambling, her early eating disorders, and her deliberate courting of risk. Her battle to overcome her problems was an achievement equal to the triumphs she enjoyed in her public life.

I obtained a priceless tip from my friend, Cecil Woodham-Smith, 'Never lose hold of the narrative,' she said. I added to this my own biographical rule: 'Keep the spotlight on your subject' –
Elizabeth Longford

From 'A Life in Biography',
(*The Brown Book* 1981)

E. M. Jourdain (Classical Mods) was Principal of St Hugh's College, 1915–24. Her publications include works on eighteenth-century furniture and decoration. She died in 1924.

ELEANOR JOURDAIN
LMH 1883

Encounter

An Adventure, *by 'Miss Morison' and 'Miss Lamont', describes 'the psychical events that overtook two Oxford ladies on a walk in Versailles in August 1901'. Ten years later they wrote of their encounter with Marie Antoinette and her entourage, and the book became a bestseller and an Edwardian literary scandal. For the women were in fact the Principal and Vice-Principal of St Hugh's, Charlotte Anne Moberly and Eleanor Jourdain (who had been at LMH with Gertrude Bell).*

WE WENT ON IN THE DIRECTION of the Petit Trianon, but just before reaching what we knew afterwards to be the main entrance I saw a gate leading to a path cut deep below the level of the ground above, and as the way was open and had the look of an entrance that was used I said, 'Shall we try this path? It must lead to the house.'

There was a feeling of depression and loneliness about the place. I began to feel as if I were walking in my sleep; the heavy dreaminess was oppressive. At last we came upon a path crossing ours, and saw in front of us a building consisting of some columns roofed in, and set back in the trees. Seated on the steps was a man with a heavy black cloak round his shoulders, and wearing a slouch hat. At that moment the eerie feeling which had begun in the garden culminated in a definite impression of something uncanny and fear-inspiring. The man slowly turned his face, which was marked by small-pox: his complexion was very dark. The expression was very evil and yet unseeing, and though I did not feel that he was looking particularly at us, I felt a repugnance to going past him. But I did not wish to show the feeling, which I thought was meaningless, and we talked about the best way to turn, and decided to go to the right.

Suddenly we heard a man running behind us: he shouted, 'Mesdames, mesdames,' and when I turned he said in an accent that seemed to me unusual that our way lay in another direction. 'Il ne faut' (pronounced fout) 'pas passer par là.' He then made a gesture, adding, 'Par ici cherchez la maison.' Though we were surprised to be addressed, we were glad of the direction, and I thanked him. The man ran off with a curious smile on his face: the running ceased as abruptly as it had begun, not far from where we stood.

From Elizabeth Morison and Frances Lamont, *An Adventure* (Macmillan, 1911)

ELIZABETH LONGFORD
1926

'In short, I was a fool'

In 1792, 23-year-old Captain Arthur Wellesley met and fell in love with Kitty Pakenham, Lord Longford's second daughter: 'her gaiety and glowing complexion, her bobbing curls and exquisite figure' enchanted him. He proposed a year later, but her family rejected him because he could not afford to keep her on his military pay. By 1805 he was a prosperous Indian colonel with brilliant career prospects, and well-meaning friends had succeeded in making him renew his offer. But Kitty panicked: 'she had lost her round pink cheeks pining for Arthur'.

'I AM VERY MUCH CHANGED and you know it . . . so much that I doubt it would now be in my power to contribute to the happiness of anyone who has not been in the habit of loving me for years . . . Read his letter again my dear Olivia is there one expression implying that Yes would gratify or No would disappoint. . . ?'

This letter clearly gave the match-maker Olivia Sparrow the chance to draw back, but her assiduous scheming . . . could not be reversed. Without having set eyes on Kitty for at least eleven years, Arthur sent her a formal proposal and was 'somewhat nervously' accepted. Another friend, Mrs Calvert, heard afterwards that 'when someone told Sir Arthur that he would find her much altered, he answered that he did not care.' So in 1806, back from India and about to become MP for Rye, 'he used the remainder of his leave to make the journey, so familiar in youth, to Ireland, there to marry her.

He had been warned. But the sight of his faded, 34-year-old bride was a shock, all the same. 'She has grown ugly, by Jove!' he whispered into the ear of his clergyman brother Gerald, who was to marry them. Arthur decided afterwards that he had not been 'in the least' in love with her. He told his friend Mrs Arbuthnot in 1822:

'I married her because they asked me to do it and I did not know myself . . . in short, I was a fool.' . . .

Mistress of a large household in Hampshire, Kitty's pious concern was with her servants and the poor. The kind of managerial genius which a future great hostess like Lady Palmerston displayed found no place in Kitty's make-up. Yet this was what her husband expected. He asked for a commissary-general and was given a domestic chaplain.

From *Wellington*, Volume I: *The Years of the Sword*; Volume II: *Pillar of State* (Weidenfeld and Nicolson, 1969, 1972) See also pp. 10. 78

M. G. Ferry (Exper. Psych.), writer and biographer, is Editor of *Oxford Today*.

GEORGINA FERRY
LMH 1973

Thoroughly un-housewifely

DOROTHY HODGKIN WAS ANNOUNCED as the sole winner of the Nobel Prize for Chemistry on 29 October 1964. The headlines were predictable. 'British woman wins Nobel Prize – £18,750 award to mother of three' announced *The Daily Telegraph*. In a feature published later in the year, just after the award ceremony, *The Observer* reported that the 'affable-looking housewife' Mrs Hodgkin had won the prize 'for a thoroughly un-housewifely skill: the structures of crystals of great chemical interest.' (More endearing was the report in the local paper of her childhood home: 'Nobel Prize for former Norfolk girl'.) These reports implied that for a woman to have done such a thing was completely exceptional (and therefore not something that other women might seek to emulate). They identified Dorothy first and foremost as a wife and mother, only grudgingly admitting that she was also a university professor and Fellow of the Royal Society.

The manner in which Dorothy received the news of her prize was in many ways typical of the slightly chaotic Hodgkin lifestyle. The telegram from the Royal Swedish Academy of Sciences arrived at 94 Woodstock Road. But Dorothy was with Thomas in Ghana, where he had been appointed by President Kwame Nkrumah in 1961 as the first Director of the new Institute of African Studies at the University of Ghana. That telegram was followed by many others, offering congratulations. It was left to Dorothy's niece Jill to decide what to do with them. Ever conscious of the need to save money, she put them all in an envelope and sent them to Africa by sea mail. (They arrived about three months later.)

Meanwhile a couple of young reporters from *The Ghana Times* had been despatched to the university to get an interview. And it was from them that she heard the news even though, as she wrote later, 'they didn't know what the Nobel Prize was'. So the first to share in her celebrations were her African friends and colleagues, one of whom was hastily despatched from Legon to Accra to buy wine for the party. A few days later, at a function for the Ghana Academy of Sciences, Nkrumah himself announced that Dorothy had been elected a member of the Academy. 'I'm sure', she later wrote, 'it was the first they'd heard of it.'

From *Dorothy Hodgkin: A Life* (Granta, 1998)

S. M. M. Hayes (History), Viscountess Bangor. After LMH she lived in Barbados, where she met many of those who have since helped with and feature in her biographies, including Princess Grace of Monaco, George VI and HM The Queen, They are to be republished in 2002. *America's Queen* has to date sold more than 200,000 copies worldwide. Sarah Bradford describes Jackie Kennedy Onassis as 'a complex woman who tempts you to see her superficially'.

From *America's Queen: The Life of Jacqueline Kennedy Onassis* (Viking, 2000)

SARAH BRADFORD
LMH 1956

The First Lady's underwear

SHE HAD LITTLE PATIENCE with women in general and with official women and newspaperwomen in particular. 'She was not responsive to the other cabinet wives,' Robin Biddle Duke recalled, 'and she made it very tough for me because I was the wife of the Chief of Protocol and at receptions before big dinners there would only be the wives of cabinet ministers and of the cabinet ministers of the visiting chief of state. And if it was a head of state that interested her, like Haile Selassie, everybody was in a cluster on one side of the room and she would be on the other side with the big wheel, hopefully speaking French because she loved to speak French, and I would have to go over and take Mrs Ball and say, "Mrs Kennedy, Mrs Ball has not had a chance to speak to His Majesty," and I'd try and be gracious about it and I knew she was just looking daggers at me. So it was kind of hard and I found those days very difficult and it was because really she thought they were all a bunch of dowdy dames.'

Jackie was not fond of 'hordes of women', and was repelled by what she saw as their intrusive interest in her. She told Puffin D'Oench of her experiences at one of these functions when she and the other Senate wives were traditionally expected to change into Red Cross uniform. 'She truly disliked those occasions,' Puffin recalled, 'because the room in which they took their clothes off had no privacy, and some of the women crowded around to feel the material with their fingers, or stole glances at her to inspect her underwear. They were looking at her slip and the lace and the rest of it and she just felt that this was unspeakably awful . . . It must have been quite a sight,' Puffin added, 'since I suspect Jackie wore especially flossy things in anticipation of being seen partially undressed. At school and college, Jackie, unlike many others, was always modest, although I often saw her in a slip. We all teased her about having the flattest chest of anyone we knew.'

On their return to the White House, Puffin recorded a touching instance of Jack's delight in his wife's appearance and his interest in what she wore. 'We got back and Jack Kennedy came upstairs from the Oval Office because he liked to see what she was wearing. And he said, "But you've taken your hat off, go get your hat and put it on." So she put on her little pillbox hat and he was delighted.'

MARY HOLTBY
LMH 1943

Beowulf

Grisly old Grendel   gulped guys in his greed;
Beowulf bashed him   and boy! did he bleed!
Hoisted his hand up   and hung it on high
So, dashed, he departed   now destined to die.

While Grendel all gory   lay gasping and glum,
Immersed in the mere   was his murderous Mum.
So soon as he snuffed it   she set out to slay
The heroes who, heartened,   were hitting the hay

The king's chief companion   she crunched in her chops,
Bedewing the doormat   with deathly dark drops.
Then back to her bolt-hole,   on breakfasting bent,
She leaves the lone lords   this loss to lament.

But down to the depths   the dauntless one dives.
He splinters his sword   but surprise! he survives;
In the water's a weapon   the woman to whack;
With the blade he bisects her   and bounces right back.

It's home he must hasten   'mid hug and hurrah,
Having mopped up the menace   of monster and Ma;
But a weird Worm awaits him   and wealth for the warrior –
Though the sortie's successful   the slaughterer's sorrier.

For the pest with its powerful   poison has pricked him
And vitally vanquished   are victor and victim
A funeral soon follows   with faggots enflamed,
And in deadliest detail   his deeds are declaimed.

How brave was this Beowulf   brilliant and bold,
Gaffed Grendel and Gammer   and gained the Worm's gold;
Let his lion-like exploits   be listed at length
For students whose stamina's   stout as his strength.

From *How To Be Ridiculously Well Read in One Evening*, ed. E. O. Parrott (Viking, 1985)

E. A. I. Pasternak Slater
(D.Phil., 1974; Lecturer,
Fellow and Tutor,
St Anne's College, 1976)
has also translated
A Vanished Present,
the autobiography of
her uncle Alexander
Pasternak; edited the
short stories of Evelyn
Waugh, and contributed
to *Freedom From Fear*,
a portrait of her Oxford
friend Aung San Suu Kyi.

From *Shakespeare the
Director* (Harvester Press,
1982)

ANN PASTERNAK SLATER
LMH Fellow 1972

Theatre properties

THE THEATRE OF EVERY AGE is tempted to sacrifice plays to properties and sense to spectacle. In 1856, Kean's playbill for *A Midsummer Night's Dream* proudly listed scenes such as the 'Workshop of Quince the Carpenter . . . the Furniture and Tools . . . are copied from discoveries at Herculaneum', and even Granville-Barker's relatively austere production of the same play is remembered chiefly for its famous golden fairies. *Antony and Cleopatra* has always presented irresistible temptations, from Beerbohm Tree's spectacular production of 1906–7, which sacrificed gobbets of text to grandiose effects, down to 'a dissolving vision of the Sphinx' opening and closing the play, to the ill-fated film of *Cleopatra* in 1963. Its makers spent as much on her barge alone as sufficed to budget the entire contemporary film of *The Caretaker* and, for all that, the epic was a flop. 'I only came to see the asp,' was Charles Addams's comment.

H. A. Cobb (English;
D.Phil., 1990; Lecturer
at University College,
London) is a writer and
reviewer for the *TLS*.
Her publications
include contributions
to *Voicing Women* and
*Shakespeare's Playing
Spaces* for the Open
University, a book praised
by Sam West as essential
to his preparation:
'a terrific part of
my homework for a
forthcoming production
of *The Dream*' (see
pp. 103, 248).

From *A Midsummer
Night's Dream* (Northcote
House, in association
with The British Council,
1997)

HELEN HACKETT
LMH 1980

Shakespeare's fairy-populated world

A MIDSUMMER NIGHT'S DREAM is very much a play in which mysterious forces, elusive of rational control, are shown irresistibly turning human events and feelings aside from their planned courses. Love, dreams and the imagination all participate in this effect, and the fairies themselves can be understood as personifications of invisible forces of nature and of fortune which overrode the attempts of humans to govern their own lives.

K. M. Briggs, an expert on folklore, has suggested that in the Elizabethan period there was an urban vogue for fairy literature, produced by a convergence between the courtly tradition of romance, which included supernatural figures, and the rise of non-aristocratic writers like Shakespeare who gave written form to the more humble hobgoblins of oral tradition. Indeed, both Puck himself and the world of cowslips, acorn cups, hedgehogs and spiders which he inhabits must have had nostalgic and idyllic connotations for Shakespeare's urban audience. Just as Shakespeare himself was a native of Warwickshire, so many of his audience would have been born and raised outside London. At this time migration from the countryside into the capital was taking place on a huge scale: by 1590 one in eight English people would spend part of their lives in London. For many in the audience, the fairy-populated world of the wood would be the world of their youth and childhood.

K. M. Briggs (English; D.Phil.; WAAF, 1941–45). Writer, folklorist and artist, Katharine Briggs ran her own folk-dancing and mime company, and was President of the Folklore Society 1967–70. Her publications include the definitive four-volume *Dictionary of English Folk-Tales*. She died in 1980.

KATHARINE BRIGGS
LMH 1918

The personnel of Fairyland

SHELLYCOAT (Scottish). A mischievous bogle, dressed in water weed and shells, whose clinking tells us who he is. Like the brag he delights in misleading night wanderers. He specially haunts the old house of Gorrinberry in Liddesdale, and there was also a fierce Shellycoat near Leith.

SHEFRO (Irish). A gregarious fairy, who, according to Hartley Coleridge, wears foxglove heads for caps.

SILT-GO-DWT and SILI FFRIT. Names of little Welsh fairies, something of the kind of the Scottish Whuppity Stoorie.

SHOOPILTEE (Shetland). This is the Shetland water kelpie. He appears as a pretty little horse; but when people mount him he gallops off into the sea and drowns them.

SIJRIKER (Yorkshire and Lancashire). A death portent. Sometimes it is called a brash, from the padding of its feet. It sometimes wanders invisibly in the woods, giving fearful shrieks, and at others it takes a form of padfoot, a large dog with huge feet and saucer eyes.

SILKY (Northern Counties). A name for a white lady. The Silky of Black Heddon in Northumberland had one close resemblance to a brownie. If she found things below stairs untidy at night she would tidy them, but if they had been tidied she flung them about. She was dressed in dazzling silks, and went about near the house, swinging herself in Silky's Chair – the crossed branches of an old tree which overhangs a waterfall – riding sometimes behind horsemen or stopping them by standing in front of their horses. But on the whole perhaps she belonged more to the class of ghosts than of brownies, for she was laid by the discovery of a treasure, which had been troubling her.

SKILLYWIDDEN (English). The name of a little fairy boy found sleeping and carried home by a farmer in Treridge.

THE SPRIGGANS (Cornwall). Some say the spriggans are the ghosts of the giants. They haunt old chromlechs and standing stones and guard their buried treasure. They are grotesque in shape, with the power of swelling into monstrous size. For all commotions and disturbances in the air, mysterious destruction of buildings or cattle, loss of children or the substitution of changelings, the spriggans may be blamed.

From *The Personnel of Fairyland* (Alden Press, 1953)

Right: Katharine Briggs by John Ward, RA, oil on canvas, 1980

Below: from K. M, W. and E. Briggs, Whispers, An Experiment in Lino Cuts (Capricornus, c.1930)

My grandam called me to her side
And said beneath her breath:
"They pluck the dangling fruits of death,
Or so the good book ever saith,
Who follow the witches' ride."

And then she paused, and cocked her head,

And chuckled still more low,—
"And if you seek, my dear, to know
Strange things, and by strange ways would go,
I'll tell you where they sped."

From Bodleian MS Ashmole 1406, cited by Katharine Briggs.

A Spell for Getting a Faery

An excellent way to gett a Fayrie: this will obtain any one that is not allready bound.

First gett a broad square christall or Venus glasse in length and breadth 3 inches, then lay that glasse or christall in the bloud of a white henne 3 wednesdayes or 3 fridayes: then take it out and wash it with holy aqua and fumigate it: then take 3 hazle stickes or wands of an yeare groth, pill them fayre and white, and make soe long as you write the fayries name, which you call 3 times . . .

A. J. Warren (Music), daughter of Dame Josephine Barnes (see p. 71), is the founder-editor of the Viking/Penguin Opera Guides, and edited the 2001 edition of the *New Penguin Opera Guide*. The leading librettist and translator of English-language opera, she won the Olivier Award for Achievement in Opera for *The Silver Tassie* (2000). Her librettos include *Figaro*, *La Bohème*, *Rigoletto* and *Faust*. Performances in 2001 have included her versions of *Aida* at the Albert Hall; *Don Giovanni* at the English National Opera, and a Chandos recording of *Falstaff*.

From Giuseppe Verdi's *Falstaff*, original libretto by Arrigo Boito, English translation, 1987

AMANDA HOLDEN
LMH 1966

Fairies can be fierce

From Act III, Part 2 of Verdi's Falstaff

FAIRIES
We'll poke him and prickle him.
provoke him and batter him,
explode him and shatter him,
attack him and tickle him.
We'll jump up and land on him,
we'll dance on his belly
and then we'll abandon him
when he's turned to jelly.
With spiders and bats to
bombard him and fling him,
mosquitoes and gnats to
attack him and sting him.

ALICE / MEG / QUICKLY
Pinch him and burn him and turn
    him about until candles and
    starlight and moonlight be
    blotted out, Moonlight and
    starlight and candles be snuffed
    out.

FALSTAFF
Ow! Ow! Ow! Ow!

ALICE / MEG / QUICKLY /
FAIRIES
Thump him and thrash him and
    tear with your claws at him,
bump him and bash him and bite
    with your jaws at him.
Nip him and knock him and tighten
    your grip on him.

SPIRITS
Attack him!

IMPS
Rattle him! . . .

BARDOLPH / PISTOL
Prepare . . .

DR CAIUS / BARDOLPH /
PISTOL / FORD
. . . to meet your doom!

FORD
Monstrous offender!

ALICE
Wicked pretender!

BARDOLPH
Mountainous bubble!

QUICKLY
Maker of trouble!

PISTOL
Sedulous drinker!

MEG
Gluttonous winker!

DR CAIUS
Stealer of chattels!

FORD
Causer of battles!

BARDOLPH / PISTOL / ALICE /
QUICKLY
Are you repentant?

FALSTAFF
Ow! Ow! I'm repentant!

ALETHEA HAYTER
LMH 1929

Who killed Polonius?

Horatio's Version explores in different form the same territory as Tom Stop-
pard in Rosencrantz and Guildenstern Are Dead. *Alethea Hayter describes
the Proceedings of a Court Enquiry, instigated by the new King, Fortinbras,
to investigate the events surrounding the deaths of Polonius, Ophelia,
Claudius, Gertrude, Laertes and Hamlet, Rosencrantz, Guildenstern, et al.
The Enquiry is chaired by the bureaucratic Voltimand.*

SHAKESPEAREAN SCHOLARS have forbidden us to guess at the number of
Lady Macbeth's children. Shakespeare's characters, they remind us, have no
existence outside the plays in which they appear. Dover Wilson, for
instance, writes: 'Horatio is not a person in actual life, or a character in a
novel but a piece of dramatic structure.' But in *Horatio's Version*, he appears
as a very real person, 'sensible and well educated, kind and brave . . .' and it
is evident that much of what happened passed over his head.

From the Preface

EVIDENCE GIVEN AT AN ELSINORE COURT OF ENQUIRY
On the Third Day of the Court's Enquiry, the Chairman calls the First Player
to the stand: he is asked to confirm Horatio's statement that the play had
been altered to entrap King Claudius.

FIRST PLAYER
It was altered all right, but none of us had the least clue what the Prince was
driving at. We wouldn't have touched it with a barge-pole if we'd known it
was political. The thing was lethal – we found that out afterwards, all right,
but we only arrived here the night before the show, and we were rehearsing
right up to the last minute, because of the lines and business the Prince
wanted to put in, so we never had a chance to pick up the local gossip, or
we'd have refused to put in all those . . . about second marriages and so on.
We sensed during the show that that bit wasn't going over very big, but up
till then we hadn't a notion.

VOLTIMAND
What were the extra passages which you were asked to insert?

FIRST PLAYER
Do you know the play *The Murder of Gonzago*? No? Well, it's not the
world's masterpiece, but it's got some nice little scenes, and it generally goes
down pretty well, the way we give it. The plot isn't much – the top roles are

From *Horatio's Version*
(Faber & Faber, 1972)
See also pp. 10, 92

an old lord, Gonzago, who's a sick man, and his wife Baptista. You have them on stage talking abut how ill he is, and how fond she is of him, and is he going to die, and will she be sorry if he does? It's really a bed-chamber scene – the Prince wanted us to make it in an orchard, I don't know why, it's not in the original script; so we had a plant in a pot to show it as out of doors, though it was much less effective with Gonzago lying on a bench than if he's on a great bed like we usually play it . . .

VOLTIMAND
These comments are unnecessary. Confine yourself to what actually happened.

FIRST PLAYER
That's exactly what I'm doing; I was just going to tell you what happened about the dumb-show.

We might as well have spared our pains, because the Prince wasn't pleased at all, and the rest of the audience just didn't attend, they were all whispering with their heads together, the King and the Queen and that old ass, what was his name? The Chancellor – Polonius, that's it. I must say, we've hardly ever played to a stickier audience. You couldn't get a reaction out of them to start with, and then you got all too much – stopping the show in the middle like that, just when the big scene was getting under way. And the Prince kept putting us out, he tried to be a compère, he kept chipping in with explanations that didn't fit the play . . . The whole performance was a mess, but you can't blame the Company – we weren't given a chance.

VOLTIMAND
Did the Prince tell you why he wanted the play changed in this way?

FIRST PLAYER
He certainly did not. You don't suppose we'd have touched it if we'd known, do you? I wouldn't have thought he'd have played us such a trick – he was always a good friend to the Company. I suppose these great men don't bother about what happens to poor devils like us who get caught up in their affairs.

VOLTIMAND
But you agree that King Claudius appeared particularly upset by the poisoning scene in the play?

FIRST PLAYER
'Upset' is putting it mildly. He stood up and started yelling for the lights to go up, and somebody else shouted for us to stop, and the whole audience rushed away – you'd have thought the place was on fire.

DIANA ATHILL
LMH 1936

On Jean Rhys

NO ONE WHO HAS READ Jean Rhys's first four novels can suppose that she was good at life; but no one who never met her could know how very bad at it she was. I was introduced to the novels quite early in the fifties, by Francis Wyndham, who was one of their very few admirers at that time, but I didn't meet her until 1964, and as a result I did almost nothing to help her during a long period of excruciating difficulty.

It was not, perhaps, her very worst time. That must have been the last three years of the forties, when she and her third husband, Max Hamer, were living at Beckenham in Kent, their money had run out, and Max, a retired naval officer, became so desperate that he stumbled into deep trouble which ended in a three-year prison sentence for trying to obtain money by fraudulent means. During that nightmare Jean, paralysed by depression, could do nothing but drink herself into a state so bad that she, too, was several times in court and once in jail. By the time we were in touch Max had served his sentence, they had crept away to a series of miserable lodgings in Cornwall, and Jean was no longer quite at rock-bottom; but she still had nine terribly difficult years ahead of her before re-emerging as a writer.

She had always been a very private person, but she was known in literary circles when her fourth novel, *Good Morning, Midnight*, came out in 1939. When the war began a lot of people 'disappeared' in that they were carried away from their natural habitat on joining the forces or taking up war-work. Jean followed her second husband out of London, so when he died, and she slithered with Max into their misfortunes, she was no longer in touch with former acquaintances and became 'lost'. Francis tried to find out what had happened to her and was told by one person that she had drowned herself in the Seine, by another that she had drunk herself to death. People expected that kind of fate for her.

It was the BBC which found her, when they were preparing to broadcast an adaptation of *Good Morning, Midnight*. They advertised for information about 'the late Jean Rhys', and she answered. She wrote to Francis Wyndham that she was working on a new book (which was to become *Wide Sargasso Sea*). Responding to Francis's and my enthusiasm, André Deutsch agreed that we should buy the option to see it – for £25.

When people exclaim at how mean this was I no longer blush simply because I have blushed so often. I tell myself that the pound bought much more in the fifties than it does now, which is true; that this was not, after all, an advance, only an advance on an advance, which is true; and that no one else in those days would have paid much more for an option, and that, too,

From *Stet* (Granta, 2000)
See also p. 127

is true. But it is inconceivable that anyone would have paid less – so mean it was. If we had known anything about Jean's circumstances I am sure that Francis and I would have fought for more, but it would be a long time before we gained any idea of them.

The trouble was, she kept up a gallant front. In the letters we exchanged between 1957, when she said that her book would be finished in 'six or nine months', and March 1966, when she announced that it was finished, she would refer to being held up by domestic disasters such as leaking pipes, or mice in the kitchen, and she would make the disasters sound funny. Not until I met her did I understand that for Jean such incidents were appalling: they knocked her right out because her inability to cope with life's practicalities went beyond anything I ever saw in anyone generally taken to be sane. . . .

I had a clear glimpse of the central mystery of Jean Rhys: the existence within a person so incompetent and so given to muddle and disaster – even to destruction – of an artist as strong as steel.

JENNY PERY
Books
wood engraving,
2001

J. M. Stuart-Williams (Modern Languages, 1958) is a writer and professional artist specialising in wood engaving. She has worked for a consultancy in Istanbul; taught French; run a Family Planning Clinic in Oban, and been an editor in the Russian division of Pergamon Press. She studied art at Glasgow, St Martin's, Exeter and Camberwell, where she took an MA in printmaking.
See also pp. 116, 145, 248

AN ARTIST AS STRONG AS STEEL

Helen DeWitt was born in 1957. Daughter of an American diplomat, she grew up mainly in South America. She read Classics at LMH, then went to Brasenose as Senior Germaine Scholar in 1983, completing a D.Phil. in Greek and Latin Literature in 1987. She was Joanna Randall-MacIver Junior Research Fellow at Somerville 1987–88. In 1988 she began work on the first of many unfinished novels. *The Last Samurai* is her first published work.

From *The Last Samurai* (Chatto & Windus, 2001)

HELEN DEWITT
LMH 1979

Non avanty il ragatso

3 MARCH 1993

17 days to my birthday. We rode the Circle Line today because we couldn't go back to any museums. It was tedious in the extreme. One funny thing that happened is that a lady got into an argument with Sibylla about two men who were about to be flayed alive. Sibylla explained that one of the men dies of heart failure at time t and the other at time t + n after having someone peel off his skin with a knife for n seconds and the lady said pas dev and Sibylla said I should warn you that he speaks French.

Then the lady said non um non avanty il ragatso and Sibylla said not forward the boy. Not forward the boy. Not. Forward. The boy. Hmmm. I'm afraid I don't quite understand, you clearly have a command of Italian idiom which I cannot match, and the lady said she thought it was not a suitable subject for discussion in the presence of a small child and Sibylla said oh I see, and that's how you say it in Italian. Non avanty il ragatso. I must remember that.

The lady said what kind of example do you think you are setting and Sibylla said would you mind if we continued this discussion in Italian, I feel that it is not a suitable subject for discussion in the presence of a small child or as they say in Italian non avanty il ragatso.

After she got off the train Sibylla said she should not really have been so rude because we should be polite to people however provoking and I should not follow her example but learn to keep my inevitable reflections to myself. She said it was only because she was a bit tired because she had not been getting much sleep and otherwise she would never have been so rude. I am not so sure but I kept my inevitable reflections to myself.

JENNY PERY: 'I love the sensual satisfaction of cutting into the silky end-grain (of a hard wood, usually boxwood), and I admire the crispest blacks and whites and the infinite range of textured greys that it can produce. I hope that in my extreme dotage I shall still be bent over a darkened block with scorper and spitsticker, letting in the light with every cut.'

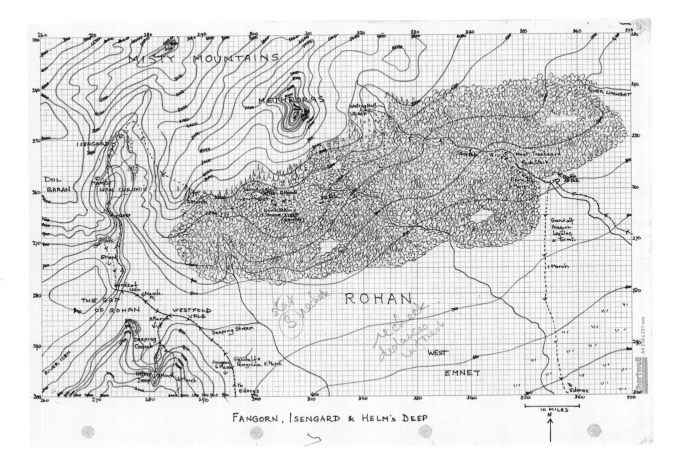

FANGORN, ISENGARD & HELM'S DEEP

Original artwork for one of the maps

BARBARA STRACHEY
LMH 1930

Journeys of Frodo

WHEN I FIRST READ *The Lord of the Rings* I wished I had a complete set of maps covering the journeys of Frodo and his companions. Finally I decided to compile such an atlas myself. This is based on the very clear and detailed descriptions in the text. I have also consulted *The Hobbit*, *Unfinished Tales* and *Pictures by J. R. R. Tolkien*. The evidence is – as one might expect – splendidly consistent. I have tried to use all the topographical logic I can summon, but I am not a cartographer and I have deliberately not tried to work on the basis of projections, but drawn everything as though the earth were still flat and not spherical. We know, however, from *The Silmarillion* that after the Change of the World it was, in fact, spherical. No doubt this is unscientific of me.

From the Preface to
Journeys of Frodo (Unwin
Paperbacks, 1981)
See also p. 95

PRISCILLA TOLKIEN
LMH 1948

Bed-time stories from J. R. R. Tolkien

FOR US THE STORY-TELLING PRESENCE of our father, J. R. R. Tolkien, was far more evident than the more remote world of College and University, to which he went on his remarkable high-seated bicycle, to lecture, give classes and attend meetings. Stories at bed-time, whether invented or re-tellings of other more ancient stories, such as fairy stories, and reading aloud, especially when we were ill in bed, of our favourite books, such as Beatrix Potter's stories – these things he gave us in abundance.

The highlight of storytelling in the year was The Father Christmas Letters, which arrived every year between 1920 and 1943, together with a large picture illustrating events at the North Pole, where Father Christmas lived with his enchantingly irreverent companion, Polar Bear. Again it was probably not fully realised by any one of us just how great was his output nor the extent of his talent as an illustrator until the Ashmolean Museum mounted an exhibition of his paintings and drawings in 1977. The other remarkable feat was how this work was kept hidden from the curious eyes of children in what was for us those heady days and weeks leading up to Christmas.

By the time he retired in 1959 at the age of 67 we had all grown up and left home. For many men at his age, even for scholars, it can be a time of retrenchment, but for my father it was a time of burgeoning international fame, following on the publication of *The Lord of the Rings* in three volumes in 1954–55. More and more, I am astonished at the feat involved in both writing and completing work on such a scale before he had retired and while involved in the extra pressures and responsibilities consequent upon the disruption of life during the Second World War.

I was at school throughout those years and can recall vividly the sound of his vastly heavy old-fashioned Hammond typewriter hammering out the text from his often indecipherable handwriting. I remember the excitement of typing out some of the early chapters myself, although I could only then type with two fingers, and the nightmares over the terror of the Black Riders as they penetrate even into the heart of the apparently solid and secure world of the hobbits.

From 'Memories of
J. R. R. Tolkien in his
Centenary Year', *The
Brown Book* 1992

H. Heroys (English) arrived in England with her family in 1918, in flight from the Russian Revolution (her father, a White Russian general, had been a page at the Tsar's wedding in 1917). At this time she spoke Russian, French and Swedish, but no English. A Scholar at LMH, in 1927 she won a prize for the best novel by an undergraduate, *Another Country*. 'She always had a certain air of mystery,' said a friend, and this was compounded by a thirty-year pause before the appearance of her epic account of the Russian Revolution, *The Witnesses*. Her publications include *The Brief Hour, Electra* and a biography of Metternich. She became a trilingual translator in Geneva, and set up the Hélène Heroys Literary Foundation, which provides stipends for promising young writers in England. She died in 1971.

HÉLÈNE DU COUDRAY
LMH 1925

'LMH undergraduate wins literary prize'

Winner of the University Novel Competition 1926

In 1926 Messrs Philip Allan & Co., Ltd, offered a prize of One Hundred Pounds in advance of royalties for the best novel submitted by October 1st 1927, by an undergraduate in residence during the year at either Oxford or Cambridge University.

Among the manuscripts was one of such outstanding merit that it was an easy task to select the winner of the competition. When the author, at the publishers' request, visited their office, she was found to be Miss du Coudray, of Lady Margaret Hall.

The descriptions of the refugee Russians agonisingly life-like; their eternal talk, their untidy helplessness, their hostility to whatever country has sheltered them, their retrospective sentimentality, their demands for incessant pity, their conceit, and the streak of poetry that informs the meanest of them, have been admirably caught and observed.

Review in The Times Literary Supplement, *1927*

What's become of Waring
. . . since he gave us all the slip?

Some thirty years after Another Country, *Hélène du Coudray published* The Witnesses *as M. W. Waring, after the quotation from Browning*

From *Another Country*
(Philip Allan, 1927)

Another country

FEODOR SERGEIVITCH APOUHTIN, president of the Society for the assistance of emigrated Russians in England, chairman of numerous committees and honorary secretary of many others, reached the door of his house, in one of the smaller streets of Belgravia, a quarter of an hour later than was his custom . . .

'You are very late,' his wife remarked, 'I had to tell George to wait with lunch till half-past one.'

'Yes, I was kept at the last minute by a woman who came to see me. A most unpleasant incident . . . She came to put her case to me and ask my advice. She lived in Malta – there are many Russians there, you know – and apparently met an Englishman, who married her and then went away to England. Having discovered that he was married already, she followed him.' He looked round with gravity.

'Mais c'est tout à fait scandaleux!' exclaimed his sister, who retained the habit, proper to what she considered Russian aristocratic circles, of speaking in French.

'My dear Princess,' (she was the widow of a Caucasian magnate) replied Andreev, a slight smile widening his well-curved mouth, 'Malta is known as a most profligate place. Ces affaires là pullulent.'

'Unfortunate woman,' said Madame Apouhtin, sticking her needle into the centre of a red silk flower.

'That is what I feel' – her husband flicked an imaginary grain of dust off his knee – 'I really don't know what can be done. As I pointed out to her our position with the English is so extremely delicate that any scandal naturally tends to influence them against us. One cannot give way to prejudice. We have no rights and we ought to exercise discretion . . .'

'Well, and what is this lady like? You have told us nothing about her. Is she young? pretty?'

'Did you have any difficulty with her? Was she very upset?' asked Andreev.

'Of course, but very controlled on the whole. She wants a divorce. We shall have to get her one, I suppose. It's a great bother, with all this difficulty about passports to China – but undoubtedly she must be helped. She does not know anyone, no parents, no relations. She broke down when she was telling me that she did not know that man's address. I did what I could. I comforted her – her smile is most agreeable.'

LIBBY HOUSTON
LMH 1960

A maze-dance

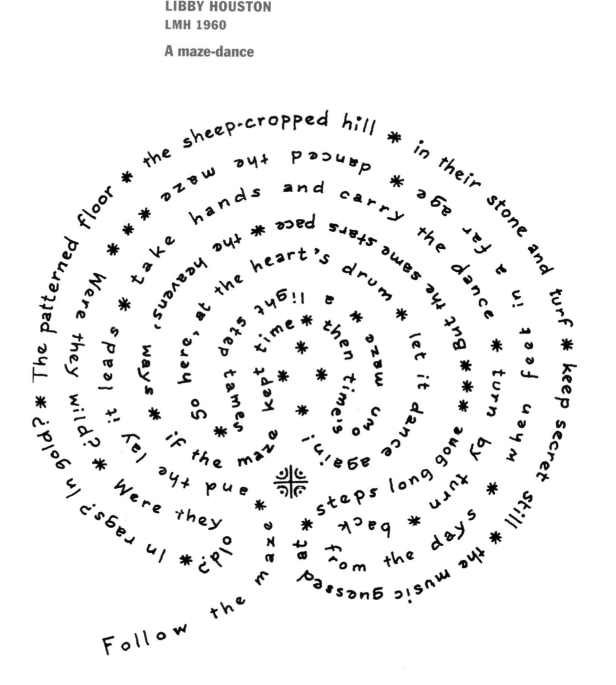

The patterned floor * the sheep-cropped hill * in their stone and turf * keep secret still * the music guessed from the days * turn by turn * back * steps long gone * from the days * when feet * far ago * danced the maze * Were they take hands and carry the dance * But the same stars pace * the heavens, * the heart's drum * let it dance again! then time's a maze * kept time * the days flight * tames * if the maze * and the [lay] it! * it leads * Were they wild? * In gold? * In rags? * old? * Were they * Follow the maze at * So here, at

From *Selected Poems:
All Change* (Oxford
University Press, 1993)
See also p. 65

P. M. Henscher (English; FRSL), winner of the Somerset Maugham Prize in 1998, is the youngest writer to be represented in *The Oxford Book of Short Stories*, edited by A. S. Byatt. His publications include *Other Lulus*; *Pleasured*; and the prize-winning *Kitchen Venom*, which drew on his experience of a clerkship at the House of Lords. He is a judge for the 2001 Booker Prize.

From *The Bedroom of the Mister's Wife*, a collection of short stories (Vintage, 2000)

PHILIP HENSHER
LMH 1983

Forbidden études

A complete short story

I MUST HAVE SEEN HER CHILDREN before I took any notice of her. They were conspicuous, those two boys, and might even have been notorious in the neighbourhood. At least eight years apart in age, they seemed to have no friends, and were always idling up and down the road in the other's joyless company. Nor did they resemble each other in the slightest, and you had to know they were brothers. The elder had a certain furtive obesity, a plank of greasy blond hair falling over his face like the unlovely New Romantics of my own adolescence; the younger was more rancid, twitchingly mobile in his emaciated and blood-drained features. Jason, the elder, you felt, longed only for a locked bedroom and limitless supplies of pornography and crisps; the younger, fancifully named Claude, his peak of ambition might have been the largest possible animal he could safely torture to death. I noticed them, but I doubt I would have connected them with a slight nervous woman who I could only have glimpsed in the newsagent's or in the garden of a house fifty yards beneath the indisputable tide-mark of respectability which so marked the road my parents lived in.

Hepatitis had come at an inconvenient time for me. I'd always more or less accepted that the career I had chosen, of concert pianist, would mean years of fruitless struggle and then failure, disappointment, the garret and an embittered old age. But it hadn't happened quite like that. I hadn't even finished the year at the music college before a concert agent heard me play and signed me up. It all seemed to be going a bit too fast. He produced a date at a hall – not a quiet one in the suburbs, but a big hall, a famous one. And it was soon. We put together a programme, and I bought a proper set of tails, and got used to the way the other kids looked at me. It was wondering, and not particularly envious. And then I got sick.

It was really bad luck. I still didn't know how I got it – it might have been a terrible holiday in Spain, or a girl called Janice who seemed nice but who, in the end, turned out to have given me a false telephone number. Anyway, it doesn't really matter. There was no question of doing the recital. I was weak and yellow, papery and hideous. 'Go home,' my agent said. 'Go to your mum's. Get well. Everything can be put off till you're better.' I kind of knew he was just getting rid of me, that he was glad to have been given an excuse. But I didn't have an alternative. I went back to my parents' to get over it.

My parents had a piano, of course they did. It was the same one I'd prac-tised my scales on when I was a boy, a nice 1920s domestic grand from a

Leipzig firm called Zimmermann. The touch had gone and the keys were yellow as my eyes but I wasn't home to practise. I was home to lie on the sofa and watch daytime TV and get better. All the same, if you carry out the same activity for six hours a day for ten years, every single day, and then suddenly stop, it gives you a pretty bad itch. I'd be sitting with my mother, working on one of the recuperative ten-thousand-piece jigsaws she'd got and suddenly she'd say, 'You're trilling.' And I'd look down and there, on the table top, my fourth and fifth fingers were executing a perfect left-hand trill in triplets, as recommended by Brahms, and I wasn't even thinking about it.

One day, a piano tuner came. My parents said nothing about it. I suppose they must have asked him to. He spent a couple of hours going up the keyboard, followed by five minutes of extravagant arpeggios, and one of the easy Chopin waltzes, the one in C sharp minor, to impress the idiots in the kitchen. Me, sitting idiotically in the kitchen, I didn't say anything, though it had been a waltz I'd been playing since I was nine years old.

So a day or two later I left the jigsaws, and went into the dining room, where the piano was. If you play an instrument – if it makes up your life – it isn't a metaphor, and won't become one. It is just what it is. So I won't say that it seemed to grin at me sardonically, with its gaping top, its crocodile-yellow grin. But a couple of weeks out of the presence of the beast is enough to make you realise how big it is; and, since I was alone in the house, I stood at the door in my dressing-gown, and looked at it for five minutes. And then I went over and sat down, and played, very slowly, just to myself, some Schumann. It was just what came into my head. It was the slowest of the variations he wrote and then removed from the *Symphonic Etudes*. The most beautiful of all the forbidden études, so difficult, so beautiful. No one knows why he took the best five variations out, but I sometimes thought I knew; they are too beautiful to listen to, they are only to be played. And I played the most private of them, to myself, in the empty house, and thought, here is Schumann, and here am I, unaudienced, and here are the forbidden études.

After that I played quite often, though never really practising. It was a few days before I realised I had an audience. The window of the dining room, at the front of the house, was behind your back as you sat at the piano, and you were not disturbed by the sight of people walking up the road. I played all the old favourites, since I could only play what I had in my head and the music I had left at my parents'. I played the first of the Liszt *Années de Pèlerinage*, the Swiss book, and the *Appassionata* and the *Pathé-tique* and the *Adieux*; I played preludes and fugues by Shostakovich and Bach; I started on the Ravel *Miroirs*, which called my mother into the room, concerned I might be overdoing it; and each day I finished with that beautiful showstopper, the Chopin *Berceuse*, which begins so sweetly, and works up to such an exquisite muted firework display, doing your passage work in thirds no end of good. The only thing I did not play were those forbidden études of Schumann. I didn't want to. They were never out of my head, and my mother had to go on with the thousand-piece jigsaw – a view of Milan cathedral, as I remember – on her own.

I had just finished the *Berceuse*, and got up, not tired but replete. I turned round. The two boys were there, on the street, gawping, one big, one small. I scowled at them, but it seemed to have no effect, and, unembarrassed, they just stayed there. They were young and idiotic; I stood there too, and stared out of the window at them. After all, this was my family's house, and it shouldn't be stared into by the neighbourhood oiks. But they wouldn't go, and after a minute I couldn't stand it any longer, and left the room. They might have been there, unobserved, for hours.

A few days later I was in the post office. 'You look a bit better,' my mother had said. 'Would you like a little walk? Ten first-class stamps.' I'd hit a bad day and a gleeful crowd of pensioners were mobbing the desk for their weekly forty quid, or whatever.

'Oh dear,' the woman behind me in the queue remarked. I vaguely nodded. 'Terrible, isn't it.'

'Yes,' I said. 'Yes, terrible.'

'Hello,' she said. 'I know you. At least I know your parents. I'm Sylvie.'

'Hello, Sylvie,' I said. I was tired; it took me at least a minute to remember to tell her my name in return.

'You play the piano, don't you,' she said. She was a small woman, dark and frail, perhaps younger than she appeared; her general nervousness, her frayed overcoat, two years overdue for replacement, may have aged her. She took one little bony hand in another, left in right, right in left, incessantly, and I thought of the American proverb, one hand washes the other, thinking that this woman would never be done with the patient washing. 'I heard you do. I know you're good. My children, my boys, they said you're good enough – well, I won't say what they said, it would embarrass you.'

'Thank you,' I said.

'I was musical,' she said. 'Once. I mean I still am a bit. I used to play the cello. I don't get much time now, with the boys and everything – '

'You ought to keep it up,' I said, conventionally.

'Do you think so?' she said, and now her hands stopped folding each other over and over, and she looked up at me, her eyes shining. 'Do you really think so?'

'Of course,' I said.

'But I have no reason to,' she went on. 'You know – I hate to ask – please just say no if you don't want to – but I would love it so much if someone like you would just strum through some music with me.'

'With pleasure,' I said. It didn't seem a lot to offer, just there, in the post office.

'I used to be good,' she said. 'I have Grade 8.'

'I'd love to,' I said, since Grade 8, to me, meant an exam for children, one I now could barely remember. 'Come round any time. I'd love to. I really would.'

'My goodness,' she said; and her gratitude, so real, so overwhelming, as if she had lost some long-preserved virginity, made you wonder about the rest of her life. 'I can hardly wait.'

My mother wasn't exactly discouraging, but it would be hard to say that she greeted the news that I had made friends with Sylvie, who lived thirty houses down the road in some nebulously different social class, with any enthusiasm. She knew quite well who she was. 'There's a husband,' she said. 'Hangs his jacket on the hook in the back of his car. And two boys. Never seem to go to school.' I shrugged; it wasn't my business.

I saw the boys the next day, though, as I was sitting in the front garden to take advantage of some sunshine, early in the year. They were mooching up the road, zigzagging from one side of the pavement to the other like stage drunks. The elder saw me first, and straightened up, and they began to walk, head down, as if expecting some punishment.

'Hello,' I said confidently as they came up. 'I think I know your mum.'

'Our mum,' the elder said, and then was overcome by a fit of giggles, in which the younger less quiveringly joined him. 'Our mum – knows you.'

'Yes,' I said. 'Yes, we met in the post office.'

'He's called Claude,' the fat boy said, pointing at his brother.

'I see,' I said.

'But he's – he's – he's – ' the younger one began, unable to get it out.

'What's your name?' I asked the fat boy.

'I'm called Jason,' he said.

'I see,' I said.

'Nothing wrong with that,' he said.

'No, indeed,' I said, and after a moment in which we all stared at each other with massive and inexplicable hostility, they continued up the road. I sat down again.

Sylvie came round the next day. My mother stayed firmly in the drawing room, and let me answer the door and take her into the dining room. She probably wanted to make a point, but you could see it was lost on Sylvie; though she started babbling, almost before she was in, about how lovely the house was, her single-mindedness was almost appalling. I recognised it; the way she checked herself, almost forced herself to accept a glass of water to keep up the fiction that this was some kind of social encounter, corresponded to something in me, the part of me that wanted only to be alone with music.

She was a musician, you could see that. And she was a musician despite being no good at all.

The cello was a horrible beast, an orange job made, at a guess, in Bulgaria, and behind it she had an anthology of the horrible epics of the cello's repertory. 'You must know this,' she kept saying, 'but tell me if you don't.' But I knew them all; the Brahms E minor and the Elgar concerto and the Debussy and the Beethoven A major. I'd played them all before with a succession of no-hopers, and relaxed into them without really thinking. She could play, she said, the easier movements, and we gave up at the first sight of a fugue. To be honest I found it best to concentrate on what I was doing. She was terribly bad; out of tune, uncertain of anything higher than the G above middle C, with an ugly, breathy, stubby sort of tone. But she was loving it, you could see that; and though a blind man would not have thought much of her abilities, a deaf one might have loved it. Her platform manner, polished in how much solitude, in how many desperately snatched hours in quiet upper rooms, was awesome, and she gestured over the tangerine instrument until you felt like throwing a tarpaulin over her. As we went from Elgar to Brahms to Haydn, I went in my head from embarrassment to silent amusement to something like pity. We said little between each piece; I just looked at her flush, and wondered at what my mother would be overhearing.

The beautiful but rather demanding coda of the Shostakovich sonata came to an end, and I looked at her, wonderingly.

'That was so good,' she said. 'You really are – '

'Yes, wasn't it,' I said.

'Did you ever play – ' she said, leaning forward, her eyes shining, both hands around the neck of her cello. 'Have you ever played – the sonata – the sonata I always call – you'll think me silly – the sonata of sonatas? Did you ever play that? The Chopin cello sonata? I never have. Only on my own. Do you like Chopin? Do you?'

'Of course,' I said. 'Yes, I do. I love Chopin. I knew there was a cello sonata, but I've never played it. I don't think I've ever heard it even. It's a late piece? isn't it?'

'Oh yes,' she said. 'Oh yes. It's very late. So beautiful. I don't know – I don't know how to ask – '

'Ask away,' I said. I was getting annoyed with these mock withdrawals, this absurd and unnecessary shyness; if she wanted something, she should just ask for it. 'I'll only say no. I mean, I can only say no.'

'I'm sorry,' she said, 'but it's my dream, really, to play the Chopin sonata with someone, someone like you who can play so beautifully. I never thought it would happen. I mean, I have the music here. Do you think – if I left the music with you. I don't want to impose, I really don't, but if you could spare the time to look at it, and perhaps in a week we could – '

She stopped, and closed her eyes. There was something behind her, you could see that; something invisible, blocking her mouth. All she had wanted to ask, it seemed, was if I would play a piece of music with her, but it seemed to me then, as I looked at this stranger, that I had given her more than I knew, that a couple of hours with me and with music was something she would carry on thinking about for years; and I thought this with a tang of shame, that it had meant so little to me, that I had given her as little as I could and would have given her less. I wondered what had silenced her: husband; children; a life she had not chosen. The strings of a cello are taut, and respond quickly to the movements of its player. She held her instrument firmly, taking a deep breath, and the strings blurred, silently, into vagueness with the perfect vibrato of her trembling.

'We could have a go now,' I said reasonably. 'It might not be very good. But I can sight read pretty well. I'd like that, to be honest. I really would.'

Sylvie, looking down, handed over the music. I opened it up and looked at it for a moment. I didn't know this piece; there is more Chopin than you know, and this had somehow escaped me. Late Chopin; rich Chopin, Chopin writing for himself, and I took a big breath and started. Someone had tried to play this piece with Sylvie before, and over the copy was written a web of increasingly desperate numbers, fingering, exclamation marks, spurious simplifications and omissions of the demanding inner parts, and, every ten bars, symbolic spectacles to remind a hopeless pianist to watch the hopeless soloist. I hadn't gone far before I realised that, with this one, I was being stretched.

We got through the big first paragraph, and I slowed a little at the tiny piano interlude. I could vaguely see the thing getting pretty black later on. She didn't come in at her cue, and I paused, looking at her, doodling a little on the chord; she looked at me, her eyes shining.

'I'm sorry,' she said. 'It's just – it's just so beautiful – and, you know – playing this, with you, playing this, so well, I feel as if well, I'm not very good, I'm really not a very good cellist, don't try and persuade me anything other, but playing with someone so wonderful, I just feel so privileged, so lucky, that I know I'm playing better than for years. And that bit, just those eight bars, you know. Could we just – I know we should press on, but if we could play them just once more – it would mean – '

'No problem,' I said. 'What is it? Seven after B?'

'Exactly,' she said. 'You see, you see. You know.'

I wasn't sure that I did; it was just a big tune in A flat. But we played it – I tried not to look at her, she was flinging herself around the dining room to such a degree – and she stopped again at exactly the same point.

'You know,' she said, a bit breathlessly, 'I'm not sure that was quite right. Could we – '

'Of course,' I said, and we started again from the same point. It meant nothing to me, just a small problem in fingering, and I was almost angry that, selfishly, for some reason I knew nothing about, she wanted to play the same few notes over and over again. 'Let's go on,' I called as, at the same point, she half-faltered, but continued. I was concentrating, and only really marking her beats, but it can't have been more than a dozen or so bars later – a minute in real time, in the sort of time which exists outside music – when I looked up at a clatter on the wooden floor, and saw that she had dropped her bow, that, stricken, she was looking at me, that big in her was some great solitary confession which already frightened me; and frightened me because in a second I could see that it had nothing to do with Chopin, or music, or, to be honest, with me.

The door opened.

'Am I interrupting?' my mother said, coming in firmly. 'I just wondered if you were near a break.'

'A break,' I said, thankfully.

'I hate to say it,' my mother went on remorselessly, 'but we mustn't let our wunderkind exhaust himself. I'm here to make sure he recovers.'

'Oh no,' Sylvie said. 'Oh, I'm ever so sorry,' and her accent, grating against my mother's like lemon on glass, made me despise, momentarily, my family. 'It's been such a treat, I've been too demanding. Let's call it a day, shall we? You've been ever so kind, more than kind, really – '

'I think that would be best, to be honest,' I said, and it was as if I had slapped her face. 'We can do it again some time.'

She flushed, more insulted than I had meant. I sat at the piano and watched her loosen her bow, put her music, her instrument, the rosin, the bow into their appointed places.

'Would you like a cup of tea?' I said eventually.

'No,' she said. 'No, thank you, that is kind, but I must be home for the boys. This has been such a treat for me. It really has. Really wonderful. I hope I haven't tired you out – '

'Not at all,' I said, and then she went.

And that was it. We didn't play again; I saw her a couple of times by chance, and we were perfectly friendly, for five minutes or so. And about a month or two later, when I was feeling much stronger, almost myself again, I was down at the park for a walk by myself. I was miles away, and didn't notice the boys until they were right on top of me. One of them was fat and blond and fifteen; the other may have been seven. They blocked my path moronically, and stared. I smiled.

'Our mum – ' the younger one said, eventually.

'You – ' the elder one said, with no seeming intent to insult, but, apparently, just trying to attract my attention. Yes, I thought, going on, walking around the unattractive brace, that's about it; you – , yes, you –

The odd thing is, I've played the Chopin cello sonata quite a lot since, and come to like it. It's a strange sort of piece. There's a peculiarity about it. It's much easier for the soloist than for the accompanist. The cellist has an easy time of it. She just comes along and does what she has to do, plays a simple sort of part. For her, there's nothing surprising, nothing awkward, just the same sort of thing she plays every single day of her professional life. Every single day of her life. Believe me, it's the pianist, the one in the supposedly secondary role, who has the hard job, really, in the end; he is given one problem after another, and has to unlock all the difficulties, has to make what he can of it, and all the time, something he has never seen before, something he can hardly begin to know how to get round, to come out of with credit.

Sometimes you play it, and almost start to think that your fingers are going to be bent into a completely different shape by the end of it, by the sorts of demands it makes, demands you never expected. But you look down, and there, at the end of your black sleeves and white cuffs, there are your hands, and they are the same hands they ever were. Of course they are.

Well, I got better, after a bit, and got my strength back. Luckily, the hall had a slot they hadn't filled, eight months after the original date, and I made my début, a bit later than planned, but with pretty well the same programme. I remember my tails feeling loose with all the weight I'd lost, that night, but it went well, and it's gone on going well since. You've probably heard of me, if you take an interest in these things. I'm twenty-six. I don't know if I mentioned that. But I am. I'm twenty-six. I've got years ahead of me.

Illustration announcing a programme of lecture-recitals at LMH by Margaret Deneke, Choirmaster, 1930

ELIZABETH MACKENZIE
LMH 1941, Fellow 1954,
Vice-Principal 1981–88

FOUR SONGS OF RETURN

I

Where suddenly the wanderer comes
The whirling air is taut and still.
The mast that turned the stars about
Stands like a tree before the hill.

The winds that wove his days are done:
Now shall the cheating shuttle stay.
The past must grow again, and night
Restore the web that died by day.

The desolate, the empty place
Which shrank as Argus-eyes forgot,
Restores itself – is time fulfilled –
Most joyful here, where time is not.

From Four Songs of Return, *1964*
music by Egon Wellesz, op. 85
words by Elizabeth Mackenzie

My awareness of the existence of role
models was a factor: the knowledge
that women could and did compose
music strengthened the willingness
to sit down and write – Susan
Wollenberg, LMH 1966, Fellow 1972

B. D. Clegg (English), actress and scriptwriter. At Oxford she acted with Kenneth Tynan and Lindsay Anderson; at the Old Vic she played Maria to Richard Burton's Toby Belch, and Nerissa to Katharine Hepburn's Portia. In *Emergency Ward Ten* she played Nurse Jo Buckley, which she combined with writing for *Coronation Street*, *Dr Who* and *Crossroads*. Her publications include a biography of the Littlewoods family.

BARBARA CLEGG
LMH 1944

Tardis materialises . . .

For some years, Barbara Clegg combined acting in television (she was Nurse Jo Buckley in Emergency Ward 10*) with writing. Her radio work includes original plays as well as scripts for* The Dales *and* Waggoners' Walk, *while her television work ranges from scripts for* Coronation Street *to* Dr Who *and* Crossroads.

FROM: HOLD
Tardis materialises - 1/17 -

34.   1 C
Group   6. INT. TARDIS CONSOLE ROOM.
DOC/TEG/clear screen/
TURLOUGH
            1C 2C
            (4A for end of Sc.)

COLUMN STATIONARY
LIGHTS OFF
SCREEN OPEN
BLACK FOR INLAY
MURK FROM
STUDIO II FOR G.O.

(THE DOCTOR AND HIS
COMPANIONS ARE
LOOKING AT THE
SCANNER-SCREEN.

TURLOUGH CONSULTING
THE ATMOSPHERIC
ANALYSER)

TURLOUGH: The air's breathable.

TEGAN: Are you going out
there?

35.   2 C
WCB DOC/TEG
with Gallop. on
L of frame

THE DOCTOR: I have to find out
what it's all about. Turlough,
get a couple of torches.

TEGAN: Make it three. I'm
coming with you.

THE DOCTOR: I need you here.

(TURLOUGH GOES TO
GET THE TORCHES)

TEGAN: Why does it have
to be me?

let TUR.in from
L to 3S TUR/DOC/TEG

THE DOCTOR: (GENTLY) The White
Guardian may try to make contact
again.

(TURLOUGH SUDDENLY,
WITH AN ATTEMPT
AT CASUALNESS)

(1 next)

- 17 -

- 1/18 -

TURLOUGH: I'll stay, if you like.

(THE DOCTOR IGNORES
HIM AND LOOKS
SERIOUSLY AT TEGAN
AGAIN)

THE DOCTOR: I want someone here
I can rely on. It's important.

36.   1 C
HCU TEGAN

TEGAN: Someone who doesn't run
away.

37.   2 C
3S TUR/DOC/TEG

TURLOUGH: I explained what
happened on Terminus.

THE DOCTOR: Save the arguing
until later.

TEGAN: What do I have to do?

crab L with DOC.
to 2S TEG/DOC
Pan DOC.L to
2S DOC/TUR

THE DOCTOR: (POINTS) Operate
that lever. His power's badly
depleted. He's having to draw
on ours to get through at all.

TEGAN: The power drain was the
White Guardian?

THE DOCTOR: Exactly.

TEGAN: What did he say?

THE DOCTOR: Apart from the
co-ordinate, I could understand
very little.

38.   1 C
HCU TEGAN

TEGAN: Shouldn't you wait?
He may try to make contact again.

(2 next)

- 18 -

V. L. Clore (Modern Languages) is Chairman of the Vivien Duffield Foundation and the Clore Foundation; Deputy Chairman of the Weizmann Foundation; a director of the Royal Opera House; and a Trustee of the Dulwich Picture Gallery and of the Jerusalem Foundation. She was awarded a CBE in 1989, and made DBE in 2000.

VIVIEN DUFFIELD
LMH 1963

Patronage and the arts

GOVERNMENT, SINCE THE National Lottery began, has now become the greatest patron of the arts and heritage that Britain has known; however, the requirement for matching funds has, at the same time, ensured that private patrons are vital players in this largely public sector. Governments and their policies may come and go, but the dependence on private money is permanent in arts funding.

In the recent history of philanthropy the traditional patrons, the monarchs, the church and the aristocracy, have been replaced by such figures as Henry Tate, Samuel Courtauld, Sir William Burrell, Joseph Duveen and the Sainsburys, to name but a few. Many of these patrons were connoisseurs; they bought the paintings they admired and bequeathed them to the nation, often influencing public taste along the way. Learning establishments have also played their part over the centuries – and Lady Margaret Hall has created rather a fine collection of paintings.

But sadly the role of the private patron, the private commissioning of works of art and music is on the decrease: today's new millionaires, and there are lots of them, may collect the token Renoir or even Clarice Cliff but gone are the days of Mozart's archiepiscopal patron.

The uneasy juxtaposition of private and public funds in the arts sector is to a great extent exclusive to Great Britain. In America the arts are almost entirely funded by the private sector, with some small city and state intervention but no central Government help. In Continental Europe it is the reverse – City, State and Government not only pay for the arts but they control and manage them and the results have, until recent cuts, been spectacular. Germany and Austria still have active opera houses in most small provincial cities and France has *grands projets* and wonderful regional museums. Private patronage (in the form of commercial sponsorship) is creeping in slowly, but individual giving is almost unheard of.

Americans have never hesitated to use their wealth to create monuments for the arts – not only do they build museums, theatres or concert halls – they endow and maintain them. They chair their boards and take huge pride in their local institutions as well as the national ones; for this they receive tax benefits and tremendous social kudos. While in nineteenth-century England patronage was, with very few exceptions, confined to the upper class, in America that philanthropy was in fact the ladder used by the emerging rich to climb to the top of the new social tree. To be Chairman of the Met is a powerful role indeed and carries a standing equal to none.

Vivien Duffield, 'The Role of Private Patronage in the Arts' (*The Brown Book* 2000)

SAM WEST
LMH 1985

New trainers or a theatre ticket?

THERE ARE SOME THINGS best left to the market, and theatre is not one of them. Standing in a queue for Tate Modern, 2,000 of us happy in the rain, I wondered why waiting to go into a theatre never felt like this: people of all ages and professions with only one thing in common – none of us paid to get in. Chris Smith's attempt to secure free entry for museums is a civilised and proper gesture, and £6 million of government money has turned Tate Modern into a true people's palace. No one seems to think the idea of modern art for free is ridiculous – should theatre be treated the same way?

In my experience, where people might consider a film or a gig as a good way to spend Friday night, most of them think theatre is shouting in the evenings for posh people. If your parents don't take you and your school doesn't organise visits to the theatre, it's very easy to grow up without ever setting foot inside one. When I can get into a club for a fiver, and buy an E for a tenner, and know I'll have a great time, no one should be surprised if I go to the club more often than a show. An entire generation has got out of the theatre habit: education, prejudice and attention span are all partly to blame, but the biggest barrier is expense. As an incentive to people who

From 'New Trainers or a Theatre Ticket?', *The Observer*, 9 July 2000 See also p. 103

**JENNY PERY
The Globe**
wood engraving,
2001

don't like theatre because they've never tried it, a proportion of seats should be free. There will always be those who save hard to afford the outrageous prices, but unless we make it easy and cheap for some of the others, those who grew up on cheap and easy visits will be dead and there will be no one to replace them.

Last year, about 11 million people watched a Premiership football match, and about 9 million went to the theatre. It's no coincidence that many ordinary fans are kept away from live football by the spiralling costs and 'executive club' feel at some grounds. Why can't cheap theatre be the new football, only putting on the 4–3 thrillers and avoiding the dull 0–0 draws on a windy November Tuesday?

No theatre can afford to have a truly inclusive access policy. Seat prices are set at a level which the marketing department think the market can take. The irony is that the better an organisation uses its subsidy, and the more inclusive its access, the less it takes at the box office. Last year the Hamlyn Foundation funded a week of performances at the National Theatre where all tickets across all three houses cost between £1 and £5. Twenty thousand people came who had never been to the National before. It clearly works – why can't these schemes be state-funded so there is a real possibility of continuity? If more money were given to those theatres which try to provide free seats, many more would be encouraged to try.

Richard Eyre says that nowadays people ask: 'Why should I spend £50 going to the theatre when for £50 I can buy a nice pair of shoes?' Fair enough: buy the shoes. You can rely on shoes. You cannot rely on theatre. Great theatre like all great art is, and should be, rare; it's up to us to try to make it as good as possible, but if we fail or you don't like it, and the experiment cost you £50, you won't come again in a hurry. Make it free, and you might be back next week.

ANN PASTERNAK SLATER
LMH Fellow 1972

Extravagance at The Globe, 1613

EVEN IN 1613 Sir Henry Wotton complained about the Globe Theatre's richly pedantic production of Henry VIII, complete with its Georges and Garters, its guards in embroidered coats, and 'many extraordinary circumstances of pomp and majesty, even to the matting of the stage' (rather than the usual bare boards, or straw).

From *Shakespeare the Director* (Harvester Press, 1982)

Honours Board

Many books, in particular works of scholarship, do not readily yield extracts. Some books we failed to find, even in the British Library. And there are many achievements that do not fit into an Anthology. So we have added an 'Honours Board', to list some of the LMH names and a selection of their work unrepresented in this, more literary, collection: a salute to achievement and a guide to further reading.

SUZANNE GRAHAM-DIXON
STACY MARKING

Editors of *The Brown Book*
1921–56 Agnes M. Fletcher (English 1904), first editor, after nursing in France in World War I (mentioned in Despatches).
1957–71 Christine Anson (Modern Languages 1917)
1972–79 Deaconess Souttar (English 1923)
1980–89 Hilda Pipe (History 1939)
1990–95 Veronica Palmer (Classical Mods 1947)
1996– Margaret Hodgson (PPE 1953)

Editors of the LMH Registers
1923, 1925, 1929, 1947 Christine Anson
1966 Joan Agate
1990 Cathy Avent and Hilda Pipe

Other Publications

History
Lucy Barbara Hammond (Bradby, LMH 1892). One of those outstanding students, with a First in Mods and Greats and an Hon. D.Litt in 1933; Captain of Hockey, Tennis and Boating for LMH; and 'the first student to introduce a bicycle to the Hall'. Collaborating with her husband J. L. L. B. Hammond, her work includes *The Village Labourer* (1911); *The Town Labourer* (1917); *The Skilled Labourer* (1919); *The Age of the Chartists* (1930); *The Rise of Modern Industry* (1926; 1966) and, unexpectedly (I wish we had found it) *Cooking Explained* (1975).
Evelyn Mary Jamison (LMH 1898–1901; 1907–37, Bursar, Librarian, Vice-Principal). *The Sicilian Kingdom* (1939); *Studies of the History of Medieval Sicily* (1992).
Anne Marie Fremantle (Huth Jackson, LMH 1927). Ed. *The Wynne Diaries 1789–1820* (3 vols., 1935); *Desert Calling: The Life of Charles de Foucauld* (1949); *The Protestant Mystics* (with introduction by W. H. Auden, 1965).
Anne Whiteman (LMH 1946–85, Tutor, Fellow, Vice-Principal). Curator of the Bodleian Library; mentioned in Despatches while serving in the WAAF; died 2000. Her edition of *The Compton Census of 1676* (1986) – the returns made in 1766 to the great inquiry into the number of conformists, onconformists and papists – took decades of work, and has been described as 'a classic contribution to historical demography'.
A. C. De La Mare (LMH 1951, Professor of Palaeography, King's College, London). *Italian Manuscripts* (1969); *Duke Humphrey's Library and the Divinity School* (1971).
D. A. Gilbert (LMH 1953, Professor, University of Maryland). *Anglo-American Politics 1660–1775* (1973).
Diana de Marly (LMH 1969; fashion historian). *The History of Haute Couture 1850–1950* (1980); *Working Dress Fashion for Men* (1985); *Louis XIV and Versailles* (1987); *Dress in North America* (1990).
Marianne Burns (LMH 1971–75, Fellow, Liverpool University). *Partners in Revolution: The United Irishmen and France* (1982); *Wolfe Tone – Prophet of Irish Independence* (1991).

Classical Studies
Lilian Jeffery (LMH 1945–80, Research Fellow, Tutor, Fellow). *Archaic Greece* (1976); *The Local Scripts of Archaic Greece* (1990).
Jane Gardner (LMH 1955, Lecturer, Reading University). *The Roman Household* (1991); *Being A Roman Citizen* (1993).
Richard Jenkyns (LMH 1981, Fellow and Tutor, Dean 1983–91). *The Victorians and Ancient Greece* (1980); *The Legacy of Rome* (1992); *Dignity and Decadence: Victorian Art and the Classical Inheritance* (1992).
Simon Price (LMH 1981, Fellow and Tutor). *Rituals and Power: The Roman Imperial Cult in Asia Minor* (1984).

Philosophy and Theology
Dorothy Emmet (LMH 1923, Hon. Fellow 1963; Professor of Philosophy, Manchester University 1946–66). *The Nature of Metaphysical Thinking* (1945); *Rules, Roles and Relations* (1966); *Function, Purpose and Powers* (1972); *The Moral Prism* (1979); *The Role of the Unrealisable* (1993). See p. 195
Helen Oppenheimer (LMH 1944–47, theologian and preacher). *The Character of Christian Morality* (1974); *The Marriage Bond* (1976); *The Hope of Happiness: a sketch for a Christian Humanism* (1983).

Science, Medicine and Sociology
Dame Margaret Turner-Warwick (LMH 1943; Honorary Fellow 1989; Professor and Dean, Cardio-thoracic Institute, London University, past President, Royal College of Physicians) *Immunology of the Lung* (1978).
Celia Westropp (LMH 1945, Tutor, Fellow, Research Fellow; physician). *Health and Happiness in Old Age* (with Moyra Williams, 1960).
Sylvia Lush (Countess of Limerick, LMH 1955; community health worker). Joint ed., *Sudden Infant Death: Patterns, Puzzles and Problems* (1985).
Dr Jill Welbourne (LMH 1956; medical specialist in eating disorders). *The Eating Sickness* (with J. Purgold, 1984).
Julia Tugendhat (Dobson, LMH 1960; family therapist and children's writer). *The Adoption Triangle* (1992), and 11 children's books.

Nature and Natural Science
Evelyn Seton Gordon (LMH 1912) was one of the first nature photographers to take close-ups of birds in the wild.
Wilma George (Crowther, LMH 1937; Fellow and Tutor 1959). *Elementary*

Genetics (1951); *Animals and Maps* (1969); *Gregor Mendel and Heredity* (1975); *The Naming of the Beasts: a medieval bestiary of natural history* (1991).

Rosemary Jellis (LMH 1937). *Bird Sounds and their Meaning* (1977).

Jennifer Bak (LMH 1955; zoologist). *The Ecology of a Garden* (1991).

David Macdonald (LMH 1986, Research Fellow). *Rabies and Wildlife: a Biologist's Perspective* (1980); *Encyclopaedia of Mammals*, vols. 1, 2 (1984); *The Velvet Claw: a natural history of carnivores* (1992).

The Arts, Music and Architecture

Mary C. Glasgow (LMH 1923; publisher, Secretary-General of CEMA, later the Arts Council, and on the British Board of Film Censors). *The Arts in England* (with B. Ifor Evans, 1949).

Dame Joan Evans (LMH 1933, Susette Taylor Fellow). *Life in Medieval France* (1925; 1957; 1969); *Art in Medieval France* (1948); *English Art 1307–1461* (1949); *The Flowering of the Middle Ages* (1985; 1998).

Alison Kelly (LMH 1933; historian of decorative arts and ceramics). *The Book of English Fireplaces* (1968); *The Story of Wedgwood* (1975); *Mrs Coade's Stone* (1990).

Mary Edmond (LMH 1934). *Hilliard and Oliver: the Lives and Works of Two Great Miniaturists* (1983).

Jocelyn Toynbee (LMH 1937, Susette Taylor Fellow). *The Shrine of Saint Peter and the Vatican Excavations* (1956); *Art in Roman Britain* (1964); *Roman Historical Portraits* (1978).

Jennifer Montagu (LMH 1949, Slade Professor of Fine Art, Cambridge). *Alessandro Algardi* (1985); *Gold, Silver and Bronze Sculpture of the Roman Baroque* (1996).

Hermione Hobhouse (LMH 1951; architectural historian). *Lost London* (1971); *A History of Regent Street* (1975); *Thomas Cubitt, Master Builder* (1971, 1995); *Prince Albert, His Life and Work* (1983); *Survey of London*, vol. 42: *Southern Kensington, Kensington Square and Earl's Court* (1986).

Patricia Howard (LMH 1955; musicologist). *Gluck and the Birth of Modern Opera* (1963).

Lucy Archer (LMH 1957, architectural historian). *Raymond Erith, Architect; The Architecture of Britain and Ireland* (1999).

Bridget Marsh (Cherry, LMH 1960; architectural historian). General Editor, *The Buildings of England* (1983, 1990); *London* (with Nikolaus Pevsner, 1983, 1991).

Literature and Criticism

Stack, V. E. (LMH 1919). *The Love Letters of Robert and Elizabeth Barrett Browning* (1969).

Robin Myers (LMH 1944; bibliographer). *Dictionary of Literature in the English Language 1940–1970* (1970; 1978); *Economics of the British Book Trade* (1985); *Aspects of Printing from 1600* (with Michael Harris, 1987).

Theresa Whistler (LMH 1945). Ed. *The Collected Poems of Mary Coleridge* (1954); *Imagination of the Heart: The Life of Walter de la Mare* (1993).

Ruth Pryor (LMH 1948, 1967–72 Talbot Research Fellow). *Sounds from the Bell Jar: Ten Psychotic Authors* (with G. Claridge and G. Watkins, 1990).

Colette Clark (LMH 1951). *Home at Grasmere: the Journal of Dorothy Wordsworth* (1970; 1978).

Tao Tao Liu (LMH 1961; Fellow of Wadham College). *Poems from Old China* (1987); *Unity and Diversity in China* (with David Faure, 1996).

Dame Helen Gardner (LMH 1966, Prof. Fellow, Emeritus Fellow 1975–86). *The Art of T. S. Eliot* (1949); *The Metaphysical Poets* (1957); *The Business of Criticism* (1963); *The Divine Poems of John Donne* (1966, 1982); Editor of *The New Oxford Book of English Verse* (1973) and *The Faber Book of Religious Verse* (1979).

Janet Montefiore (LMH 1967). *Feminism and Poetry: Language, Experience* (1994); *Men and Women Writers of the 1930s* (1996).

Margaret Harris (LMH 1974). *Inspiration in Milton and Keats* (1982); *A Strange Way of Killing: the Poetic Structure of Wuthering Heights* (1987).

Morag Harris (LMH 1974). *Emily Dickinson in Time.* (2000).

Valerie Sanders (LMH 1978; Senior Lecturer, Buckingham University). *Reason over Passion: Harriet Martineau and the Victorian Novel* (1986); *Eve's Renegades: Victorian Anti-Feminist Women Novelists* (1995).

Miscellaneous

Ida O'Malley (LMH 1983) was Editor of suffragism periodicals *Common Cause* and *Women's Leader*.

Elizabeth G. Withycombe (LMH 1920). *The Oxford Dictionary of English Christian Names* (with J. C. Ghosha, 1945; 1963; 1973); *Annals of English Literature 1475–1950* (with J. C. Ghosha, 1961).

Joyce Pearce (LMH 1933) did relief work with refugees after World War II and founded the Ockenden Venture for Refugees in 1955.

Masha Poustchine (Lady Williams, LMH 1933, Reuters correspondent 1941–44). *White Among the Reds* (1980); *The Consul's Memsahib* (1985); *Exiled to America* (1987).

Margaret Flannery (LMH 1940). *The Penguin Book of Dogs* (1962).

Irene Hindmarsh (LMH 1942) was Pro-Vice Chancellor, Durham University, 1982–85; Visiting Professor, New York State and Shanghai universities, 1979, 1980; delegate for university women at UN conference on human rights and the status of women.

Mary Hanlin (Marshall, LMH 1953). *Bozzimacoo: Origins and Meanings of Oaths and Swear Words* (1975).

Sharon Churcher (LMH 1966), a journalist working in New York, was the first British woman to be made a Fellow of the World Press Institute, USA. *New York Confidential* (1986).

Joanna Kennedy (Ormsby, LMH, 1969) was the first woman to be elected to the Engineering Research Council.

Alphabetical Index

Chronological Index

Acknowledgements & Credits

The publishers would like to thank all those who kindly gave permission to reproduce copyright material and who provided illustrations. Specific credits and copyright acknowledgements only are listed here. Every effort has been made to trace copyright holders; errors or omissions are inadvertent and will be corrected in future editions if information is given in writing to the publishers.

Allison & Busby, London, reproduced by kind permission: Katharine Moore, pp. 29, 30;

Anvil Press Poetry: Sally Anne Purcell, p. 133;

Ashgate Publishers: Susan Reynolds, p. 209;

© Autocar Magazine: Alistair Weaver, p. 102;

BBC Archive: Bridget Kendall, pp. 154–55;

BBC Worldwide Ltd: Mary Seton-Watson, p. 123;

Blackwell Publishers, by permission: Katharine Briggs, p. 224; Sheila Fletcher, p. 26; Carole Pateman, p. 90;

Bloodaxe Books: Anne Stevenson, p. 180;

Bodleian Library, University of Oxford, by kind permission: A Spell, p. 225;

© The British Council/National Book League/Longmans Green: Alethea Hayter, p. 92; Phyllis Hodgson, p. 209;

Cambridge University Press, by permission: Anne Hudson, pp. 69, 208; Margaret Aston, p. 211;

© Camphill Village Trust Ltd: Barbara Strachey, p. 232;

Constable & Robinson Publishing, reprinted by kind permission: © Georgina Battiscombe, p. 93; © H. F. M. Prescott, p. 210; © Rachel Trickett, p. 32; Helen Waddell, pp. 200, 207;

Cooper, Leo, by courtesy: Lettice Cooper, p. 66;

© Country Life: Barbara Scott, p. 141;

© CT Publishing: Gwendoline Butler, p. 89;

Curtis Brown, by kind permission: © Robyn Sisman, p. 107;

Darwen Finlayson, c/o Phillimore & Co. Ltd, Shopwyke Manor Barn, Chichester, West Sussex, reproduced by kind permission: Sister Gertrude, p. 70;

© Davis, Lindsey 1973 and 2001. All rights in Fingers Mulligatawny reserved;

André Deutsch Publishers, reprinted by permission: Diana Athill, pp. 127–28;

Duckworth Publishing, reproduced by kind permission: Mary Warnock, p. 194;

© The Economist Newspaper Ltd, London: Martin Giles, p. 104;

Evening Standard: Patrick Hennessy, p. 105;

Faber & Faber Ltd: Ruth Padel, p. 106;

Fourth Estate Ltd: Kathryn Hughes, p. 18;

Victor Gollancz: Lettice Cooper, p. 66; Diana Collins, p. 179; Barbara Strachey, p. 95;

Granta Books: © Diana Athill, pp. 229–30; © Georgina Ferry, p. 220; © Suzanne Franks, p. 96;

Grub Street London, reproduced by kind permission: Margaret Costa, p. 117;

© Guardian Newspapers Ltd: Naseem Khan, p. 170; Stacy Marking, p. 81; Ann Widdecombe, p. 186;

Dr Helen Hackett and Northcote House Publishers, by permission: Helen Hackett, p. 223;

HarperCollins Publishers Ltd, by permission: Amanda Foreman, pp. 215–17; Teresa McLean, p. 116;

George G. Harrap: B. Flower and E. Rosenbaum, pp. 112, 118;

Hodder & Stoughton Ltd, reproduced by permission: Margaret Jessy Miller, p. 183;

© A. Holden 1987, p. 226;

Independent Newspapers (UK) Ltd. by permission: Mary Dejevsky, pp. 130–32;

Lady Margaret Hall: C. V. Wedgwood, pp. 203–6;

Macmillan Publishers London Ltd: Anne Chisholm, p. 120; Dorothy Emmet, p. 185; Lynn Nicholas, p. 59; Sheila Sullivan, p. 134; E. Morison and F. Lamont, p. 218;

The Merlin Press, by permission: Margaret Lambert, p. 135;

Methuen Publishing Ltd: Caryl Churchill, pp. 188–94; Charles Drazin, p. 111;

Norwich, Viscount, by kind permission: Lady Diana Duff Cooper, p. 15;

© Observer Newspapers: Nicci Gerrard, p. 108; Kate Kellaway, p. 137;

Oxford University Press, by permission: Janet Courtney, p. 90; G. MacFarlane, pp. 72–73; Joy Hendry, p. 169; Mary Jacobus, p. 201; Maggie Keswick, pp. 143–45; Eleanor C. Lodge, pp. 42, 56, 156;

The Penguin Group UK: © P. M. Matarasso, p. 208; © Sarah Bradford, p. 221;

Pluto Books: Teresa Hayter, p. 157;

Prospect: Sarah Hogg, p. 185;

The Random House Group Ltd, reprinted by permission: Helen DeWitt, p. 231; Philip Hensher, pp. 237–44; Nigella Lawson, pp. 114, 115; Lucasta Miller, p. 97; Ruth Padel, pp. 147–49; Ellen Thorp, p. 121; Gillian Tindall, pp. 212–13;

© Lavinia Robinson: Priscilla Napier, p. 57;

© Save The Children Archives: Eglantyne Jebb, pp. 153, 156, 199;

Souvenir Press Ltd: Elaine Morgan, pp. 74–75;

Summa Publications, Inc., P.O. Box 660725, Birmingham, Alabama 35266, by courtesy: Professor Barbara Bowen, p. 134;

I. B. Tauris & Co. Ltd: Victoria Schofield, p. 166;

© The Telegraph Group Ltd 2001: Benazir Bhutto, p. 166; Mary Warnock, p. 13;

© Times Newspapers Ltd: Vanora Bennett, pp. 195–96;

Michael Gove, pp. 132, 187; Sam Kiley, pp. 100–1, 162–63;

© University of Michigan Press: Anne Stevenson, p. 97;

© Virgin Publishing: Eileen Elias, pp. 38–39; Guy Browning, p. 77;

Weidenfeld and Nicolson: Antonia Fraser, p. 17; Elizabeth Longford, p. 219;

Yale University Press: © Fiona MacCarthy, pp. 40–41, 61–62.

PICTURE CREDITS

Clive Barda: p. 226;

Joyce Baronio: p. 112;

© Jerry Bauer: p. 92;

BBC Written Archive Centre: p. 246 bottom left and right;

BFI Stills, Posters and Designs: p. 131;

© Bodleian Library, Oxford: p. 159;

© The British Library: pp. 57 top, 119, 139, 225 left;

Dinah Drazin: p. 111;

Nick Dyer: p. 133;

Studio Edmark Oxford: pp. 202, 256 second from left;

Fritillary: pp. 11, 14, 15, 38, 49, 102;

Gillman & Soame Oxford: p. 137 below;

Nick Hale: p. 213;

Claude Harris: p. 40;

George Havell: p. 256 third from left;

Imperial War Museum: p. 60;

Lenard: p. 141;

© Neil Libbert: p. 97;

Dick Makin Photography: pp. 1, 2–3, 4, 36, 41, 52–53, 91, 98, 138, 198–99, 225 right, 250, 251, 255;

Stacy Marking: pp. 142 below, 146;

John Moreton: p. 83;

Brendan Neiland: p. 4;

C. R. W. Nevinson, by courtesy of the artist's estate: p. 181;

© PFD: p. 103;

© Val Rylands: p. 190;

Stanley Spencer, by courtesy of the artist's estate: pp. 41, 60;

W. Suschitzky: p. 73;

P. Tinslay: p. 113;

Thomas Photos Oxford: pp. 8–9, 27, 47 top;

John Ward: p. 202, 225 right;

Anthony Wilson: p. 185 top.

Editorial
assistance by
Cathy Avent
(English, 1939)

and Suzanne
Graham-Dixon
*(Modern
Languages, 1950)*

Designed and
produced by
Jane Havell
(English, 1972)

Fundraising
by Anna
McNair Scott
(English, 1964)

Proofread by
Rosamund Howe
*(Modern
Languages, 1961)*

With special
photography by
Dick Makin

Published 2001 by Lady Margaret Hall
Oxford OX2 6QA | www.lmh.ox.ac.uk

This collection © 2001 Lady Margaret Hall
For original publication details see the entries
For individual copyright holders see p. 254

Printed by Conti Tipocolor, Italy

British Library Cataloguing-in-Publication Data
A catalogue record for this book is available from the
British Library

ISBN 0 9540929 0 2

The LMH Fellowship Fund would like to thank
the Editor and all those above who made this
book possible by generously giving their time
and expertise free of charge.

Our debt to the talented editors of *The Brown
Book*, with their records of annual achievements,
is evident throughout. The LMH Registers have
also provided essential information and set the
highest standards of accuracy and detail. Our
thanks also go to the past and present Directors of
Development at LMH, Sheridan Gould and Peter
Watson; to Nigel McNair Scott; to Roberta Staples
for help in searching out texts; to LMH Archivist
Julie Courtenay for help with illustrations; to
Marion Weston for her tireless help with clearing
copyright permissions, and to the generous (but
self-effacing) benefactors who have enabled this
book to be published.